One Unknown

One Unknown

A powerful account of survival and one woman's
inspirational journey to a new life

GILL HICKS

RODALE

First published in 2007 by
Rodale International Ltd
7–10 Chandos Street
London
W1G 9AD

Gill Hicks has asserted her right to be identified as the author of this work

Printed and bound in the UK by CPI Bath using acid-free paper from sustainable sources

1 3 5 7 9 8 6 4 2

A CIP record for this book is available from the British Library

ISBN-13: 978-1-4050-9989-9

This hardback edition distributed to the book trade by Pan Macmillan Ltd

Notice
The events of July 7 as they are recounted in this book have been pieced together from a collection of the author's and many other people's memories and accounts of that day. The author and publisher apologise for any small inconsistencies that may have arisen as a result of this.

RODALE
LIVE YOUR WHOLE LIFE™

We inspire and enable people to improve their lives and the world around them

Dedication

This book is dedicated to all the extraordinary people who have entered my life since July 7 2005: the special few who saved me that day; the many more who have helped me on the long road to my 'new normal'; and those inspirational friends and mentors who have encouraged me to take a new path into the future.

I would like to make a special acknowledgement to a fellow countryman, who suffered great personal tragedy in his own life, but then chose to devote himself to making a difference in the world. Anyone who knew him was enriched by the experience, and he touched the lives of countless people like myself who wanted an understanding friend in their time of need.

His humanity, his dignity and his courage in the face of adversity have shown both Joe and I how we should try to live the rest of our lives.

With admiration and love to:

Maurice de Rohan, AO, OBE, 1936–2006

Contents

Acknowledgements

I would like to offer my deepest gratitude to the following:

MY FELLOW PASSENGERS FROM CARRIAGE 1

ALL AT RUSSELL SQUARE TUBE STATION
TOM
THE BRITISH TRANSPORT POLICE
THE METROPOLITAN POLICE
LONDON AMBULANCE SERVICE

THE HICKS FAMILY
THE KERR FAMILY
THE MINEAR FAMILY
MY DEAR FRIENDS

THE AUSTRALIAN GOVERNMENT
THE AUSTRALIAN HIGH COMMISSIONER
THE SOUTH AUSTRALIAN GOVERNMENT
QANTAS
CENTRELINK

ST THOMAS' HOSPITAL
BOWLEY CLOSE REHABILITATION CENTRE
ROYAL NATIONAL ORTHOPAEDIC HOSPITAL, STANMORE

JULY 7 ASSISTANCE CENTRE
LONDON BOMBINGS RELIEF CHARITABLE FUND
FRESHFIELDS BRUCKHUAS DERINGER SOLICITORS

THE PEOPLE OF LONDON

THE DESIGN COUNCIL
THE ROYAL COLLEGE OF ART
ARRIVA BUSES
THE WAPPING PROJECT
PEACE DIRECT
LEONARD CHESHIRE

BBC
CHANNEL NINE AUSTRALIA
RODALE
CLAIRE SAWFORD PUBLIC RELATIONS

ALL AT ST ETHELDREDA'S CHURCH

AND ALL THOSE WHO WROTE TO ME, WHO PRAYED FOR ME AND WHO
WISHED ME WELL.

Dear Gill

I have known you since May 2006, have worked with you and we have hatched film scripts together, so I thought I knew something of what happened on July 7.

But I didn't.

You tell the story with such power and pace that I simply could not stop reading.

And it's hard to keep reading when you have a lump in your throat, and your heart in your mouth, at the same time...

Most of all you show us again and again how the PRESENT is everything.

How precious it is.

How precious life is.

How precious are those we love.

And those we don't even know.

This is an astonishing book. What you have written has the capacity to save lives, literally. This is because you understand so clearly what happened to you, and why it was essential that you stayed conscious. The same is true for all of us, but usually in less dramatic ways. It is essential for our survival and that of the planet, that we stay conscious – that we are aware of what we are doing – to ourselves, to others, to the earth. And that we act on that awareness.

In this book, by example and by examination, you show us how.

Thank you.

Dr Scilla Elworthy
Founder of Peace Direct, recipient of the Niwano Peace Prize in 2003 and nominated three times for the Nobel Peace Prize.
www.peacedirect.org

Prologue

It just didn't matter.
I was insignificant, a nobody – I was simply one more commuter travelling in London on a Thursday morning. I was just on my way to work, one more 'sardine' squeezed into a rather un-symbolic tube carriage.

It just didn't matter.
I was unaware, completely and utterly unaware of who was pressed up next to me. We were all just a bunch of people, a random sample of Londoners. Yet each of us was important to someone, each of us had our stories, a past, a present – an uncertain future; each of us was uniquely significant in our own way. We made a difference to the lives of people who knew and loved us.

It just didn't matter.
We all had our reasons for being in that carriage on that day, at that time. We didn't know each other; you keep yourself to yourself – these are the unwritten rules. There is an understanding, a code of practice – no eye contact, no communication; it's organised silence, everyone in sync', following our habitual paths, 'auto pilot' switched to 'On'. This is commuter ballet – each part played out, each character in blissful anonymity.

It just didn't matter ...
... if I had a faith – if I was a Christian, a Jew, a Muslim or agnostic. I could have been male, female, young or old. My skin colour could have been black, brown, white, yellow red or green. I was important. I was head of a department, trying to make my way to an important

Head of Department's meeting. I was dedicated to my work. It meant everything to me – my focus to achieve professional success.... I was running late.

It just didn't matter ...
... that the phone bill was overdue, that I was getting married in five months and the preparations were not coming together, that Joe and I were arguing – we were both very dedicated to our work, perhaps not dedicated enough to each other. We had made a commitment though.

It just didn't matter ...
... that I was trying to make ends meet, spending way too much on my credit card – fashion, shoes, make up, shoes, fashion – convincing myself that I needed yet another black, 'creatively cut' top, oh and more shoes. I was agonising over the decision whether to grow my hair or cut it short – two very different looks, very different statements.

It just didn't matter.
I didn't matter to anyone on that first carriage that day. They didn't know me, they probably didn't even see me, wouldn't be able to identify me if they saw me again. No one knew that I was significant, that my life counted, that I was valued and loved and cherished. They didn't know that I had a family, a brother, a fiancé, dear friends. I was funny, I loved to laugh and make other people laugh. I was also a shoulder for many to cry on. I loved and was loved back – I had a role.
   I had hopes and dreams. I wasn't different; I was just like them.

It – I didn't matter ...
... to Germaine Lindsay/Abdullah Shaheed Jamal, the suicide bomber. He didn't set out that morning to kill or maim me, Gill Hicks. I didn't do anything to him, I didn't know him, he didn't know me. He didn't know the person I was, what I felt, what I thought. He didn't know what was in my heart. And I would never have dreamt what was in his.
   I was just a body, a representation of – in his eyes – the enemy. I was a symbol of all he deemed to be wrong in the world.

I wish he had made the effort to know me before he detonated his bomb. I *wish* I could have looked at him in the eyes and had the opportunity to say – I am not your enemy, I wish you no harm, I am not the enemy.

I am a person, a human being – just like you, just like you.

None of this mattered ...
... when I was faced with my own death on a Thursday morning in July 2005.

Chapter 1

Letting Go

I WAS WITH MY MUM WHEN SHE DIED. We all were – my brother Graham, his wife, Johanna, my then fiancé Max and I. There was a harpist playing in the foyer of the hospice and the music was coming through faintly into Mum's room. I was holding her hand. I didn't want to let go, but I didn't want to squeeze too tight either – I was worried that I would hurt her. I know she knew we were there. We each kept telling her how much we loved her, how much she meant to us, how sorry we were that she was leaving us.

Then her hand slipped. Gently, it fell from mine. She was gone.

I remember how numb I felt, empty of feeling or emotion. Just numb. Something in me had just died with her and I would never be the same again. My world would be unrecognisable without her. She had been the centrepiece, the constant, the one thing that I could rely on to never change. I would feel her loss like a wound that would never heal – I was a part of her, and she of me.

It is a certain type of loneliness, a void that can never be filled. I had Graham and I was fortunate and blessed to be surrounded by people who loved and cared for me, but I had lost the one person who could give me complete and unconditional love. It is the love that only a mother or father can give. The love that makes you feel able to face the world again when everything has gone wrong, the love that is excited and proud of your every major and – more importantly – minor achievement, the love that can kiss a cut finger and instantly make the pain go away. It's special and powerful and I guess I just expected that it would always be there. I expected that she would always be there; she was my mum – I took it all for granted.

We had twelve precious weeks, from her diagnosis to her parting. Just twelve weeks – I used to think about counting time for a long while during and after her death. Some days, when we were all optimistic and searching for a cure, twelve weeks seemed like a long time – we'd call it three months because using the word month gave us the sense that there was more time. Then, when the prognosis looked bleak, when we were given an expected time frame by Mum's medical team – time was counted in days – ten Mondays, or five Tuesdays. Even though I was with her every day I still don't know how she felt – how it must feel to know, to have some knowledge of the length of time you have left before facing your death.

Six months prior to being diagnosed with aggressive pancreatic cancer, my mum had been working full time in the fashion accessories department of a well-respected Australian department store. She had been there, following the same pattern, the same routine for over a decade. Not dissimilar to most of us, she was up at the same time every day, prepared the same breakfast, consisting of a cup of tea and a bowl of muesli or bran flakes. (Concerned at the increasing number of people struck with bowel cancer, she would sometimes add prunes!) She would then walk briskly up the street, catch the bus, clock in, and there it was – another day selling belts and bags, gloves, stockings and scarves and then home again, exhausted.

Over several cups of tea and toasted cheese and tomato sandwiches (our favourite dinner), we would chat and laugh about the funny things her customers said, or did. I would give her a foot massage, whilst she settled in front of the television, then I would get ready to go out. I was always busy. There was always somewhere I had to be or someone I had to meet. I was singing in a jazz band at the time and we were planning to hit the 'big time'. Rehearsal schedules were demanding and, at twenty, I was still young, very young – I didn't think about Mum being home alone, night after night, year in, year out. I didn't think about how she was burying the pain she felt by the recent loss of Dad – even before his death. I didn't know. Actually, I didn't realise until recent times just how much she needed me, how much she needed someone to be there, to care, to share life with.

She would listen to the radio as she lay in bed, talkback shows mainly or easy listening music. Mum always fell asleep with the radio on and I never went in to turn it off. I guess I too grew to like the sounds of life going on somewhere, of people discussing what seemed to me absolute nonsense, yet in a rather passionate manner.

My room was next to hers. Sometimes when there wasn't any noise – when everything was still and quiet – I could hear her praying. It always made me cry, because although I couldn't quite make out exactly what she was saying, I knew she was praying for me, for Graham, for Dad and for all who were in need of a little extra help. She prayed for a better world, for an end to poverty and famine; she never asked for anything for herself, ever. She was the type of person who was only truly happy if everyone else was – that was just her. She didn't upset anyone, she never spoke ill of anyone, she was gracious and harmonious. She was my mother, a beautiful soul, the most honest, genuine and warm-hearted person I have ever known.

But we were going to have to say goodbye to her, she was leaving us, leaving me. I will never know if I did enough; I never asked her in the end. I only hope she knew how much I loved her. I hope she was proud of who I was then and who I have become now.

It was a very different case when Dad died, just a little over a year before Mum. They were separated, not divorced; Mum was the product of an age in which if you married, you married for life. Dad was a kind of lovable rogue, never really the family man that Mum (and I) had hoped for, but she loved him anyway, despite all his faults. I guess secretly she thought he would change, settle down, mow the lawn and do what ordinary partners did, whatever that was. He was her husband, for better, for worse.

She must have had great strength to endure all of his many inconsistencies, the broken promises, the missed Christmases and birthdays. I can only look back and recognise that strength now as an adult and as a married woman; her tolerance was far greater than mine.

The final blow came, however, when I discovered that Dad had a long-standing secret family. Mum just couldn't continue trying to make our rented house a home; she had to walk away for her own self-preservation. She left with dignity. It was just Mum and me – no forwarding address.

We didn't know where Dad was living or with whom – he travelled around Australia as part of an acting troupe, so he lived on the road, we guessed.

Then one day it was Graham who got the call, asking, 'Do you know a Don Hicks?' The Royal Adelaide Hospital were on the phone, telling Graham that Dad was there and that he didn't have long. He was in a coma. The sister at the hospital had called every Hicks in the phone book trying to locate the relatives, if there were any, of Donald Harvey Hicks.

My Dad. There, alone, dying.

He died, never waking from the coma. We did manage to all be there, around his bedside, talking to him, never really knowing if he could hear us. I told him how much I loved him and that I was sorry our lives had gone this way. I said how desperate I was to understand – that if he woke up everything would be all right, he could explain. I just wanted him to pull through, for me. His eyes were wide open, still a deep blue. But his stare was vacant. He looked right through me, as if I wasn't in the room. I held his hand and kept talking, hanging on, waiting for a reaction, but nothing happened.

His heart eventually stopped beating and, just like that, he was gone, taking with him all the unanswered questions, the keys to the past and maybe to the present.

I had been, as most little girls are, my dad's princess. We were very alike, both in character and in our appearance. He was one of those people who could light up a room the moment he walked in – always something to say, a joke or a story. But behind all that was a man who was deeply troubled. His life had been plagued by illness; I have no memories of Dad being 'well'. There was a stock of medication in the bathroom – various pills and potions for this or that ailment and, looking back, it really was quite sad. Once again though, I didn't really see all this – I was too young to understand his plight, too young to notice the pain; all I saw was a man who was always withdrawn from family life, resting or sitting and watching cricket for hours and hours.

Funny, cricket is a game that I have come to hate, probably because I hold it directly responsible for all the lost years I could have had with my dad. Cricket, that is, and every other sport that was televised back then. And let's not forget British comedy, Benny Hill being a real favourite. Oh and let's see, yes, there was *Parkinson* and the nightly news – and when all the television was over, there was always a book or two to be read.

I missed him then probably as much as I do now.

To watch someone you love leave you and the world you know is the most difficult thing to face. It's the very notion of being absolutely powerless to change the outcome. There is absolutely nothing you can do. Sometimes tears are all that is left, there is nothing else you can do but cry. You cry for all the life they will never see, and for yourself because you are left; left behind to carry on without them, to continue with life in a world without them in it. It seems impossible.

...

It was the combination of both my parents' lives and their rather early deaths that made me question everything about my own path. The realisation that we are all here for a given amount of time, that no one escapes death, made me rethink. Was I making an impact, a difference? What could I achieve? How far could I push myself? What were my boundaries? I was certain of one thing, when I died I wanted the world to know – I wanted to be remembered, to be noted for doing something. I wanted my life to count.

At that time I was engaged to Max. He was a very beautiful person, both inside and out – the epitome of the Italian/Australian man, embodying all the flair and style of the Italians and the ruggedness of the Australians. He and his mother, Sara, introduced me to red wine and good food. He was my best friend and, to this day, we still remain very close. I remember the Italian inscription on my engagement ring – '*Amia moche sempre*' which, translated, means 'We will love each other always'. The funny thing was that we got the spelling wrong, so it actually didn't mean anything at all, although it did mean everything to us.

I met Max when I was 20. It was love at first sight for us both. Life was good, it was safe and we were going to build the 'Australian Dream'. We would get married, buy a house, have two, maybe three or more kids, a dog and watch television (cricket stuck on Channel 9). It was wonderful and good and we knew we would be lucky if we managed to fulfil this dream, this 'rite of passage'.

But Mum's death was a catalyst that changed my life's direction. I didn't want to stay in Adelaide. I knew I wouldn't be able to live in a familiar world without Mum in it. I couldn't settle. My soul was restless.

I felt compelled to change everything in my life – to shake it all up like a giant snow cone and see how it would settle. I didn't really know who I was any more. I knew that I wanted a huge family and all the things that usually go with that, especially the large home with rolling green lawn, eventually, but something was calling me now, an inner voice that would not let me rest until I acknowledged it, until I listened.

I couldn't explain why I wanted to pack just a suitcase and head off. I didn't understand it myself, so how could I explain to Max and Graham that this was what my heart was telling me to do? My little nephew Alex had just been born and life was continuing, as it should – but still I couldn't stay. Still the call to leave was the loudest voice.

In the end Max decided he would join me, although in many ways it felt like we were embarking on separate journeys. He too felt he needed to leave Adelaide and see what the wider world would present him with. He agreed that what we both needed was a chance to see who we were and who we could be.

The UK was our chosen destination. I guess this was partly because the language spoken was English, but also, for me, because I would be closer to Scotland – closer to my Mum's roots. There was no single reason; it was blind faith really.

Graham wasn't happy. He didn't say much but his silence was indication enough of the depth of his unhappiness. He wanted to look after his little sister, to shield me from the 'unknown' – but he couldn't. He had to let me go and trust that I would survive all that a city like London would throw at me. He organised a truck to collect all my furniture and bits and bobs and supervised their arrival at a lock-up storage unit. I signed a six-month contract, thinking this would allow me enough time to discover whatever I had to and return 'home'.

We were both very quiet. I didn't know what to say. My heart was breaking, but it was my own choice so I didn't feel I had the right to cry or show my brother how sad I was at leaving him and his new son behind.

...

The scheduled flight time was 24–26 hours – every other passenger knew this, which is probably why they arrived, 'suitably' dressed in comfortable trousers or tracksuits and flip-flops. I, on the other hand, wore blue suede, high-heeled boots that suggested a hint of fashion indulgence whilst complementing a smart, two-piece wool-blend olive trouser suit. My very long, dark hair was blow-dried perfectly straight and kept in place by a pair of Gucci sunglasses strategically positioned on my head. Lips were 'daytime' red. Max's hair was slicked back with wet gel. We thought we looked the perfect jet-setting couple.

I was brought up to be well dressed, on the basis that it is far better to be overdressed than underdressed and that there is never an excuse not to be well presented. Mum always told me that you only get one chance to make a first impression – that you are judged according to how you look – and I believed her. Clothes offered me an added air of confidence so I would always indulge myself whenever I needed a boost. You never know what will happen, who you will meet, or what situations you may find yourself in.

I carried my vanity case with me throughout the flight. It was filled with creams and lotions, as well as lipsticks in every imaginable shade of red. I was reluctant to place the case in the storage locker above my head, preferring to place it in front of me, in full view at all times.

As we flew over Europe, making our way to Britain, I remember calling to one of the cabin crew, a woman, and asking what I thought was a perfectly valid question. 'Excuse me,' I said, 'but when we land, will customs be searching my suitcase?' She looked at me rather strangely. 'I only ask,' I went on, 'as I have folded everything in a certain way and I am concerned that if my bag is searched some of my clothes may get messed up, and crumpled.' She smiled, a funny smile where only one side of the mouth curls up and said, 'You haven't travelled before, have you?' Then she turned and walked down the aisle, leaving me to ponder her response.

Surely I looked 'professional' and 'experienced' – I had a two-piece expensive wool-blend suit on, after all. Surely she could see I was a woman of the world? What gave me away?

The plane began its descent. The co-pilot was giving his instructions over the intercom – 'Cabin crew cross check; doors to manual, please take up positions for landing' – and down we went, dropping through the air, through the clouds to reveal the city below. Max and I were bolt upright in our seats, faces like little deer in headlights. I squeezed Max's hand tightly, muttering my flying prayer. 'Dear Lord, please watch over this plane and be with us as we land; please keep me from harm, in Your name, Amen.' Then the wheels touched down. Relief. Thank you dear God, thank you.

What would London be like? All we had to go on was London's reputation as a tough city that would 'eat us alive' if we didn't grow some thick skin. I'd packed thermal wear so at least I would be warm! But would I be ok? Would I make my name as a jazz singer? A thousand questions and doubts rushed around my head. I knew I would be fine. What could possibly go wrong? I could at least speak the language so that was one major hurdle already crossed!

Heathrow was enormous and I felt like a tiny child in a very large department store. Everyone was rushing around; they all seemed to know where they were going. The sheer volume of people was striking – I had never seen so many people in one place. It looked like the entire population of Adelaide was right there in the airport. I tried not to look amazed – think traveller, think business traveller, I said to myself, trotting on my suede heels.

I'd never seen armed police before. They were carrying what looked like submachine guns. They walked in pairs, up and down the concourse, looking around, eyeing every passenger. I felt like I was on a movie set, although there was nothing remotely 'Hollywood' about the situation in reality. It was intimidating and I really was quite scared, already wondering if leaving my safe, beautiful Adelaide was such a good idea after all.

Was this show of police force necessary? Were they targeting drug traffickers, I wondered. Max told me that it was all about the terrorist threat. What terrorist threat? It was the early 1990s – who would be terrorising London? Maybe it was just that Heathrow was a major airport and terrorists have been known to hijack planes?

Well, we'd landed now, so there was no danger of our plane being hijacked. Still, I was keen to get out of the airport as soon as we could – if there was a threat of some kind, I didn't want to be around to see it. I was lucky to have been born in a country that had had no experience of terror on its shores, so all of this was new and rather frightening.

I didn't feel personally threatened – who would want to harm me? – and I understood that this threat was about the government, the target was government interests, not fresh-faced Australian travellers. I'd be fine.

I remembered what had been drummed into me about London life – don't make eye contact, keep your head down at all times and 'blend'. So that's what I did, not looking at anyone as I made my way through the airport, dragging my luggage behind me and working out the cheapest route to central London – trying desperately not to bump into anyone or anything!

I look back on this now with a degree of horror and, of course, embarrassment. But mostly I reflect on this time of my life with a fondness for the innocent Adelaide girl who was dealing with the death of her parents, trying to make sense of it all, trying to find her way, to find who she was, what she was really made of and, most importantly, hoping to make a lasting mark on the world – to leave a legacy.

There is still a lot of her in me today, she's just a little older – well, a lot older in fact – and a hell of a lot wiser. But the wide-eyed, childlike optimism is still there, sending me charging into new challenges with open arms, embracing all in my path. I am glad that life's events haven't hardened me. I am tough, but I am not hard. There is a difference.

. . .

I'd left Australia in 1992 in my very early twenties. Then, my plan of being away for six months, even a year seemed radical. There was a grand plan; Max and I would return, get married, settle down and have those six children that I longed for. We *would* do all those things.

But then he left. London didn't present the same opportunities for him as it did me and he had had enough. I could see it coming – his discontent, that he was missing his family, his old life – but I refused to acknowledge that it was real, never believing that he would actually go and leave me behind. I remember closing the front door behind him, standing with my back against it and sliding down, crying, feeling scared and alone.

I could have called out, I could have opened the door and yelled to him to stop and wait. I could have said that I would go home with him. But I didn't. As much as the immediate loss of him and of our relationship actually felt physically painful, something would not let me go. Something kept me from following him.

I knew what I would find if I settled back in Adelaide, I knew that life would be great – as close to paradise as anyone could get. However it held no surprises. I needed to chase the unknown; I needed the thrill of not knowing what an unforgiving city like London might have in store for me, and I needed to stay prepared, on my toes, alert and awake. For me this was being alive – feeling alive. I had made my choice. I wanted to make something of myself. I was still on a journey of self-discovery and it hadn't ended for me; I wasn't ready to leave.

I was passionate about living in London's cultured and diverse society, about British art, architecture, fashion and design – I represented it, I promoted it, I lived and breathed it. I was climbing the professional ladder – just starting to achieve recognition and status. How could I leave?

I sat with my back propped up against that door for hours, plotting Max's departure in my mind – 'He'll be on the tube now ... he'll be at Heathrow ... he'll be boarding the plane ... he'll be over Europe'. Eventually, I fell asleep there, crying.

...

To this day, I still don't quite know where all the years have gone – how one Christmas has blended into another. I became notorious amongst friends and family back in Adelaide for making promises that were never kept, promises of returning home – next Christmas, next Easter, next birthday. Something always had a habit of getting in the way, like a new job, a promotion, a new adventure that I couldn't resist.

I remember when I first arrived in London. My dreams were still fresh, undeterred, raw and somewhat innocent – yet at the same time I was full of bravado. My strategy to find a job was, I would admit, slightly mad, but I believed it would work and to all intents and purposes, it did: I would travel to a part of London that I wasn't familiar with (which was most of it!) and look around at all the buildings, trying to get a 'feeling'. I believed in following my gut instinct and that wherever the right job for me was, the building would 'call out' to me, luring me inside, to a meeting with my future employer. That was the plan. I had very little money left and I was concerned that time was running out, I was desperate for work – not just work though: a career, a path, my reason for being here.

And one morning, it happened – a tall building caught my attention. It was Kings Reach Tower, the home of IPC magazines, publisher of the then recently launched, 'thinking woman's' glossy, *Marie Claire*. I couldn't believe it! This was it. This was my future. I marched in, as if I was the Chief Executive, and, with a huge smile, went straight up to the front desk. 'Hello, my name is Gill Hicks. I don't have an appointment, but I would like to speak to someone who works in editorial on *Marie Claire*. I would like to work here.'

Ten minutes later a young, model-like figure appeared – she didn't walk, she glided across the marble floor of the reception – and stretched out her arm to reveal a tiny wrist for me to shake her hand. I was scared I would break her, but I had to maintain my assertive manner. I explained in great detail how I had had the 'feeling' and couldn't believe my luck when I saw that this was the building that housed all my favourite magazines, and how this could have been a complete disaster. ... I was talking faster than my brain could think, about to dig myself into a very large hole when she – her name was Tamara – put me out of my misery. 'We are not hiring at the moment,' she said. 'Thank you, please leave your details with reception.' Then, without thinking, I blurted, 'I'm brilliant, I'm amazing, I'll prove it to you – I'll work for free and by the end of a month, you will wonder what you ever did without me – promise.'

So, that's what I did! I went in every day, working on the beauty editorial pages, making my excuses at lunch to sneak out and eat my homemade peanut butter sandwiches as I couldn't afford to buy lunch with the other girls. I found a lovely spot – a small jetty – where

I would kick off my shoes, dangle my feet in the Thames (the building was just on the river) and eat my lunch, daydreaming of all my 'possibilities'.

I have a fond memory of buying a very large-brimmed hat, a dark blue felt – very regal! It was my attempt at looking English, or at least my idea of English. But whilst I may have looked like a 'proper' English lady, I was still very much an Australian – and this came through loud and very clear whenever I would catch public transport. Despite my drills in how to behave when out in London, my natural instincts would still somehow take over. I would never miss an opportunity to gain knowledge and 'friends' – smiling and opening up conversations with my fellow commuters. I wouldn't hesitate in asking someone what they did for a living, how long they had been in London – the usual 'ice-breaking' questions that you would use in any normal social situation. Except, that is, on the tube in London. Gradually people would move away, one seat at a time. I caught on eventually and would read a book, just like everyone else. But there was always the odd occasion when my passion for human intervention would rise up and suddenly I would find myself chatting away!

Within the space of five years, I had managed to rise to the very top of the magazine game. I was now Publisher of *Blueprint* – a revered publication with a global readership, the most-respected architecture and design magazine.

I worked hard, came in early and stayed late. I deserved my promotion and loved each and every minute of every day. I was 'married' to the job. I wasn't interested in men and had no time for them – they would only get in the way of all I had to do. However, secretly I longed for a partner, someone to share the madness with. In my heart I thought no one could replace Max; I wondered sometimes if I should just return home – Max and I did talk of getting back together many times. But still I was drawn here. Something was keeping me in London.

...

Joe wrote for *Blueprint* and even though I had read many of his contributions, we had never actually met one another. We finally met at that sought-after, 'romantic' venue/hot spot – the Royal Institute of British Architects. Who would have thought that would be where I'd meet my future husband!

Blueprint hosted a very special evening, gathering the great and the mighty from the architecture and design disciplines in honour of a world-renowned architect. I noticed that our Editor had been chatting to someone for a good part of the evening and I was furious. He should have been 'working the room' – talking to all our many invited guests and not just concentrating on this one person. I marched over to them in my full-length, black leather coat, trying to think of an appropriate way to break up the conversation and discreetly ask our Editor to move on. Anyway, to cut a long story short, Joe says he fell in love with me at that very moment – he was impressed by my fury, which gave off a certain power, I guess – and the next day he called and asked me out.

We met for dinner. I was so nervous as I hadn't been on a 'date', so to speak, for a long, long time. What would I say? All I could talk about was architecture and maybe graphic design at a push, or maybe art. Gosh, I wondered if we both liked the same sort of art. Oh, what the hell – I would just have to go with the flow.

Before the entrée arrived, Joe looked at me and said, 'I have something I must tell you.' That sounds intriguing, I thought and said something stupid like, 'Oh, are you a post-op' woman? That's ok, I understand!' Luckily he laughed and said, 'No, I have a daughter; she's ten, nearly eleven. Her name is Lily.' I reacted in a way that he had never expected, saying, 'Wow, that's fantastic, what a shame you only have one child – I would like to have six myself!' And with that we settled into a lovely evening.

Joe walked me home, holding my hand all the way. We were never really apart from then on.

Even though I was now in a growing relationship, which was lovely and offered all the extra benefits of a life that I had missed, I was still dedicated to the 'job', still driven and defined by what I did. I started my own publishing company called Dangerous Minds and worked every hour that God sent and then some more. I was exhausted most of the time but still strived for more. Although I thrived on the pressures and commitment of running my own company I was tempted by a position at the Design Council, the UK's strategic body for design.

The project that I was to head was enormous – the first of its kind. It was taking design to the general public throughout the UK. How could I resist such a position? I would be able to work at a level that I had longed for. Everything was coming together for me professionally – I was made a Fellow of the Royal Society of the Arts, I sat on various arts panels, I was appointed to the board of the Women's Playhouse Trust. These accolades were everything to me; they surpassed my wildest imaginings, went beyond my hopes and dreams from all those years ago when I would sneak away on my lunch break at IPC magazines to eat my peanut butter sandwiches, whilst dangling my feet in the Thames. I had arrived – it felt like it was all just beginning, that this was the start of many riches to come.

When I thought about going back to Australia I realised I couldn't leave now – not now that I had finally been recognised and accepted. I would miss the grit, the grind of London, the way that colour contrasts with the grey backdrop. I would miss a city that had given me so much – and that I was just starting to give back to. My life was emerging here, I really felt like I was 'me'. I could indulge my creative spirit, wear beautiful tailored black head to toe, interestingly cut designer pieces with flat, black zip-up Prada boots, standing at all times with one foot in front of the other, like a dancer, poised. I worked in an environment that encouraged radical and fantastical ideas and was even able to turn them into realities. It could all happen. Whatever I dreamed could happen, it could happen here.

I still felt like an Australian abroad – an outsider on the inside – but I liked that. I was admitted into the 'inner design circle', yet retained my Australian core. And through everything, I hadn't lost my ability to see the funny side, always allowing myself some 'play' room even though my work was serious.

But things were starting to change. It was becoming increasingly difficult to remain the happy-go-lucky Aussie. The weeks would fly by and time was slipping through my fingers. I was feverishly busy at work – the first in and the last to leave. It felt like I was always there, just popping home to change clothes and freshen up. I started to bring more and more work home, having breakfast, lunch and dinner meetings – it was getting harder to keep laughing.

I was tired, but I kept going. There was so much to do, my project at the Design Council was just about to launch and the next few weeks would be crucial to its success. I was excited by what this piece of work could achieve and had to ensure that I was doing all I could to allow it to succeed.

I would always look at my diary before leaving the office at night to check what the following day had in store, often using the evening to prepare for certain meetings. Thursday, July 7 – Head of Department's meeting first thing, followed by a design meeting for our brochure, then launching project July 14 ... so much to do within the next week to ensure that all went to plan. But I'd just have to worry about that on Friday and use the weekend to get done some of the reports that I was running behind on ...

Chapter 2

'Priority One'

'HEY, WATCH IT!' I say to an aggressive commuter as he pushes past me to squeeze onto the packed train carriage. 'Do you mind? We all have jobs to get to!' I am furious; I've been waiting for that train along with everyone else and he has no regard for anyone but himself. He makes some remark under his breath as the doors close, his cheek pressed hard up against the glass. Then the train slowly pulls away from the platform.

...

I was tired having slept only fitfully. Joe and I had argued the night before and whilst, of course, it all seems silly now, at the time I thought it was serious enough to question whether or not we should go ahead with our plans to marry in December. We had let the sun set on that argument – something we had promised never to do on previous occasions – and I had got into bed next to Joe, rigid with fury. Eventually I had drifted off, angry and frustrated.

In the morning I got up and stood blankly in front of my wardrobe, not knowing what to wear. There were quite a few appointments in my diary for that day, kicking off with the heads of department meeting. I started banging things around – shoes, bags, anything that might wake Joe up and annoy him. Although the weather had been very hot, this particular morning was drizzly, making my decision of what to wear even more difficult. Any woman reading this will know instantly what I mean – and that's not to mention the frizzy-hair hazard!

After much deliberation, I grabbed my jeans and turned up the cuffs (very cool, you know – the bigger the cuff the better) and put on my favourite flat, white, pointed, 50s-style, patent leather shoes. (I loved them so much that I bought the same style in three colours – one black and white striped, one rough gold and the now infamous white.) So that took care of the bottoms, but what to wear on top?

By now I was running late – a new concept for me, usually a real stickler for punctuality, early for everything. In the end I just threw on a white T-shirt, a suit jacket and ... it just needed something else. I was bored of wearing my trademark silver fob-chain necklace, so I rummaged through my drawer under the bed (yet another ploy to wake and annoy Joe) and found a blue chiffon scarf – that would do!

It's funny how all these decisions, or rather indecisions, were adding to the minutes, the seconds that ensured my place on 'that' carriage. It's all about timing. Had I been just five minutes earlier, or indeed later, just five minutes, my story would be very different. I only changed from my usual route because there were problems on my regular branch of the Northern Line, so I went in via Kings Cross to make up some valuable time.

I could drive myself mad contemplating time – if I had been a second earlier or later boarding the carriage, would that have put me in a different position in relation to the bomb?

A minute, a second, can change the course of your life. I was never meant to be there – but, circumstances, somehow, ensured that I was.

. . .

I can't believe how many people there are here this morning, of all mornings, when I am late already – I guess it is rush hour and this is Kings Cross Station, gateway to several tube and overground lines.

More and more people are now lining the platform. It's quite dangerous – I'm at the front and I don't want to be pushed onto the tracks. That's what the yellow line's there for; we are all meant to be *behind* the yellow line. I hate being short, particularly now as I'm going to get pushed back and miss my opportunity to get on the next train. That's what always happens. I must be assertive. C'mon Gill, stand your ground – attitude, it's all about attitude. C'mon, be strong.

Hang on, there's a slight breeze. That's a good sign. It means a train is on its way down the tunnel. And about bloody time too! Good thing it is only a few minutes since the last one. I am so late; shit I am so late. Come on train. Please come on.

And here it is at last. The doors open and people pour out, trying to push past those of us who are waiting, wedged together like a human wall on the platform. No one wants to make a clearing for people to get through. I'm certainly not going to – the last time I did that some-one slipped in ahead of me.

Phew. I'm in. It's a tight jam, but I'm in. I can't believe even more people are trying to get in – it's so full. At least I don't have far to go – only a few stops. But there'll be no time for a coffee-and-quick-puff-at-my-cigar stop for me today.

Why do I always end up sandwiched between tall people? At five foot nothing I always get directional air on my forehead from some stranger's nostrils. Come on Mr Driver – can we just go? Shut the doors – we are packed in here. Please shut the doors and let's go. Yes! The doors shut and we're moving.

I must remember to talk to Margaret when I get in about what we are going to do about the Olympic win. Hmmm – maybe a celebra-tion? An event to mark ... Oh, and I mustn't forget to tell Ruth that ...

.... *Click your fingers* ....
It was as quick as that – we had only just pulled out of Kings Cross Station. It could only have been seconds, just seconds. It was as quick as a click of your fingers and that was it. The lives of all of us in that carriage changed forever. But I didn't know it then. I didn't know what had happened. It was as dramatic as being on a sunny, sandy beach, drinking and talking with friends one minute, to suddenly, like the click of a finger, finding yourself in the bowels of hell. In a breath everything had changed. The whole world changed.

· · ·

I was falling, falling, falling. I was falling into blackness. It was timeless – a moment that transcended time and space. My imminent death was neither slow nor fast. It was in a frame that didn't configure with reality; my body was falling in slow motion whilst my feelings and thousands of tiny thoughts were racing around in my mind. My life was flashing before my eyes, flickering through every scene, every happy and sad moment, every conversation, everything I have ever done, said, experienced. It was all being played like a film running on high speed in my head. I was confused. How did I know that I was facing my death?

I was certain I was having a heart attack. I couldn't breathe. I couldn't feel, hear or see anything. It seemed to be my own private experience. I could just make out muffled screams, very faint – as though I was under water. My fellow passengers were screaming – at me, horrified that I was dying. They knew that I was in serious need of help. I was sure that they were trying to pull the emergency stop button. They were trying to help me. I could just hear their screams, surrounding me. They were everywhere but nowhere to be seen.

I was going deeper and deeper into an abyss. It was slow. My body falling slowly down. Timeless, spaceless, black. The darkness was so thick; it was tangible. It was hard, yet it was also soft. And it was hot, as if I was drowning in a sea of hot tar. It permeated through me, through every pore. The blackness was expansive, embracing and engulfing me entirely. I felt I was being cushioned by it, protected – wrapped up and delivered by the blackness to the ground, like a feather gently drifting in the air from side to side. When would it end? Where was the ground? Was there a ground? I didn't know. I didn't care. I was dying. Or was I now dead? Was this dead? I didn't know. I just didn't know. Oh God, oh dear God was I dead?

Millions, billions, trillions of scattered thoughts filled my head as my life continued to flash before me, images interspersed with white flashes, like twinkling Christmas lights, flickering on and off, on and off. It was all staggered, flipping from one fragmented image to the next.

Then the falling stopped. I was motionless. I was dead. My body was dead. It had stopped. I could feel nothing – I was completely numb. I couldn't feel my arms or legs. I was dead; this was what dead was like. This was *my* death. It was over. Dear Lord, please be with me, please hold my hand, guide me through; please dear Lord.

My eyes opened. It didn't make any sense. The void that had taken me, that I had fallen into – all that I had just experienced, all that was black around me, in me – was real. It was everywhere – on and with everyone. I wasn't alone. It wasn't my own private black hell and the screams weren't about me. They weren't screaming at me. They were all screaming, but for themselves, not for me.

I wasn't dead. Something had happened – something dreadful. I didn't know what and I didn't care. I couldn't think about the details – only that we were all there, all sharing this together. They weren't alone. I wasn't alone. And I wasn't dead. This was not death.

Above the screams were faint but distinctive voices shouting. I could hear one saying, 'Stay calm, it's ok. Stay calm.' Still the screaming continued.

What had happened? Where did the train go? Where were we all now? And what was this I was lying in?

I didn't have the energy to think. Time was catching up. There was chaos, commotion, confusion. People were walking over me, near me, past me, around me. They were crying, silent, screaming, talking. It was real. This was all a reality.

Instinct was beginning to take over, telling me to get up, get up, get up. I raised my arms. I was weak, confused and I couldn't breathe. The air was still black. Help ... help me. I didn't know if I was whispering, yelling or just mouthing the words. I didn't know if anyone could see me, if my own plea could be heard through all the other terrified appeals for help. I wasn't alone. I kept saying the words over and over again. Help... help ... help me. Help.

A man reached down. I could see his arms coming towards me. I stretched out to him. 'I need to stand up. Please help me up, I need to get up.' I still didn't know if I was actually making sense, if I was really talking. Could he hear me? The screams around me were louder than before. There was an atmosphere of panic and it was seeping through to me. Over and over I said, 'I need to stand up. I can't breathe. I need to stand up. Please, please help me.' The man bent down. I was slipping away. I couldn't feel my legs; I just couldn't feel them. And I couldn't see in all the black dust and mess. My whole body was limp, numb, weightless, nothing. I couldn't keep my eyes open ... the lids were heavy. They were closing ... everything went quiet.

...

I awoke. I was still there, still in that horrific place. But it was different now. It was quiet, eerily quiet and still. The man was gone. They all were gone. The commotion had stopped, the chorus of screams had dampened and the sense of panic lifted. I was on a bench seat. I didn't know how I'd got there – he must have pulled me up and carried me over to the seat – but it didn't matter why or how; that was just how it was. I had to accept that I was part of this – whatever *this* was.

It was now a 'room', no longer a carriage and definitely not a train. It was its own unique place – a blend of total destruction and devastation beyond belief.

The atmosphere was thick. There was an acrid smell and it was trapped down there with us, contained in the twisted metal shell. The 'air' was too heavy to breathe, too saturated with the rubble, the particles and burning electrical wires.

I felt so weak. It was hard to hold my head up, hard to look around. Too hard to make sense.

The blackness was gradually lifting, being replaced by various shades of grey. This was due to a light – a security or emergency light – on the wall of the tunnel, shining through what had once been the carriage windows. It offered an opportunity to gauge the severity of what had happened – to get an awareness of where I was and how I was going to get out.

There was not enough light to gather more than a dim view. There was no colour or contrast, only grey, dark grey – but this was enough for me to verify what I had already sensed but hadn't wanted to acknowledge. The carnage was all around, motionless, quiet, next to me.

I could see them but I couldn't reach, couldn't move, couldn't touch them. Every fibre, every atom in me wanted to scream out but I couldn't speak. I was frozen – unable to comprehend what had happened. It was quiet and I knew why. I knew why they were all so quiet, I couldn't scream for them. I couldn't breathe.

There were a few lone cries in the darkness, one to the left of me, one to the right. They were begging for help, praying to be rescued. I couldn't help them. I couldn't respond. Where had everybody gone?

Was it just us left down here? The dead, the dying, those who couldn't move? As individuals we were alone, but somehow – it is very difficult to explain – we were together. We were all sharing this, all waiting and supporting each other.

'Please God. Help me, I'm dying,' a voice close to me kept saying. It was a woman and I couldn't see her but her voice was so clear, so close. There was a reply, from the other side, facing me – another woman's voice saying, 'It's ok; help is coming. Stay with us – what is your name? Stay with us. Help is on the way – they won't be long. Stay with us.'

For a while these conversations continued. A cry for help, followed by reassurance, comfort. Then one by one the voices fell silent. There was no more reassurance – just quiet, the eerie sound of nothing.

Everything was still awash with grey smoke, thick grey everywhere. I stopped looking around me and I looked down at myself. I could see myself, or rather, I could see what seemed to be me. Oh dearest Lord, dear God, what had happened to me?

The light was shining almost directly through the carriage over to me – to my legs. They resembled an anatomical drawing. I could see the insides, the muscle, the tendons, the bone. And attached to these were my feet – still perfect, still looking like my feet, but just dangling, as though they had been severed, cut clean through where the ankles used to be and left hanging by a thread. My feet were just hanging. This couldn't be real, it couldn't be happening. My legs are gone, I thought. My dear God, my legs are gone.

Something kept me calm. An inner voice – Divine intervention? I don't know, but something took hold of me. Something rose up inside me and took control as I began to register just how desperate my situation was. I knew that to stay alive I had to remain calm. This was crucial because if I panicked, if I screamed or cried out, my heart would be pumping more blood. The more blood my heart pumped, the more I would lose – it was streaming from my wounds, flowing from what resembled my legs. I had to be rational. If I allowed myself to be emotional I would die. I had to 'remove' myself emotionally from the scene, from my body.

I had to act fast to reduce the blood loss, to try and stem the flow. There was no time to think. I just had to react. But I was weak.

I wanted to close my eyes, but I couldn't. Not yet. I still had my scarf on and some clothes. They were in shreds but they were there. I had to stop the bleeding. I raised my arm – it hurt and was bleeding and all I could see as I lifted it was red skin. I managed to grab hold of my scarf and slip it from around my neck. I then brought it up to my mouth – trying desperately to rip it in two with my teeth to create tourniquets. It was difficult cutting through. I was trying not to pass out, but my eyes closed. My only thoughts were to hold on, hold on.

I opened my eyes and reached down to tie the left leg first, up around my thigh. Then I reached for my right leg, trying to lift it a little. As I moved my hand up to my thigh my hand sank, disappearing deep into my leg. My inner thigh was missing. It was gone. How did this happen? *What* happened?

I had to stay calm, focused, breathe, breathe. I tried again, tying the scarf higher, attempting to convince myself that it looked worse than it really was, talking myself through it and trying to stay calm. It took my last bit, my very last ounce of physical energy to gather both torn limbs and elevate them over the armrest on the seat. That was it. That was all I could do.

I was battling the drowsiness. My eyes wanted to close, to block out all they had witnessed. But I tried to stay awake. I had to stay in an upright position – I couldn't allow myself to lean back, to give in to the need to close my eyes. I reminded myself that this wasn't a bad dream, that it was real and that I wouldn't wake up next to Joe and tell him of this nightmare. I needed to stay alert, to wait for a light, for the signs of a torch.

The light that filled the carriage, that revealed the haze of smoke and grey – everything was grey – was coming from the tunnel wall and shone directly on me. I looked at myself again.

'My legs are gone, my legs are gone,' I repeated, over and over. I didn't know who I was talking to or if anyone was listening. I just needed to convince myself, to believe what was there. I didn't know if I was screaming these words, speaking or whispering. Maybe I just thought I was saying them. I just didn't know.

I became aware of two people sitting upright, just opposite me. They were awake, alert. One of them was in trouble though – he too was screaming out that he had lost a leg. It wasn't just me. We were both trying to hold on. He was being comforted by a woman. They sat there together – she was calming him, telling him that he would be all right, reassuring him that help was coming, that we would be all right, that it wouldn't be long now.

She saw me and called over to me, 'What is your name? Are you ok?' 'My name is Gill,' I replied, but I don't remember saying much more; I didn't want to talk, to say anything else – what else was there to say? She told me her name. It was my mother's name and I remember thinking how strange that was, wondering if it was a sign that Mum was here with me, helping me. I didn't want to say or do anything. I turned my head, away from her – I didn't want to see her, to look. I had to concentrate on myself – on not dying. I needed to slow my heart rate, control my breathing – out, out, in, out – and just focus on staying alive until help got there.

They will be here soon, I thought. I need to be alert, to let them know that I am here, that I am still alive. They will come. They will come with a torch ... they will come. It will be ok. They will come. I need to wait for the torch.

I had to distract myself, to focus on something other than blood and legs and death and dying. I looked at my watch. I kept my eyes transfixed on the watch's face – looking at the numbers, the hands moving around, minute after minute. I took deep and measured breaths, slowing my body down to a state where the vital organs were just doing the minimum – not over-exerting themselves – just enough to see me through, to keep me alive until I was rescued. They would be here soon, I told myself. It wouldn't be long.

I had to stay calm.

But did they know we were there? God, what if no one knew? What if everyone above ground had no idea that we were down there, trapped, waiting, maybe waiting for no one! I couldn't panic – I just had to trust that this being London, a major city, they would know. Of course they would. They would know and they would be trying to reach us.

I was still losing a lot of blood and I was getting weaker. It was becoming harder to stay awake, to wait for the torch.

I could hear two loud and powerful voices in my head. One was willing me to hold on, to remember those who loved and needed me; the other was encouraging me to let go, to drift away into a peaceful and permanent sleep. The voice that was calling me to sleep was beautiful and sweet in its tone. It was comforting, welcoming, warm and inviting. It was saying just what I wanted to hear and I was entranced by it. I wanted to go to sleep, to lay back, close my eyes and let go; to just stop being there. I wanted to, but somewhere deep in my heart I knew I couldn't, that this was not the voice I should listen to. I needed to resist, but I was weak and I was tired. I wanted to sleep.

Both sides were stating their case – putting more and more pressure on, asking me to choose. 'Come with me, sleep, sleep, sleep.' 'No – come with me. Stay awake. The torch will come, stay awake.' I was being asked to decide between life and death. It was as though the world had stopped and everything in it had paled into absolute insignificance. I had to choose, there was no time left – Life or Death? LIFE or DEATH?

The struggle to keep my eyes open made it increasingly difficult to deny the option of going to sleep. The 'voice' of Death was comforting, I could feel myself slipping into 'her' arms. It was getting harder and harder to resist. I knew I had to make a final decision.

But then I thought about all the things that mattered to me – Joe, my brother Graham, my family, my dear, dear friends – all the people I loved and who loved me. I wanted to spare them the pain. I didn't want them to grieve my horrible end. I knew only too well what life was like, what living was like when someone you love dies and you are left to carry on – nothing is ever the same again, something of you goes with them. I knew what the early death of Mum and Dad had meant to me – the sadness in my heart will never be lifted; every birthday, every Christmas, I wish for them to be here, to share all those times with them. I didn't want to do this to the people who loved me – not if I had the choice, not if I could avoid that pain, not if I had an option.

It was Graham's pain that I could anticipate the most. All we had left from our childhood was each other. I knew it would break his heart to lose me as well. I knew he wouldn't recover, not from knowing how…

. . .

And then it hit me, in a moment of absolute clarity in the darkness and silence around me: my death was not about me – I would be ok. I would be delivered – the 'voice' of Death had convinced me that there was nothing to fear. No, my death would be about all the people left behind, all the broken, shattered hearts, the unanswered questions, the unspoken words. It actually wasn't about my sense of loss at all. It was ok for me to die. Suddenly, I wasn't scared, I wasn't afraid of going – it would be peaceful, a passage out of where I was, away from what had happened. I could rest. Forever.

But then I looked again at my body. I looked at the two people opposite me, the person next to me, in front of me. An unexpected rush of energy filled me – 'I don't want to die. This is not where I die. This is not the end for me.' I think I shouted these words as loud as I could, or at least it certainly felt that way – like a declaration of intent. I wanted to live, to choose life and whatever lay ahead.

Dear Lord, please let me live, I prayed. 'Please keep me, in your name. Please dear Lord, I want to live.' I don't know if I shouted, whispered or maybe just mouthed these words. What I am sure of though, is that I did think them – I made a conscious decision to stay alive. It was such a profound moment, one that is with me still today.

I thought again of everyone I loved and of how much I wanted to see them, to say just how much I loved them, to hug and squeeze them. It was them that gave me the strength to make that crucial decision – the decision to stay alive and deal with whatever lay ahead, but to stay. They were a part of my rescue, a crucial part of my survival.

The conversation in my head ended abruptly. Only one voice remained and it was all about survival. It was talking loudly, clearly and slowly, telling me what to do, reassuring me and keeping me calm. 'They will be here soon. You can do this. You can hold on. Not long now, not long now ... Breathe, slowly, slowly, slowly. Out, out, in, out...' It was hard to breathe. The 'air' was still too thick to take in. They will give me oxygen when they come, I thought. I can wait for that, I can wait .... 'Out, in, out, out, out.'

Was that a light? They were there – it was them. It had to be. I could just about wave and say, 'My name is Gill, my name is Gill.' And then I heard two words, two of the best words that I could ever hear – 'Priority One' – and a tag of some sort was placed on me. That sounded fantastic! I was saved! I knew they would come, that it was just a matter of time. I was a Priority One. That was good, very good, very...

I started to let go. I had done all I could to keep myself alive and now I had to put my trust and my faith in them. But I was weak, very weak. I surrendered my body.

I was placed in what felt like a makeshift stretcher – structureless, not hard. I think it must have been a blanket, or blankets strung together; it felt similar to being in a hammock. They needed to get me out of the carriage, down the tunnel and out, to get me to hospital. To save me.

I fell in and out of consciousness. I could hear men talking but it was muffled, like it had been before, when I was falling. It seemed like they were having a hard time getting me out. They would put me down, then pick me up again. Someone was saying that he was losing his grip.

I was confused again, unsure of where exactly I was and how I came to be there. But I was fighting to hold on, I was not going to die. I could hear them. They were worried – their voices sounded concerned. They needed to hurry, to get me out before I slipped away.

One man held my hand. He didn't let go. I was so cold but I could feel his warmth. He was calling to me, telling me to stay with him. He knew my name and held my hand, tight. He said to me over and over, 'Stay with us Gill. Come on love, come on Gill, you have got to stay with us.' I needed to know he wouldn't let go – his hand kept me connected, kept me there, kept me alive.

. . .

I had left for work that morning tired and angry. Joe hadn't needed to get up early as he was working from home. This had made me even more furious – I had to get to work, I had an early meeting and I had a heavy day ahead. We would make up eventually. We always did. It was just a matter of time. But we were both stubborn, neither one of us wanting to back down and admit defeat. Not me. Never!

. . .

I blanked out, hovering somewhere between life and death – holding on to this world by a thin thread. I put my trust in them, my life in their hands. I couldn't do any more. I let go completely. It was up to them now. I felt safe with them. They wouldn't let me die. They would do everything they could. I just knew that, somehow. I just knew.

Chapter 3

Keep the Lines Clear!

'HELLO? HELLO? YOU ARE IN ST THOMAS' HOSPITAL. You have been involved in a major incident. We need to find out who you are.' It was a woman's voice – that's all I could tell – but it was muffled, like the voices in the carriage had been. It was as though I was listening to the world from the inside of a fish bowl.

My eyes must have flickered, opening long enough to see bright lights and people around me. I knew I was safe, but I didn't really understand where I was, how I got there, what had happened.

'Can you blink for me? Blink once for "yes" if you can understand me, ok?' I blinked, closing my eyes as tightly as I could, then opening them again, staring back into the light. 'I am going to go through the alphabet, ok my love? When we get to the first letter of your name, blink once. Everything will be all right my love; we will find out who you are.'

This wonderful reassuring voice was all I could focus on. I felt so safe, so loved by whoever was there, whoever it was that was talking to me. I wanted to sleep, I wanted to close my eyes, but I knew I had to let them know who I was.

'A, B, C, D, E ... Let me know, my love, when we get to the first letter of your name. Big blink to let us know, all right darling? F, G–' I blinked. 'G, is it G?' I blinked again. 'Great, that's great, the first letter is G. Ok, now we'll start again for the next letter, A, B ... It was so hard to stay awake, to find the strength to listen, well to hear what was being asked of me.

I was confused and I was scared even though I knew I was now safe and they were talking to me all the time, reassuring me, telling me where I was and what was happening. I just didn't understand. Once again, it was as though time had stood still. This new world I was in made no sense. I felt no pain. I felt nothing. I was numb all over.

'C, D, E, F, G, H, I–' I blinked. 'I. GI – that's great. You're doing so well. Just a bit more; we need just a bit more, ok my love?' I wanted to talk, I wanted to shout and scream, even to whisper – just to communicate, let them all know who I was and how to find Joe. But I couldn't. A large tube went all the way down my throat. I couldn't move. I couldn't feel my arms. I couldn't remember what had happened. I couldn't even think any more; I just wanted to close my eyes.

'… J, K, L' – was that an L? I couldn't hear. Had the voice said L? I murmured, trying to let her know that I wasn't sure, that I thought she'd said L, but I wasn't sure. 'Is it L? Can you blink?' I blinked. 'It's L. The third letter is L – is your name Gill?' I blinked and blinked again. 'It's Gill, her first name is Gill!'

There seemed to be a lot of people around my bed waiting for news of who I was. I wanted to cry. I can't remember if I did then or if I already was. It was just so brilliant to be called Gill. Brilliant that I was Gill, that I was there and that my name was Gill.

'Ok Gill, now we need to find out what your last name is and where you live. You're doing so well, just a bit more. So, I'll start with A again and just blink when I get to the right letter, just like before …G, H–' I blinked. 'Is it H, Gill? Does your last name start with H?' I blinked again. 'That's great Gill. Ok, next letter … H, I–' I blinked. 'I?' she asked. I blinked to confirm. 'Ok, next letter, you're doing great Gill, just great …'

I was exhausted, I didn't know if I would have the strength to finish my name. But there were tubes everywhere and my eyes were the only part of my face that could move. I had no choice. I had to continue. I had to let them know, so they could get Joe.

'Gill, my love,' my face was being stroked, in a gentle, tender way – it felt like Mum. 'Gill, just a bit more. We need the next letter. So far we've got H I C – blink when we get the next letter, ok?' and she started again. '… I, J, K–' I blinked. 'K – is that right Gill?' I blinked again. 'Are there more letters?' I blinked and she continued, 'Is it S?' I blinked with relief. Yes – blink, blink, blink. 'Is that it Gill? Is your last name Hicks?' I blinked, shutting my eyes tight – that was it, they had my name. I was Gill Hicks. They knew I was GILL HICKS!

I don't remember much after that. I was so tired, I just wanted to go to sleep – maybe it would all turn out to be a bad dream. What else could explain what was happening? Sitting in the wreckage of the train carriage, then lying down blinking at the letters that spelled my name, unable to move, unable to speak – it was surreal. I would wake up and it would all just be a bad dream, a very bad dream. I drifted off.

. . .

Memories of that day fade in and out. There were long stretches of time during which I lapsed into an unconscious state so that the vivid but brief snatches of memory I am left with are like beads strung on a necklace, continuous and now in order, but with large gaps in between. I remember at one point stirring, hearing voices all around me – maybe I had died and gone to Heaven? Then I would drift off again. Those gaps, those 'missing' moments, I guess I will never remember, but many of the details of what happened when I was 'out' have subsequently been filled in for me by other people who were there that day.

One thing I do now know is that at roughly around 10.30 that evening, more than twelve hours after Germaine Lindsay self-detonated, I was finally reunited with Joe.

. . .

Joe's account of that day is very moving, I can only imagine the pain and desperation of someone who is waiting for news of a loved one – it's horrible even to think about it.

When the news first broke, Joe had no idea that I was involved. Why would he – after all, I never used any of the stations that were being reported. What are the odds? It's never going to be you or someone you care about. You just read about these things, you hear about them, you watch reports on the television. What you *don't* do is sit by the phone waiting for a call to say that the person you love is dead or just about alive.

That's all that Joe did on July 7, 2005. He sat by the phone and waited for me to call to say that I was ok and in all the chaos I had taken refuge in a swanky department store and passed the time with a café latte until the mobile phone signal was restored so that I could call him. That's what Joe was hoping. He was hoping that at any moment I would come breezing in and he would be angry but relieved to see me. He was running the scene over and over in his mind, like a movie – 'Where have you been? Do you know what's happened? Why didn't you call or somehow let me know that you were ok – I have been worried sick. ' Then I would apologise, we would give each other a hug and I would make us a cup of tea. That's the scenario that Joe was hoping and praying for.

But with each hour that went by Joe's optimism faded and he began to prepare himself for the worst. Every minute without news brought him closer to facing a truth that he couldn't bear, that he couldn't allow himself to even contemplate.

The phone kept ringing all afternoon. People were calling just to check that all was ok, that both Joe and I were fine. They weren't expecting to hear the tone in Joe's voice – desperate to free the line in case I was trying to get through, whilst at the same time trying to reassure, maintaining the 'official line' that he had no news as yet, but that he was sure I was fine and that I'd just been unable to get to a phone.

. . .

Joe is Head of Critical and Historical Studies at the Royal College of Art – to hear him lecture, well, it's like poetry – and his knowledge and enthusiasm for his subject are infectious. Often, I'll be listening so intently to his words that I'll forget that the speaker is Joe – my Joe.

As well as working at the RCA, Joe also drives a bus – a red double-decker bus – allowing him to indulge his passion for transport or, more specifically, London transport. Buses, trains, tubes, ferries – he is mad about them all, but somehow it's the buses that are closest to his heart. Maybe it's because a bus offers a certain freedom that trains or water transport cannot, being fixed to a track or a river.

When he first learned that the old Routemaster buses (the red Hop-on Hop-off models) were to be phased out, Joe was distraught.

He contacted one of the main companies and asked if he could learn to drive one, to become a part-time bus driver. And so he did. Joe completed his training and passed with flying colours – taking on the 38 route, through some of the most interesting yet less well-known parts of London. He could hardly contain his joy each time that he set out at the crack of dawn in his beautifully pressed uniform, to join his crew and drive his beloved Routemaster all day long.

Joe is also passionate about London. An architectural historian both by training and by nature, he is fascinated by every path, brick and cobblestone that makes up this magnificent city. He is often re-ferred to as 'Mr London', delighting friends, family and colleagues with tales of London town, as well as trivia on just about every build-ing in the Square Mile, if not further afield. I guess its Joe's passion for London that has prevented him from being tempted to live in Australia – that and the fact that it is just so far away. He couldn't leave Lily and his parents so far behind.

...

'That' day, Joe was working from home which he does sometimes if he needs to mark students' work uninterrupted. He was also working on a radio programme idea; he often presents and/or comments on architecture related programmes.

Like me, Joe is prone to procrastinate now and again, so before settling down to work, he decided to take a stroll, get the morning paper, maybe a coffee and take things from there. He was also think-ing about our argument and how long he would leave it before call-ing me. Or would he wait for me to call him? Who would back down first, admit defeat or, worse still, apologise? Perhaps he would just allow the tension between us to continue – say nothing, avoid me and avoid talking. That was a ploy that always seemed to work. But he would deal with all this later, he decided – we had a lifetime to sort out our differences. Right now he had a lot of work to do and I probably wouldn't be in until late anyway.

Joe's first encounter with the events that were unfolding was when he saw that our local tube station was closed, but he thought little of it at that point. It was after 9am and he was approaching the coffee shop with his newspaper whose headlines boasted the Olympic win for London in 2012. It now seems incredible to think that while Joe was having his coffee, reading the paper, blissfully unaware of what was happening, I was just a few miles away, underground, somewhere between Kings Cross and Russell Square stations; somewhere ...

Joe returned home and flicked on the television. Breaking news on the BBC reported several power surges on the underground train network, with many passengers trapped inside trains, stuck in the tunnels. That would explain why our station was closed, he thought, and leaving the television on in the background so he could keep half an eye on the news, he started to tackle his work.

Suddenly, the story changed. A bus had just blown up in Tavistock Square in central London. There were now fears that the earlier incidents were not the result of a power surge but that the underground system had been hit by a series of bomb attacks. Reports were coming in of walking wounded from Kings Cross, Aldgate, Liverpool Street, Edgware Road and Russell Square. The city was under siege!

Joe was furious, cursing at the television, angry at whoever had done this. London was his city. How dare anyone harm this place? He now sat glued to the news. It was like seeing the Twin Towers fall all over again, watching as each update brought news of even more devastation, more carnage, mayhem and destruction.

But it was the image of the double-decker bus, its top blown off completely, that haunted Joe the most – reducing him to tears, wondering why, why and how could this happen. The terrorists had attacked the very symbols of the city. He was raging.

At just gone 11am the phone rang. It was Rebecca, Head of Human Resources at the Design Council, enquiring if I was at home as I hadn't turned up for work. She was going though the list of all those who had yet to come in; she needed to ensure that all staff were safe and accounted for.

Neither Rebecca nor Joe was overly alarmed or concerned about me at that point. All the roads in central London were blocked, so getting a taxi would have been near impossible. The underground system was closed and all the mobile phone networks were down. The city had come to a virtual standstill. They both expected that I was safe in a café somewhere, watching or listening to the news.

Anyone who knew me and my usual route to work would have had no real cause to worry. Why would I be in danger? They all knew that I would turn up sooner or later. Everyone who made it in to the office kept reassuring each other – it was almost a mantra: nothing bad would have happened, nothing would happen to Gill or anyone else we know; nothing would have happened.

But the hours ticked by and Joe began to feel he needed someone with him. The pressure was tearing him in two. He needed someone with a clear head, who would not get overly emotional or hysterical – someone who would be practical and make calls, and who could do whatever was necessary whilst he waited for news. He called our dear friend Debbie who teaches with him at the Royal College of Art. She and I were close and she only lived down the road. She came immediately.

It was early afternoon. Rebecca's calls from the office were becoming more frequent and Joe's response more desperate. I was now the only staff member out of eighty who was still unaccounted for.

Panic and fear were gradually taking hold. Speculation was rife. Some people suggested that I had flown out, back to Australia – just left without saying goodbye. Others were saying I must be shopping in a department store somewhere, oblivious to the mounting concern as to my whereabouts. This was somewhat easier to believe than the possibility that somehow I had been involved in the bombings and had perished in one of the underground trains, or the bus. This was unimaginable.

The phone kept ringing. Each time he answered it Joe expected to hear my voice at the other end; each time his heart sank when he didn't, when it was just a friend calling to see if we were both ok – 'Hey you. God, it's terrible about the bombs; there's someone who knows someone who he thinks might have been at Edgware Road. Can you imagine? So you guys are ok?' Joe tried to sound convincing, as much for himself as for those who were calling: 'Yeah, I'm ok. We just haven't heard from Gill yet, but I'm sure she's not in danger. She's not on any of those trains usually, so I'm sure she just can't get through. Sorry, I don't mean to be rude, but I must keep the phone line free – just in case.' The callers all obliged, ending the conversation as quickly as possible but probably feeling that Joe was overreacting. How could Gill be killed by a bomb?

Joe received several e-mails during the day, enquiring after us both, but mostly commenting on the horror of what had happened. One e-mail focused on the image of the bus, its metal frame peeled back. The intention was to console Joe, in the knowledge that he would be deeply affected by the fact that a bus had been targeted. Little did the sender know, however, nor Joe himself, how close his connection with events actually was.

A wave of despair now engulfed all who knew that I was missing. The television was constantly on, both Debs and Joe glued to the reports – they were now saying that there could be as many as ten targets, maybe more. It looked more than likely that this was the work of suicide bombers, but just who or how many were involved was still unknown. There were interviews with terrorism experts, police, politicians – all talking and speculating on who was responsible and whether there might be more attacks to come. But as yet there were no answers; no one claimed responsibility.

News updates kept flashing across the screen – more people feared dead, death toll rising, survivors' accounts of walking down dark, smoky tunnels. The hotline number was on the screen as well as a list of hospitals to which casualties were being taken – Royal London, University College Hospital, St Mary's ...

My mobile phone was now responding – at first there was no connection, no sound, then it would ring, and now it actually gave out a message: 'I'm sorry, there is no room for your message at this time, please try again later', or words to that effect. Messages were piling up from my sister-in-law, Jo, my friends at work, other dear friends and family and Joe, each one sounding slightly more concerned than the last. 'Gill, please call me, please. I need to know you are ok. Please. I love you' – was the last message Joe could leave before the box was full.

'Engaged, engaged, bloody engaged – how do they expect us to register her, the number keeps flashing up, saying "to register call ...", but how can we when it is constantly jammed?' Joe slammed the phone down. Debs kept trying the number on her mobile but her signal kept cutting out – there had been problems with the networks all day.

Both Joe and Debs felt as though they were in a black hole, powerless, unable to *do* anything, only sit or pace, or keep calling. Then

Debs suggested, 'I'll go to the hospitals. I'll go and find her while you wait here. What do you think of that as a plan?' She just needed to get out, to do something more constructive than just sitting anxiously in the house. 'I'm just going to pop home and get some supplies. Back soon. Call me if you hear,' she said and headed out.

Debs was relieved to be out of a confined space – two rooms, one television, one phone. They'd both become more and more tense as the hours passed and now it was time for action.

On the short walk back to her place Debs bumped into an old friend. He was not prepared for her sudden outburst: 'We can't find Gill, we can't find Gill. We haven't heard from her. We can't get through on the phone lines. We can't find her!' She told her friend of her plan to drive to each of the hospitals listed and describe me, see if I was there, just do *something*. He immediately put paid to that plan, explaining that he had just got back from near where it all happened and had seen at first hand how London was virtually shut down. There was no way she would get through – police had cordoned everything off. The best thing she could do now would be to go back and support Joe.

Debs knew he was right, but hated feeling so helpless. She no longer believed that I *was* ok. She knew something dreadful – unthink-able – had happened and she was powerless to help me. There was no way of even knowing where I was.

...

One of the directors at the Design Council, Richard, was one of the many concerned callers that Joe spoke to that day. Joe explained that he had been trying, unsuccessfully, to register me on the miss-ing persons list but that the line was jammed, constantly busy with people all trying to do the same thing. Richard and I worked closely together. He knew that I wouldn't be sitting on a plane heading for Adelaide. Plagued by the nagging feeling that actually something was very wrong, he assigned anyone in the office he could to keep dialling the hotline number to get me registered. Then he called Joe back to check if there had been any word but Joe's reply was the same – 'No news. I'll call if there is. I must keep the line free. Sorry. Thank you.'

Joe kept trying and trying to get through to the hotline to no avail.

He was irate, knowing that the first step towards finding me was letting the authorities know that I was missing, yet being unable to do so. He was desperate to let someone know – I could be all alone somewhere; someone needed to know. Meanwhile in the office, people continued to try the hotline, speed dialling the number, whilst across town two other friends were doing the same, all in a fraught race to get me registered.

One by one they got through.

They were asked a series of questions: 'Name, relationship to the missing person, address and contact number'. It was all very businesslike with no room for emotion, or chat; it had to be that way with so many people still trying to get through. Then they were asked for some personal details relating to me – height, weight, skin colour, hair colour, eye colour, distinguishing features or marks. The list went on.

It must have been an extremely emotional experience: to have to sort mentally through the intimate details of a friend or loved one – to remember if their eyes were blue or grey, or blue-grey with a slight tinge of green – then worry about whether they had given enough detail? Enough for me to be found based on the information they had given. Would it be enough to find me? To identify my body?

We all faced our own personal horrors that day – albeit from the safety of their homes or offices, far removed from the force of the blast, my friends and family were suffering, traumatised by what was happening. Sometimes the not knowing is even worse than being there, knowing only too well what is going on. All they had to hold on to was their hope and faith. Until they heard otherwise they had to believe that I was alive; that I would be found.

. . .

Rebecca called Joe again and again throughout the day. I was the only member of staff still unaccounted for. Her last call was around seven that evening. 'Sorry Joe. Any news? Have you heard anything?' 'Nothing, nothing,' Joe replied. 'I won't stay on. I must keep the line clear in case Gill's trying to get through, ok? I'll call. I'll call you.'

Joe was preparing himself, mentally and emotionally – he was waiting now for the call that would change his life for ever, waiting for someone to confirm his worst fears. It was nearly ten hours since the bombs had gone off. Could he really still tell himself that I was held up somewhere, having a coffee to pass the time? He was trying to control his desire to scream and shout, cry and wail. He had to be strong. He had to hold it together so that he could deal with any eventuality.

Debs and Joe tried desperately to hold onto hope. They laughed, saying how they would both be hopping mad, furious with me when I nonchalantly walked through the door, clutching some shopping bags, blissfully unaware that they had both had the day from hell trying to find me. It would be that classic moment where we all cry then laugh and open a bottle of wine, chatting through the day's events. This was their dream – the fantasy that they prayed would become reality.

But it was now gone 8pm – over thirteen hours since I had left the house, slamming the door as I went so that Joe felt the shudder all the way up to our bedroom in the loft. He was finding it increasingly difficult to stay positive.

Neither Joe nor Debs had eaten all day – so that's what they did. Debs prepared some dinner and poured them both a glass of wine. 'We need to keep our strength up. You get the plates, I'll serve.' They had just managed a few mouthfuls when the doorbell rang.

It was nearing 9.30pm; Joe knew it was the police. He looked at Debs. 'Shall I get it?' she asked, looking out of the window to see if there was a squad car. Joe's heart was racing. He could feel the blood draining from his face, then rushing back again, washing up and down his body. He was charged with emotion, but knew he still had to be strong. He had to open the door. He had to face the news – this was what he had been preparing himself for.

When Joe answered the door he saw a man and a woman standing there. He knew they were plain-clothed police before they even had a chance to show their identification and say why they were there.

'You're here about Gill, aren't you? Is she dead or alive? Please tell me.' 'Are you related to Gill, her partner?' they asked, still standing on the doorstep. Whilst they knew that I lived at that address, they didn't know with whom; they didn't know who Joe was.

'Yes, yes, I'm Gill's partner. My name is Joe; we're engaged, getting married in December. Is she alive? Please, just tell me.' Joe needed an answer. Every blood vessel, as Joe describes it, was screaming inside of him. It was as if every fear, every terrifying thing that had ever happened culminated to create one surge, one rush of pure terror – waiting for the words, waiting for the confirmation that life would be changed irrevocably, for ever.

'Can we come in? We need to talk to you inside.' As Joe opened the door wider, his mind was racing: Why did they need to come in? Why couldn't they tell him from where they stood? What had happened? Where was I – maybe I was alive? He gestured for them to go up the stairs ahead of him – our living room is up the second flight of stairs – then he closed the front door and followed them, each step heavier than the last, his knees threatening to buckle at any moment. He wanted to curl up in a ball and put his hands over his ears but he couldn't – he couldn't deny what was happening. He had to be strong. This was his responsibility – I was his responsibility. He had to hear what they'd come to tell him, then deal with the consequences.

He entered the room after them, as ready as he could be, with a composed and calm exterior, breathing in and out and in and out. Calm, calm. This was no time for hysterics.

'My name is Treena and this is Adrian,' said the woman. 'Please take a seat. We need to tell you about Gill. She was involved in this morning's bombings.'

Joe's heart was pounding, every hair, every fibre, raised in anticipation, as though hanging on each and every word. 'Please, tell me. Just tell me –'

'We need you to sit down. You need to sit down first and then we will tell you what has happened. Come on, please sit.'

Joe sat down. He sat down on our red cord sofa. Both Treena and Adrian were professional – they were no strangers to delivering difficult and often painful news. Looking directly at Joe, straight in the eye, Treena spoke slowly, clearly and sympathetically, saying 'Gill is seriously injured. She is in a critical condition at St Thomas' Hospital.'

Joe interrupted, 'Oh my God, is she ok? What exactly happened? What state is she in?'

'We don't know if she's going to make it or not. We're going to take you to the hospital now – we'll know more then.'

Joe stood up. He wasn't shaking, he wasn't crying – he was icy calm. He had been preparing for this news since he first realised that I was involved. With an incredible presence of mind that characterised Joe's behaviour that day he recognised how difficult this situation was for the two officers; he didn't envy them their job and he certainly did not want to add to their pressures. But whilst Joe acted with typical British stiff-upper-lip composure he still needed a little 'Dutch' courage for what lay ahead. He walked over to the dining table, picked up his wine glass and drank the contents all in one gulp.

. . .

Reliving these moments, many months later with Joe, I felt there was something quite remarkable about how he acted that day. I was amazed at how selfless he was, maintaining a mindset that rose above his own distress, his primary concern being to find out what had happened to me and deal with it appropriately, then to relay information in a calm and coherent manner to friends and family.

Whilst he made light of this, claiming he was just fitting into the British stereotype, his eyes none the less filled with tears as he continued to tell me that one of the thoughts he'd had that evening was the prospect of having to identify my body.

We didn't discuss this again, preferring to focus on the positives – on how elated he was at hearing that I hadn't died instantly, and on the belief that where there is even a glimpse of life, there is hope.

. . .

It was an unmarked car, not a squad car. There were no sirens, no flashing blue lights, no high-speed driving. It was just an ordinary car driving four people on an extraordinary journey. Adrian did his best to drive as fast as possible without breaking any laws, but to Joe and to Debs it was agonising, thinking that each red light, each pedestrian crossing could mean the difference between getting to me before I died or after.

Joe stared out of the window as they drove through Kings Cross, then Holborn and across the Thames. He was desperate to shout directions. This was his city, *his* London, the place he loved. He knew every street, knew that there were several short cuts through the busy intersections. But he couldn't talk, he couldn't shout. He left the navigation to Adrian and thought about me. About how he hoped that I would still be alive when he saw me.

On arrival at St Thomas' they were met by a Metropolitan Police liaison officer assigned to the hospital. She showed both Joe and Debs through to a waiting area and Treena and Adrian joined them. The four sat, in virtual silence and waited and waited and waited.

. . .

London had never had an attack of this kind, even during a thirty-year history of being under constant terrorist threat from the IRA. However, this was a new order of terror – a suicide bomb that deliberately targeted civilians en masse, aimed at London's overcrowded and extremely vulnerable public transport system, and, in my case, deep underground. This was the essence of terror, there was no prior warning. No one could have stopped this. We – the entire population of London – were all bracketed together as 'enemies'. No discrimination, no pity, no compassion. Just cold-blooded murder.

Outside, as they drove to the hospital, it had still been a scene of 'organised' chaos: streets cordoned off, emergency service workers down in tunnels or on the streets combing for forensic evidence – something that would tell them just what had happened and hopefully a little more on who was behind it.

. . .

Neither Joe nor Debs was thinking about that then. They were in limbo, in a waiting area where they couldn't be close to me, couldn't see me, where all they could do was wait. Wait and contemplate, try to contain their emotions just a little bit longer, then wait some more.

As our Family Liaison Officers (FLOs) Treena and Adrian were responsible for ensuring that we had everything we needed and for giving us information as and when they could. 'I'll go and see what's happening,' Treena said. 'Are you ok here for a while?' She headed out, looking for someone who might know what my condition was.

Joe was by now in overdrive, on auto-pilot. He sat with Debs and made a list of everyone who should be told what was going on, and those who could act as messengers to the wider group. He called all those family and friends whose numbers he had on him. His tone was cold, matter-of-fact, as he ran through the many 'one-way' conversations with expert precision: 'Gill has been terribly injured in the bombings. We don't know yet if she will live. I haven't seen her, I am waiting to go and see her now – I won't stay on the phone, I need to call others. Can you please let people know? Oh, and tell them not to call me, call Debs ... call Debs. Speak later, bye.'

In the meantime Treena and Adrian had organised a squad car to collect Lily – she was on her way to Scotland to protest along with hundreds of others at the G8 Summit. (She went on all the marches and all the protests, being passionately against the war in Iraq.) It must have hit her hard, as I am always the one to remind *her* to be careful, to 'take a cardigan', to 'prepare for every eventuality'. Both she and Joe would laugh and joke at my expense for hours and Joe would always say, 'Gill, the world isn't that scary. Nothing bad will ever happen to you. Relax!' Lily endured what must have seemed like the longest drive into London that day, not knowing what she would find, not knowing whether her 'step mum' was dead or alive ...

'You can come through now,' the hospital liaison officer said. 'Please, follow me. We will take you to the ITU – she's in the Intensive Care Unit.' Joe was ushered with Debs into another waiting room. He was getting more tense now, petrified that I would die and that he wouldn't be there for me. He finally snapped, calling over to the officer, 'If Gill dies whilst I'm in here, well ... I am ... I will be absolutely furious. Please, can I go through!' He'd made himself clear. The officer agreed and went to gather the medical team who were responsible for me.

'Hello, Joe, is it? We are the team who have been looking after Gill. She's certainly been through a lot. Now before we go through, we must talk to you about her condition.' It was the first time that Joe learnt of my injuries, and, yes, that both my legs had been amputated.

They went on to explain that my life was hanging on a very fragile thread; that they were hoping I would make it through the next 24 hours.

Joe tried to digest all this information, looking up at ceiling to hold back the tears. 'Can I go through now, Doctor?' Joe thought the briefing was over, but there was more. They feared that I could have suffered significant damage to my brain, severe cognitive loss, having arrested twice and been starved of oxygen for extended periods of time. There would be no real way of telling until I woke up and was able to converse.

The seemingly short distance from the waiting area, down a corridor and around a corner, to me, felt like the longest and most difficult walk Joe had ever taken. It was greater than the steps he'd taken to meet Treena and Adrian at our front door, greater than any walk he had ever done. You could walk the distance in thirty or so seconds, but to Joe, it could have been minutes, hours, days. It was as though he occupied a separate time, not of this world, like an astronaut walking on the moon – each step deliberate, yet slow, almost floating in motion.

He was scared, genuinely scared of seeing me, of seeing what I had become, of what I now was – of seeing me with amputations, without legs. Only recently Joe confessed that one of his strongest, secret fears was of the loss of limbs. He said he had often contemplated what it would be like to lose a limb, how he would cope without an arm or a leg. So now, as he turned the corner to approach my bed, he was filled with visions of scenes straight out of a horror film, knowing he was being forced to confront this fear. What did someone without legs look like? What did someone who was effectively 'blown up' look like?

Sometimes, I wish that someone had photographed me so I could know, so I could see myself. But then I think it is probably best that this is not an image I can hold – it is hard enough to hear someone you love tell you of how unrecognisable you were.

My face was shapeless. All the muscles were displaced, having lost all their tone, so there was no contouring. Angry dark bruises covered my usually pale, flawless skin. I had no eyelashes or eyebrows – they were all singed from the heat of the blast – and my hair was filthy, a bloody, matted frizz. Apparently it looked as though I had been electrocuted.

I was pumped with so much fluid that both my face and body swelled, leaving me looking somehow out of proportion and giving the impression that I was much larger than I actually was. I am sure that I would have been very difficult to identify, and whilst I am pleased, ultimately, that I was spared this sight of myself, sadly, it is imprinted in Joe's mind. He has very vivid memories of the moment that he first came to my bedside.

He knew it was me. He knew it was me under the jungle of tubes – there were too many to see where they all went or what they all did but some were connected to monitors that gave off regular bleeping sounds. These strange new noises and sounds somehow confirmed that there was life, setting the ambience for the scene Joe now found himself in.

It was only seconds. He'd had just seconds to take all this in, yet to him, it felt like he had been staring at my face for hours. He was in a vortex. The world had stopped. His eyes scanned me, slowly, yet quickly, flickering, tracing down my body, trying to see past the tubes and dressings, to find my hand. Then he saw. The sheet that was covering me came to an abrupt end, simply falling flat onto the bed, highlighting the inescapable facts of the medical briefing. There it was – the end of me. And now, with absolute dread, Joe was having to face his fear.

Every nerve end, every synapse in Joe's body was screaming with anguish, pain and despair. 'My God, please' – Joe was asking for strength, not only for himself but for me.

Then, in an instant, a wave of complete calm washed over him. It was as if until that moment he was not properly 'there', not in the room, but now, suddenly, a dreadful, terrible moment of fear and horror changed to one of profound revelation. It hit him directly in the heart. What was he thinking? It didn't matter – it just didn't matter how horrific my injuries were, or that I was hardly recognisable, or that I might be facing a life of both physical and mental disability. It didn't matter. Suddenly it all made sense. Everything felt right in the world again and Joe knew his role. I was still his Gill, his lovely, beautiful Gill and he just wanted me back. He would do whatever it took. He would spoon-feed me and care for me around the clock if that's what I needed. All that mattered, all that was vital was that I should live, that I should come back to him, in whatever form.

Joe never wavered from this overwhelming principle. His every action and every conversation from this point on were with one clear intention: to save me – to keep me alive, to keep me fighting.

. . .

'Joe, how are you doing?' One of the medical team in charge came over to sit with Joe for a moment, as he held my hand, gently stroking each finger. 'We will know more when she wakes up. It's hard to really know at this stage whether she has suffered considerable cognitive loss or not. She lost a lot of blood and oxygen to the brain – her pupils were fixed and dilated.' The doctor put his hand on Joe's shoulder. 'We'll keep a close eye on her tonight – we're all hoping that she will make it. She's obviously a fighter!' Joe just nodded, he was looking for a reaction, any reaction from me, but there was none. My eyes remained closed, shut tight.

Joe's mind was drifting. He was thinking about happier times, like when he proposed and how content he had been feeling. It took many years for Joe to realise that being married and settled was a good thing – he had a restless soul. Like a lot of people, he was scared of commitment. How could he be sure – really sure that I was 'the one'?

He was holding my hand. It felt to him like we were the only people in the room – there was no hospital, no nurses or doctors, just us. Joe prayed quietly, his eyes closed, his head bowed, his plea becoming more urgent as the chorus of bleeps indicated that I was barely being kept alive.

Minutes turned to hours, my eyes still shut tight and Joe still holding my hand, listening to the melodic bleeps that came regularly from my life-support machine. The argument we had had the night before was now meaningless. It didn't matter. Nothing mattered. It was just me and him – and he was doing all he could to be strong.

'We've sorted somewhere for you to stay Joe' – an ICU nurse, Jamie, interrupted Joe's thoughts. 'It's an apartment on the grounds.

We use it for patients' families. You could do with some rest.' Nurse Jamie led the way, making sure Joe got settled before heading back to Intensive Care. It was by now nearing 4am – almost twenty hours since the bomb was detonated.

Chapter 4

Journeys of Uncertainty

WE ALL LIVE IN THE KNOWLEDGE THAT ONE DAY WE WILL DIE; life, living the time that we have, is never long enough – we grow, we learn, we love, we hate, we argue, we laugh. It is all a gift. And suddenly it can all be taken away. Suddenly it can all end and, just like that, we die. What is left then? What do we leave behind?

These are questions that I have wrestled with, trying to find meaning, answers as to why so many lost their lives that day. I think about them all, especially those who were in my carriage. I think about the impact their absence is having on their families, on the people that knew and loved them. And once again I am filled with utter despair – a sense of complete powerlessness at having been unable to predict or change the outcome of that morning, unable to save anyone.

...

Like so many people around the world that day, my brother Graham and his family were watching the news on television, a flash report every fifteen minutes or so. Naturally, they felt a connection because I lived in London, but they were not overly concerned. Why would they be? What were the odds that I would be involved? It's just never going to be someone you know, especially not someone close.

Again, like so many others who had friends or family in London, my sister-in-law Jo called, expecting me to answer the phone. She left messages on my mobile and my work line. She still wasn't really worried; she was sure that I would call them soon enough, just to say

LEFT: Looking to the future. Mum and Dad in 1958, just after they were married. The house they were building had just been finished and they were making plans to start their family ...

BELOW: .... And 10 years on. Mum holding me, at only a few months old. Being my mother's angel, she wanted to call me Angela, but Dad insisted I was a Gillian. That was only fair as Mum chose Graham's name.

TOP: First steps. My baby book, opened on the date when I first walked. Graham was there to teach me then, but I never dreamt he would help me learn to walk again, some 30 years later! (© Mike Prior)

ABOVE: A family day out, up in the Adelaide Hills. Dad took this photo, which is a shame as it would have been complete if he had been in it.

RIGHT: Prima ballerina? I always believed I would be a professional entertainer. I spent hours working on dance routines.

ABOVE: **One thing he couldn't teach me!** Graham was a natural at the beach, unlike me; I never learnt to swim which is most unusual for an Australian child living near the ocean!

RIGHT: **Urban sophisticates.** Max and I in earnest conversation at a party in Adelaide. We left for London just a few months later.

LEFT: **Always the bridesmaid.** Graham and Jo's wedding, April 1986. I am standing far left. The tears have dried after my disastrous singing performance in church.

ABOVE: **Not such a wicked stepmother.** Lily and I with Joe's dear friend Maggie, at a May Day festival in Devon, 1999. Joe, Lily and I would often go away for the weekend – mainly to Herefordshire where Joe's parents live.

RIGHT: **All change!** Joe standing proudly in front of his beloved bus, in the last weeks of Routemaster buses in London. Joe drives part time – when he is not lecturing at the Royal College of Art! (© Andrew Cross)

RIGHT: **A momentous day.** The very first picture taken of me after the bombings, whilst still in Intensive Care. This first outing in a wheelchair took me to the hairdresser's, the coffee shop, and then out into the garden. I treasured every one of these 'firsts' in Life Two.

LEFT: **'One Unknown'.** This is the label by which I was identified on July 7, before I became Gill again. I was not overly happy when I realised that I had been booked in as an 'estimated female', born in 1960! It's a rather sobering confirmation of the state I was in when first admitted. But I'm still fascinated by this reminder of the brief period of time when I had lost not only my identity but also any resemblance to the person I had been only a few hours before. (© Mike Prior)

BELOW: Standing proud! A truly memorable occasion, standing for the very first time since losing my legs. Prosthetist Lynsey is gently helping me to take my first steps in 'Life Two' – although only having one new leg made walking rather difficult at first!

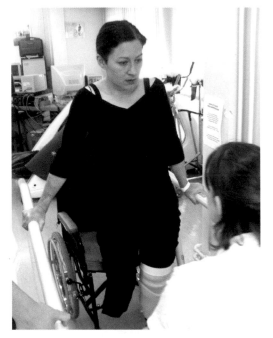

ABOVE: Showing off one of my boys, a month after July 7. This leg was the most seriously wounded, but I was trying my best to bond with it.

BELOW: The Horse Whisperer. Under the expert guidance of physiotherapist Matt, I'm gingerly trying to walk on my two new legs, without bars or a frame. If truth be told, I was completely petrified.

BELOW RIGHT: My balancing act. Matt and Carol teaching me a new trick! But seriously, learning to balance on the ball was essential preparation for learning to walk again.

ABOVE LEFT: Total concentration. Nichola working on my coordination and balance. My posture is definitely improving!

ABOVE: A spring in my heels. This is a rare view of what my 'Elite Feet' look like under the cosmetic covering.

LEFT: Playtime! Actually, Matt has set me a serious and challenging task. Looking at my face, it's clear I was both exhilarated and terrified.

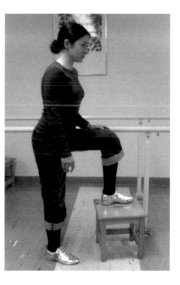

ABOVE: Leg before wicket! My physiotherapists always managed to make the gruelling training enjoyable and varied.

ABOVE: A leg up. Yet another exercise designed to boost my skills and my confidence.

TOP: A break from routine. We would spend as many hours as we could enjoying the sunshine and spectacular views of London by 'our' fountain in the hospital gardens.

ABOVE: The two Jo(e)s! This was the first time that I managed to transfer from the wheelchair to the bench by the fountain – by myself! We were all celebrating this big step towards greater independence.

that I was all right. If not, she would try again in the morning. (Australia is ten hours ahead of the UK.)

They went to bed. Just a few hours later their phone rang – they had just those few precious hours of rest before learning that their lives too had changed for ever.

The operation of getting my brother and the family over to my bedside was in full swing in no time. Graham needed to renew his passport, as did Jo and their kids.

The Australian government's response to the London bombings was immediate; they already had experience of this sort of thing from the bombings in Bali in 2002 where so many Australian nationals had either lost their lives or were terribly injured. Officials were now primed and at the ready rallying with support that was all-embracing – I was one of theirs and they reacted like parents. There was no time for 'red tape' – fast-tracking the passports was only the start; Graham's journey and arrival in London were fully orchestrated within a matter of hours.

For Graham, the support that he and his family received from the government was much needed and greatly appreciated, as was the knowledge that his sister was being treated as an important and valued citizen. At the same time, Graham was cautious – he didn't want Jo and the kids to come to London until he'd been able to see me for himself and ensure that it was appropriate. He didn't want to add to their distress and was trying to protect them as best he could. So they agreed he would come on his own and that they would join him later, once he gave them the go-ahead.

Graham endured what can only have been the most tortuous 24-hour flight, imagining the unimaginable, hoping that I would still be alive when he got there, hoping that I wouldn't die, wishing, praying for everything to be ok. It was all a dream. It had to be. This couldn't really be happening, could it? He was alone, completely isolated in the air, not knowing what was happening on the ground below, not knowing if he would be too late. He was powerless to do anything but sit and think and check the time, and sit and think. He couldn't eat – he just drank coffee. The flight attendants knew his story; they knew why he was headed for London and didn't ask questions – just reassured him as best they could.

Within 60 hours of learning what had happened to me, Graham was in London at my bedside.

...

Joe had had little sleep, maybe a snatched hour or two. For the most part he had been there, by my bed, holding my hand and willing me to live, to fight. I was still on the critical list, my eyes still closed tight.

I woke up, in a panic. Where was I? I couldn't breathe. I wanted the tubes out. I couldn't talk. Where was Joe? Subconsciously I knew that my legs were gone. I knew that when I was in the tube carriage. It was still there – the image of my legs, my poor legs just hanging onto me was etched in my mind. But maybe they were saved? The panic washed through me, as I was gesturing, pointing at my lower body. Every nurse and doctor there knew exactly what I was asking – 'Are my legs still there? Are they ok?'

I remember a voice, softly spoken, telling me, 'I'm sorry Gill. I'm so, so sorry, they couldn't be saved. I'm so sorry.' I then gestured to my arms, asking them to hold each arm up to my face so that I could see that I had both arms. I was terrified, in total shock. What was I? What had happened? Was I just a torso – did I have any limbs at all? How would I live? Would I still die? What was I, what was I now ... oh God, God what has happened?

I was hysterical, rejecting their efforts to console me. I didn't want to breathe through a tube and there were wires all over me – I didn't want them either. I wanted to curl up in a tiny, tiny ball and go to sleep. I wanted to be left alone, to be told that I was having a nightmare, that I would wake up and everything would be as it was before.

But it was all too real. They were confirming my fears – my limbs were gone, forever gone. It was real, it was real, it was all real.

They tried again and again to pacify me, giving me more morphine and stroking my face. Nurse Jamie ran to get Joe. They thought that if I knew he was here I would be ok, I might calm down if I saw a familiar person, someone who loved me.

Joe woke up, startled, unsure for a moment as to where he was – then it all came flooding back. 'Joe, she's awake, she's in a real state. She knows about her legs. I think it's best if you come and sit with her.' And with that Jamie and Joe rushed to my bedside.

'Gill, Gill darling, it's ok my Boo Boo. It's ok. I'm here, I'm here. I love you sweetheart – it's Joe, I'm here.' The morphine was starting to work. That and the fact that Joe was there, that I knew he was there, calmed me down. Once again my eyes closed.

Joe sat by my bed, holding my hand. He learnt quickly how to talk to me by observing the nurses: each time they did something, whether it was changing a line, injecting me or just coming to give me a wash, they would clearly and rather loudly explain exactly what was happening and what they were doing. They had to speak loudly as I had suffered significant hearing loss as a result of the bomb blast, and whilst initially Joe was uncomfortable with the idea of doing this – saying intimate, loving words of encouragement for all to hear – he soon got used to it, feeling at 'home' and at ease with the medical team. They were not only caring for me but also for him.

'Squeeze my hand. Squeeze my hand and let me know that you love me too.' I would give Joe the hardest squeeze I could. It quickly became 'our' thing, comforting him as much as it did me. At least there was now two-way communication.

But the bleeps from my machine were now changing; my vital signs were not good, which is what the medical team had feared. My body wasn't sustaining itself. I was completely reliant on machinery and drugs to stay alive, and my body was now 'giving up'. Maybe receiving the news about my legs had been too much for me to bear, or maybe it was because I was just exhausted. I, my organs, my body were too tired to carry on. No one knew why, why now? I had already got through the crucial twenty-four-hour period, but now I was giving up. The situation had to be turned around. I had to be encouraged to keep going.

...

It was the early hours of Saturday morning, just about forty-eight hours since the explosion. 'Hi mate, you must be Joe. I'm Steve.' Joe was pleased – thrilled to see Steve there, knowing that he was a very old and dear friend of mine from Australia. Steve was upbeat, cheery and positive – that was his nature – even though he had just flown in from

Queensland, Australia! Joe hoped that Steve's very presence would gee me along. He was running out of ideas to keep me fighting.

Steve and I had long been planning his visit to London. He was stopping by to see me and meet Joe en route to Amsterdam where he would be giving a lecture. Steve is a very well-respected academic in his field, specialising in hearing impairment – a Professor for Ears, as I would put it. He certainly hadn't planned on seeing me like this. We'd had other plans: we were going out on the town and Joe and I were going to show him the real London. The art, the architecture and design, the special hidden places that few people know about.

Steve and I were very close, sharing a sense of humour, a love of people and socialising. And of course we both loved Stella. Stella is Steve's wife and my closest friend, so close that it seems almost wrong to describe her as a friend – she is more of a sister to me. She is, in fact, Max's sister and is very beautiful, with that Italian effortless elegance. She could throw on a plain white shirt and look a million dollars in it – I would often stare at her in bewilderment, wondering why it never worked that way for me. Stella always wore White Linen, a fragrance I still buy to this day because when I smell that crisp, clean perfume it takes me right back, right to when we would sit, chatting and laughing in our pyjamas on her bed.

Stella was always there for me. I could always depend on her, and I hope the same was true of me for her. Living on the other side of the world from each other didn't seem to matter; it didn't weaken our friendship. We would write and send each other beautiful cards and she would send orchids every birthday. What we had was special, unbreakable.

I lived with Stella after Mum died. She would comfort me when all I wanted to do was let out all the tears that I had kept in, not wanting to cry in front of Mum. I'd tried to show Mum how strong I was, what a great job she had done raising me, and most of all that I would be fine. I would take the world on ... and I would win! Stella would stroke my hair and curl up with me as I cried myself to sleep.

A smell of homeliness always filled Stella's apartment, with rosemary wafting throughout and Edith Piaf playing on a cassette recorder in the kitchen. I would often belt out a verse or two of 'strange Gill

French' (actually English with a French accent!). Those were special times. I still think of Stella whenever I eat potatoes roasted with rosemary. I can almost smell it now as I write these words. How strange that something as simple as a smell has the power to take you right back to a special moment in time, as though it is happening all over again.

For Steve, hospitals, medicine and medical jargon were all very familiar. He dropped his bag and headed straight for my bed. 'What amount is she on? Mmmm, right, yeah, no that's good – so you're checking her stats every what, half hour? Mmm, good. That's good.' Steve chatted with the medical team and Joe was happy to let him take this role on. After all, he knew what he was talking about, so he could speak to the doctors, gain an accurate perspective and then relay it all to Joe in terms that 'we' would understand.

I had totally relapsed. I was beginning the process of letting go. Joe knew it, Steve knew it and all the medical team knew it. When I woke, I would be in such extreme distress that they would have to administer a heavy dose of morphine and a general anaesthetic to sedate me. It was extremely painful for Joe to witness; he and all the team had been so hopeful just twenty-four hours earlier, and now ...

It was time for action. Steve spoke to the doctors. Their concern was that as long as I was so heavily sedated, my body would not be fighting – I would be at the mercy of the situation, and the situation wasn't looking at all good.

Joe called an emergency meeting with his sisters Rose and Bella and Steve as well. It was decided that they would each take on a job. Joe delegated everything, freeing himself up to concentrate completely on me, on rallying me around. There were phone calls to make, people to talk to, the house, Lily – someone needed to look after Lily. Even though she was nearly eighteen she would still need someone to reassure her, organise food, money and so on. Joe wanted to be able to clear his head and do everything in his power to bring me back.

Steve was on one side of the bed, Joe on the other, each of them talking loudly to me, telling me how life would be fine. Joe was saying how much he was looking forward to getting married, how the wedding would be beautiful, whilst Steve was telling me that Stella and he loved me very much, that Stella would be over soon, she would come and see me. 'Graham should be here tomorrow. We are all here Gill, we are all here – you must come back, do you hear? You must.'

Something got through – the vital signs started to improve. 'It's another miracle Steve, I thought we were going to lose her then,' Joe said. But I still wasn't in the clear. I was still unable to breathe on my own – the next five days would be crucial.

...

The Qantas flight landed at Heathrow and an overhead announcement was made. 'Would Mr Graham Hicks please make himself known to staff? Mr Graham Hicks. Could I also ask passengers to remain seated until Mr Hicks has disembarked. Thank you.'

Graham was met at the plane by Australian Government officials who had a car waiting. They were ready to set off immediately to the hospital, fast-tracking him through all the usual procedures.

Graham had never been to London; he'd never even been on a long-haul flight. He didn't know anyone – not Joe, nor any of my friends, although he had met Joe's sister Bella very briefly when she and her family had visited Australia.

So when Graham arrived at the hospital in the early hours of Sunday morning, Bella was a very welcome sight, standing at the end of a 'restricted access' corridor in the hospital. They hugged and she confirmed that I was still alive, that there was still some hope.

Joe was beyond exhaustion. He was taking a break from my bedside, at his familiar resting spot, the floor of the patients' waiting room – he knew that carpet intimately. He was roused from his partial sleep by someone walking in the room and instantly recognised my brother, even though the two of them had never met. Joe knew the eyes – Graham had my eyes; there was no mistaking that we were related.

Joe stood up and without uttering a single word the two of them embraced, hugging each other tightly as they both wept. Joe wasn't expecting this. He thought that Graham would blame him; he was expecting my brother to be angry, furious, to demand answers. He'd anticipated resentment – that Graham would see him as the reason why I had stayed in London. He knew how strained my relationship with Graham had been – his sadness had been made clear in every phone call or sporadic visit. He was disappointed that we had missed out on so much of each other's lives, that I hadn't returned home to Adelaide and that I'd made the decision to spend so many years away from him and his growing family.

He never really knew my reasons. Maybe I didn't even fully understand them myself. But I'd always had the best intentions. Every time I said I'd be back, for good, definitely at Christmas, I meant it. But then November would come bringing a new twist with it – another reason to stay on, just a few more months. The months turned to years, slipping through my fingers, leaving over a decade's worth of broken promises on my part and disillusionment on Graham's and Jo's. Now, familiar with the pattern, they would respond to each new decision on my part to leave London in the same way: 'Oh that's good. When did you say you were coming back? Great, yeah ... so what's the weather like there at the moment?'

London had a hold on me. I was gripped by its strange beauty and power. I could do things here that I would only dream of in Adelaide. Besides, I couldn't face going home, going back to reality, partly because then I would be confronted with the harsh reality that Mum and Dad were dead.

In London I had lived in my own private fantasy world, able to believe whatever I wanted. I could pretend that both Mum and Dad were still happily pottering away in Adelaide, together, very much alive and in love, living in our grand home in the Adelaide Hills, overlooking the city lights. I never wrote, never even sent a Christmas card; I was far too busy doing all the things I did here. But they didn't mind. They didn't call me – they didn't want to bother me or to intrude.

It was a wonderful fantasy, a defence mechanism that allowed me to cope – or to not cope – with my loss. I just didn't realise that my imaginary world was jeopardising the relationship I could enjoy with the family I still had, who were very much alive and who felt my absence daily.

'She's still barely conscious,' Joe told Graham. 'I'll take you through, but I must warn you, she doesn't look like Gill. Her face is ... well there are no burns to her face ...her eyelashes and eyebrows are singed quite badly, but ... well, she's still critical, but she's fighting. She's fighting.'

Joe led Graham to my bedside. It was a route, and a routine, that Joe now fitted into: 'You wash your hands with this and you have to put an apron on. Basically, the main worry is that she will get an infection – it could be innocently carried in from anyone who visits and an infection now could kill her. They've drummed the sterilisation routine into me.' Graham did as he was shown. He didn't say much. He was eager to see me, to see for himself what had happened to me.

'Here she is. You need to talk loudly – we think she understands everything but we can't be sure until she is off the ventilator and speaking. She squeezes your hand; that's how we communicate.'

'Gill, Gill, Graham's here, Graham's here darling. Are you going to wake up to see Graham?'

I opened my eyes and looked over. I couldn't move my head, just my eyes. He knew I recognised him and although I tried to offer a smile, a sign, the tubes concealed it. All I had to communicate with were my eyes and the fingers on my left hand (my right hand was a bundle of bandages, covering all the burns). I was desperate to reassure Graham, to reassure everyone for that matter – I didn't want the people who loved me to feel helpless. I wanted to give them a sign that I was back in control, that I was fine and that as soon as I could, I would be chatting about 'nonsense' and ...

It broke my heart to see the pain and distress in their faces. I closed my eyes.

Graham sat at my bedside, holding my hand, telling me not to die, not to leave him. He looked at me, all tiny and broken in the big hospital bed and remembered how desperate he had been to have me in the world – a buddy to play with. Before I was even born he'd told all his mates at school that he had a little baby at home and – boys being boys – they hadn't believed him. 'Yeah right', they'd said. 'Sure you do.' In his wisdom Graham had blurted, 'If you don't believe me, come and see for yourselves after school.' And so they did – a long line of boys followed Graham home. 'Can they see the baby?' Graham had asked our bemused mum, and she, in her gentle manner, had taken Graham aside and explained that the baby was still in Mummy's tummy. Graham had frowned. (This is a family facial expression that we all share, so much so that when Alex – Graham's son – was born, Jo said, 'Oh no, he has that bloody Hicks frown!') Clearly he was faced with a problem. What could he say to all these boys? How could he produce a baby? Then he'd had an idea: 'Mum, if they can't see it, can they feel it?' And, with that, Mum had stood patiently as each boy placed his hand on her stomach, then left, amazed at actually having felt an unborn baby. Graham had delivered! He was so proud.

Graham's memories of our childhood all came flooding back to him. He thought of how he had helped Mum to take me home from the hospital when I was born. It was a very clear memory for him as it was seen as quite controversial at the time – seven-year-old boys were just not considered responsible enough to carry new babies. Matron was not pleased! But Mum knew how eagerly Graham had been awaiting my arrival, how much he already loved his baby sister. She knew he wouldn't drop me, that he would carry me like a precious gem, a delicate piece of porcelain. She wrapped me in my special 'leaving hospital/going home' blanket and passed me to Graham. He was so proud. He was this little person's big brother; he was going to look after me, protect and watch out for me, always. I was *his* little sister.

It wasn't long before I was able to reach the kitchen counter. It wasn't long either before Graham realised the true wonder and beauty of having a small slave – someone to act on his command. 'Look,' he would say, 'this is how I like my vegemite sandwiches made: lots of margarine, spread it properly ... are you watching?' And I was expected to make them like a pro' from that day on.

As I got bigger, the tasks and the 'tortures' became more elaborate. A particular favourite of Graham's was to place a beanbag over my head and sit on it! He would watch my legs kicking frantically, and hold me down whilst I squirmed, desperate for air. Gradually the kicking would slow down and Graham would get off – catching me just before I fell unconscious! Of course, I knew deep down he loved me; he just had his own 'special' way of showing it!

Graham was father, mother and brother all rolled into one. He felt he had to be as both Mum and Dad were at work. He was always there for me, going to secondary-school parents' evenings, picking up my report cards, getting cross if he thought I was going off the rails or hanging with the wrong crowd – you know, that adolescent stage that we all seem to go through! And I respected Graham's opinion. I looked up to him and wanted to do well at everything in an attempt to impress him. I really wanted him to be proud of me; I remember feeling how important it was for me to let him know that his efforts weren't wasted.

. . .

I think it was the strength of family that made all the difference at this tragic and very fragile time. Whereas Graham and I only have each other, Joe is one of four. He has three siblings – Rose and Bill who are older, and Bella, his younger sister. Rose is married to Steve, they lead busy lives, mostly travelling the world as Rose consults on Chinese art; Bill is married to Alicia and they have two children, Julian and Jasmine; and Bella's partner is Lyndon and they too have two kids, Will and Mez. The family is scattered throughout the UK, but bound together by their artist parents, Antony and Elizabeth. Both of them are in their early eighties, yet still painting, undaunted.

Their home, in rural Herefordshire, is a beacon to which, like migrating birds, the family comes together every Christmas, Easter and on other important occasions to celebrate. We have shared many a happy time there.

Graham too married into a large, vibrant family – Jo is one of eight children! It was quite overwhelming for him, coming from the quiet and humble Hicks family, to marry into such an outrageous and delightful bunch.

I remember being a bridesmaid at their wedding and also the honour of being asked to sing. The day was one that Mum had dreamt about, I'm sure, ever since Graham was a small boy. She was beaming and Dad had even made it to the wedding too. There they both were, proud parents watching together as Graham and Jo walked down the aisle. The time came for the signing of the register – my cue to perform a truly fabulous rendition of 'Evergreen'. The nun started playing the organ, filling the church with chord after chord, waiting for me to sing. But it sounded wrong. I didn't know what the nun was playing, but I knew it wasn't 'Evergreen'! What could I do? I couldn't let the side down. Mum and Dad were smiling at me, waiting. The pressure was mounting. So, with a deep breath, I started: 'Love, soft as an easy chair, love fresh as the morning air.' In an effort to drown out the sound of the organ, I sang louder but it was hopeless. I kept on though, right to the bitter end, by which point the tears were streaming down my face and Mum's head was bent down, I guess in shame. I ran from the altar, hysterical, mascara lines streaked all down my tear-stained cheeks.

Singing was my passion, my dream. I always imagined that I would either be a dancer or a singer – an entertainer of some description. Although I went to many a dance class it was singing that I seemed best suited to. So, never one to do things by halves, I went off to study voice with a coach who tried to teach me the beauty and wonder of the *classically* trained voice. But I always felt an urge to add my twist to a classic and whilst my teacher was desperate for me to master being a soprano, my heart wanted to sing soul, the blues, jazz. Our relationship was, at best, turbulent, but we managed to stretch it out for at least two years before parting company.

I learned a lot from those lessons though – how to breathe properly, how to use my diaphragm, how to gain greater control over my body. And, as Graham drove me to my classes, it became 'our' time. He would always play the same cassettes – the Eagles, Fleetwood Mac, Brian Ferry, or maybe the Sweet's 'Ballroom Blitz'. Many a time we could be seen, driving along head-banging and playing air guitar! Well, it was mostly me actually – Graham was always the responsible one and he was the driver, after all.

...

'You look like you could use some rest.' Joe could see that Graham was shell-shocked and exhausted. 'This is my sister Rose,' he said. 'She'll take you back with her tonight. She has a cottage in Richmond and you can stay there as long as you like, ok?' Graham reluctantly agreed, passing my hand back to Joe. He kissed the top of my head and said, 'See you in the morning Gill, ok? See you in the morning.'

Already there was a real comradeship between Graham and Joe. They were brothers, united by their fierce love for me, brought together by this horrific event. Joe knew at once that the bond they had formed would last a lifetime.

...

I still had no idea of what had happened. I knew I had lost my legs. I knew that I was very near death. I knew all of these things. But what I didn't know was how? What? It was Monday, my fifth day in intensive care. I was still on the life-support machine, still tangled in a maze of wires and tubes, but I was getting slowly stronger, becoming more and more responsive, more alert and more expressive.

Joe was still concerned though, still worried that I had suffered brain damage. From what he could tell, I had no short-term memory. He would be telling me something, continuing from an earlier visit, but I would offer a surprised expression, as if I was hearing it for the first time. He was trying to find ways to communicate with me, other than squeezes of my hand, or blinking eyes. He thought getting me to write something down might be a good idea so he went to get a sheet of paper and a pen. He could see that I was eager to say something, to get something off my chest. He placed the paper down and helped to guide my hand as I formed letters on the page. The first letter was D, the second, I, the third letter was wobbly but it was an E and the last was D. DIED. Joe scrunched the paper up, afraid to interpret what I had meant by this. Did I *want* to die? Had I died and was I now trying to tell him something about death? Joe and I have never discussed this since.

I motioned to Joe, pointing at my legs – where they used to be – then tried to shrug my shoulders. Joe understood that I was trying to ask what had happened. 'Do you know what happened?' I turned my head a little from side to side. 'Darling, my darling Gill, you were in a bomb, a terrorist attack. It was a suicide bomber darling. That's what happened.'

My eyes opened as wide as they could – I was completely shocked. A bomb. It was a bomb! How could I have been in a bomb? Me? I suddenly felt like I was choking. It was very difficult to breathe. Tears rolled from the corners of my eyes. I just couldn't process this information – it was too difficult to believe. I was in a bomb. It was a bomb that led me to be in this state. A bomb. A suicide bomber. Someone had blown himself up – deliberately, willingly, ended his own life and tried to end mine.

My heart and mind were both trying to understand, to remember, to recollect the event. But all I could do, my automatic response, was to cry. I cried and I cried in utter disbelief. I was trying to remember but I couldn't. My mind was still protecting me, shielding me until I was ready to deal with the truth. Joe squeezed my hand. 'It's all right. You're all right. You're alive, you're safe now. I'm here and I love you so much. I love you my Boo Boo. I'm so happy to have you back. I'm so happy that you survived darling. I love you so very much.'

I was overwhelmed. So many emotions were hitting me, ripping through my very core – I wanted to scream, to pull out all the tubes and run away, yet, at the same time, I wanted to be still, to absorb, to digest, to mourn and to feel sad. I also wanted just to pretend that I hadn't heard what Joe had told me. To pretend that he was wrong, that it wasn't a bomb. But I couldn't make a sound as I had no voice, I couldn't run as I had no legs and I couldn't hide. All I could do was to squeeze Joe's hand back. This let Joe know that I loved him too, that I needed him and that I understood what he was saying. I knew I was safe.

My throat was raw. I had a rasping cough and I was still bringing up large black fragments of whatever it was I had ingested and inhaled in the tunnel. I was desperate for the tube that was wedged into my throat to come out. I hated being so restricted, unable to talk or to drink from a cup. I badly wanted something to soothe my throat – I could have drunk an ocean dry.

I would motion over to the nurses, through the mass of lines, tubes and wires and will myself to say, 'Water, water'. But I couldn't say the words. I couldn't say anything because of the tube in my throat. I had to use my eyes to communicate, and somehow the nurses would always know exactly what I wanted or what I was trying to tell them. It was almost like a telepathic connection.

'Here's some water. That's it. Is that better?' The nurse would drip some water from the tip of a giant cotton bud into the side of my mouth. The drops would just glide past the tubing, down to my throat. It was so wonderful; those tiny drops of water were my greatest pleasure.

'More, more, more,' my eyes would say, expressing my unquenchable thirst. Joe called the cotton buds lollipops and he would laugh at me wanting another and yet another. The nurses taught him what to do, showing him how to drip the water into my mouth, then wipe around my lips – they were still black from the carriage – and the inside of my mouth. I would close my eyes and think about a time when I would be able to drink a whole cup of water. It seemed almost unimaginable but it kept me going. It was one of the things that helped me to stay positive, my own personal goal: to drink an entire cup of water.

I knew then that I would appreciate every cup of water I would ever drink for the rest of my life. I would never take anything as simple as this for granted again, ever. And to this day I never have. Every sip is still valued and savoured and I am grateful that I am able to enjoy the very pleasure.

At this point it felt like I was only conscious for an hour or so each day. But I was building on this daily, stretching my waking state out, until I reached four, maybe five hours a day.

I still didn't know *exactly* what had happened – I guess my memory of the event was being preserved somehow. I must have had a permanent look of confusion and distress on my face, but the nurses and doctors never for a moment wavered in their care or concern. It takes very special people to do what they do and I think the very best of those special people were caring for me during this time. And whilst for me, as the patient, this was just a period of time I had to 'get through', with the prospect of leaving, moving on always there, for them it's different. They continue, caring for the next person and the next, just as they did for me.

July 11, 2005

Dear Friends and Colleagues of Gill

By now you probably will have heard that Gill was injured in last week's bomb attacks. Gill's condition remains critical, but she continues to make good progress.

Gill's family is extremely grateful for the extraordinary support of the medical team treating her, the London Ambulance Service, the Metropolitan and British Transport Police, and the Australian High Commission.

We have decided to set up an e-mail group in order to keep you informed about Gill's progress and we intend to provide updates as regularly as possible. We are aware that at this short notice we might not have included the addresses of all Gill's friends and colleagues and would be pleased if you were able to pass this information on to others who are concerned for Gill's welfare.

However, we should add that there has been a good deal of inaccurate speculation and unpleasant press intrusion into Gill's case. Please be aware of this, as apparently innocent enquires from unfamiliar sources might not be what they seem. We would ask you to understand that our overriding concern is that as Gill is not yet able to decide on what information is released, we have no choice but to be circumspect with the detail.

As we lack the means to handle numerous enquiries at the moment, this e-mail is intended as a one-way communication, but any really important messages or queries can be returned to this e-mail address. We fully appreciate that you wish to offer your support and will be anxious to see Gill, but we have been advised by the medical team that now is not yet the time for Gill to receive visitors. We can assure you that Gill is receiving superlative treatment and that the medical team is meeting all her needs at present. Gill certainly will appreciate your help and support in the future, so please be patient.

We will send further updates as soon as we're able.

With best wishes

Joe Kerr and family

I so wanted those tubes to come out. I longed to be able to drink, but most of all I wanted to talk. I had terrible fears that I wouldn't talk again, that maybe my throat and my lungs were burnt in the explosion – I had inhaled a lot of smoke, dust and dirt. But I couldn't allow myself to dwell on it. We would know soon enough.

Debs said she knew that I was still Gill and that that I would be fine when she realised that I seemed more concerned for the welfare of the nurse who was checking on me, than for myself. I would be seemingly in a deep, deep sleep when a nurse would come along and say, 'Gill, I am just going to check your feeding tube, ok?' I would suddenly come to life, eyes wide open, trying to nod and make 'contact', then, once the nurse in question was gone, I'd be off again, straight back into a deep, deep sleep. Debs would smile because, she said, that was so 'me', so 'Gill' – worried about everyone else, making sure that everyone was being looked after, despite all the obstacles.

But by Tuesday morning I was one major tube free! I could only whisper, but this was enough to at least have a conversation. Joe filled me in on what had been happening over the last five days. My memory was sketchy; it was like remembering a dream, with bits out of sequence, floating in and out of my conscious thoughts. I couldn't believe that so much had happened, and yet, once I was told, snippets of my memory did return. I had a vivid recollection of our priest, Father Kit coming in, preparing to console me and pray for me at my bedside. However, when he came close I sat straight up, stared him right in the eye and declared, if in a weak, thin voice: 'I will walk down the aisle in December Father, you can be sure of that.' To say he was shocked is an understatement! He looked at my little bandaged body, saw the obvious ending where my legs had been amputated, but didn't doubt that he would see me walking on December the tenth! It was from this moment that we formed our relationship – one of mutual respect and love. He referred to our meeting in his next service, observing that he had left the hospital strangely uplifted by the experience, an emotion he hadn't expected to feel. He had felt my strength and my optimism.

Being able to communicate, albeit in a whisper, was an important step for me and all those who were around me. I was now able to converse with the nurses, the doctors, even share a joke (I still had the same stupid sense of humour and I had a whole new captive audience!). I was really becoming Gill, properly meeting those who had cared for and loved me as an unknown patient. And I was proving to Joe, to Graham and to all concerned that I was not severely brain damaged, that I was coming back – that I was the 'old' new Gill.

• • •

It hit me like a lightning bolt. Suddenly, all the events of that morning flooded back. I wasn't prepared for it. No one was prepared for what I was about to tell them. The smell. It was the smell that came first. Stuck in my nostrils like nothing that was familiar, indescribable, acrid. Death. I started to panic. Before my eyes, right before my eyes it was all there. I was back in that carriage, sitting there, propped up against twisted metal, I could see my legs, I could hear the screams. Oh God, I knew. I knew exactly what had happened. I have never felt such despair. Every emotion rushed through me like a fireball. I wanted to know every detail now, everything – to see the pictures from the newspapers, to see who did this, his name, his face. There were four, four! My train was just one of the sites hit – it was beyond comprehension. Joe showed me the newspapers; he had kept them all.

I skimmed one article, staring mostly at the picture of the suicide bombers – there was Germaine, he was nineteen years old. I stared and stared at his face, trying to see behind his eyes, trying to get a sense of why. I looked at the pictures, the faces of all those who didn't make it out, those who were killed. I was transfixed on those who were in my carriage, who were there at Russell Square station with me. I wanted them to know that I knew: I remember, I know you were there, I thought. I was there with you – I know. I won't forget your faces, your names. I won't forget because I was with you. I sat with you. I was so close to you, I could feel you. I am so filled with complete sadness, with a deep sorrow for you, for those you left behind.

The days seemed to blur, to join into one continuum. I couldn't keep track of the day or the time. Just the moving of the sun and the shadows in the room let me know if it was late afternoon or early evening.

• • •

'It's time to get you moving, Gill – to get those reflexes going!' Claire, my intensive care physio was extremely caring, but very firm – she would have me up at any cost!

The world looked very different once I was sitting up, and after the dizziness stopped I was able to take in my surroundings: the proportion of the bed in relation to the wall, where the nurses' desk was and the machines – all the machines I was hooked up to looked smaller and less intimidating once I could see them. (From lying down I could only hear all the bleeps and not see what was making them.)

I couldn't sit up for long – I was still too weak and my body wanted to rest. Claire came to get me up two, even three times a day. She became central to my daily care and I was growing very attached to her (and, I suspect, she to me).

'Right, now what's your catching like?' Claire was getting balls of bandages ready to throw before I had a chance to answer. Graham started laughing, explaining to Claire, 'Let's just say that Gill isn't exactly gifted when it comes to being a sportsperson. She was always the one who was picked last on any team, not really known for her natural ability to catch or throw for that matter, so this should be interesting!' I smiled but I was determined to concentrate on this task. I knew it was all part of my recovery plan – they weren't just making me catch things for no reason – and right from that early moment, I was dedicated, ready to listen to all I was told and to do my best to follow instructions exactly.

'Ok, Gill, are you ready? I'll just do a slow one. See if you can catch, ok? Ready?' I nodded, and reached out to catch the bandage ball. 'Excellent, good. Now let's try some more.'

I caught every one and Graham was dumbfounded. He raced out, saying 'I've just got to go and make a phone call.' He called Jo and the kids. 'Guess what?' he said. Jo was concerned, thinking Graham was calling with bad news. 'Gill can catch! Gill can catch!' They both screamed with joy and laughter on either end of the phone. Jo too knew the significance of this report. It was amazing – I couldn't catch before, and now I could! Maybe I would be sporty after all? Then again no, no, let's not get carried away!

Graham came back in the room to find me reaching high up to catch the most difficult of throws. Claire's face showed her amazement – she was thrilled at my skill and Graham and I decided that I was obviously now empowered by some strange source, like Spiderman or Superman. Or something – maybe a chemical from the bomb, or one of the drugs that I was being given in hospital – was giving me this 'superhuman' ability.

Secretly, I loved being able to catch – and I loved it that Graham was there, that he was proud of me.

July 13, 2005

Dear All

I'm delighted to bring good news. Gill is still on the critical list, but is making excellent progress and is in good spirits. She's fully conscious and is talking with her family and the medical team. Last night when Joe arrived she was sitting up in bed drinking a cup of tea, watching 'Newsnight'. The advice of the medical team, however, is that she's still not able to receive visitors; so please be patient. It's clear that Gill is looking forward to seeing her friends and colleagues again, but appreciates that this can't happen yet. In the meantime we can't begin to convey how grateful we've been for all the kindness and support we've received from everyone in the last few days.

We're deeply saddened to read reports of reprisals against British Muslims, and have absolutely no wish to see retribution inflicted on innocent people.

More news to follow as soon as it becomes available.

With best wishes

Lyndon Jones and Bella Kerr, on behalf of Joe Kerr and family

I was desperate to get out, to see the outside world again, to feel the sun on my face. I felt like I had been in my hospital bed for a lifetime. My hair was still filled with the evidence of the explosion, I badly wanted to have it washed, to feel more like 'me' and less like a patient, or a victim of terror – just Gill.

It was becoming important, suddenly very important, for me to let the medical team know who I was, who I *really* was. I felt a great need to be accepted, re-introduced if you like, as one of 'them' – a young, sassy, fashionable woman who would never dream of leaving the house without lipstick, or worse, with filthy hair! Normally my hair was cut in a sharp, sleek bob. I liked it blow-dried straight, so that the sheen and gloss would be more apparent and I loved to smell clean and perfumed. I knew I was getting better, turning the big corner of recovery, because these things were now starting to matter to me.

'Is there a hair salon here?' I asked Claire. 'And if there is can I go and get my hair washed?' I was expecting Claire to laugh and say 'No, sorry, there is just no way we can move you,' but she didn't! 'I'll go ask the doctor, but I don't see why not. The only problem is infection, but if we covered your wounds and watched you every moment, limiting the contact you have with others, well, it might be possible.' I couldn't quite believe it – this was actually going to happen.

Jamie and Claire 'customised' a wheelchair: Jamie fastened a food tray to the front of a standard chair and padded it with several pillows. My stumps had to remain straight – I wasn't allowed to fold my knees, but they were wadded so heavily that this would have been near impossible anyway. Claire and Jamie then carefully lifted me down from the bed onto the chair. It was incredible. My heart was just about ready to leap out. I was so excited!

Graham, Joe and Steve all stood in amazement. 'Let's go!'

This was the first time that I had seen the entrance to Intensive Care, the first time I was in a lift, the first time I was exposed. I didn't care. I just kept my gaze down, trying not to catch anyone's eye. It was so exciting.

I was wheeled into the salon. It wasn't huge so with me in my wheelchair, the three boys, Claire, Jamie and another intensive care nurse; we filled the room and spilled out into the corridor. Treena, our FLO, turned up too. I don't know how she knew – must have been that brilliant detective mind – but there she was, peeping over Graham's shoulder and waving at me.

My hairdresser was called Ariana. She was a Kiwi and she was just fantastic. She didn't bat an eyelid; she made the whole event very 'normal' – so much so, that I was half-expecting her to ask at any moment if I was going somewhere nice for my holidays!

This was the first time that I saw myself in a mirror – I looked drawn, tired, ill, bruised and battered. I didn't look like me at all. I showed Ariana where I normally part my hair, then I looked down. I didn't want to see myself any more. I closed my eyes and just focused on enjoying the thought of clean and professionally blow-dried hair. Ariana noticed a large burn on my scalp. The area – about the size of an apple – was bald. She covered it over and asked, 'Would you like it turned under, or flicked out?' What a wonderful question, the best I had had to answer since July 7. I just said, 'Do whatever you think looks good.' Whether it was flicked out or in didn't matter – I was there and that was the triumph. I was there, alive and with *clean* hair, in a salon.

July 17, 2005

Dear All

Gill is still getting better every day and although she tires very easily she has managed a visit to the hospital hairdressers – yes, girls, there's never an excuse to look less than your best!

She is, of course, still being monitored extremely carefully and is still seeing only a limited circle of people, including police family liaison officers with whom she is talking and helping to work out what happened on the 7th. Family liaison officers working with another Australian patient have visited with kind donations thoughtfully requested from the Australia Shop, so Gill is enjoying Vegemite and other exotic delicacies from home. She has also met up with another patient who was injured on the no. 30 bus. Members of the family attended the Trafalgar Square vigil and were moved by their private conversations with Ken Livingstone who spoke with real humanity to all the families involved.

If you are praying, add one for the dedicated staff who are looking after Gill, and maybe a little one for slightly cooler weather – the hospital doesn't seem to be coping well with this surprising heat ...

Thanks for your replies – it means a lot to Gill and to us.

With best wishes

Lyndon Jones and Bella Kerr, on behalf of Joe Kerr and family

The triumph of being out – of being able to get my hair 'done' was just the start of the miracles that would unfold that day. Jamie and Claire were so impressed with my 'new' look that they decided we should all celebrate. So before I knew it, there we all were, all outside, in the grounds, looking out at Big Ben. With the sun on my face and a gentle breeze wafting over it was truly the most amazing experience – a first.

Joe bent down, squeezed my hand and asked 'Darling, Boo Boo, would you like a café latte? Do you think you could cope with some coffee?' It was as if he was reading my mind. 'Could I? God, this is amazing. Am I allowed?' Jamie nodded and Joe disappeared, returning minutes later with cappuccinos and coffees for everyone! As I took my first sip the smell of the coffee knocked through the senses, wiping away in a moment all the clinical smells. It represented everything that was 'normal' to me. This was what I did, every day. I was the queen of coffee and here I was, after everything, after dreaming and imagining being able to drink water, after having the drops slide down from the cotton bud into my mouth – here I was having a café latte on the river bank, looking at the London skyline, with my brother, with Joe, his sister Rose, Steve, Treena, and of course the two extraordinary people that made this moment possible, Claire and Jamie.

It brings tears to my eyes just writing about this. I guess I will never be able truly to articulate what it meant, and indeed what having a coffee outside, or even just being outside meant! I have Jamie and Claire to thank for this – for taking the risk, for putting the rules to one side and for giving me, in the process, much more than they could have imagined. I would go so far as to say that what happened that morning made me feel 'human' again.

They had no idea of the magnitude of what they had given me. They had given me so much - they gave me a holiday from being a patient, but more than that they had taken on the responsibility of giving me back my life: Life Two. How could I ever repay them? I felt a great need to show how much I appreciated them, how I would never forget, how I would treasure this intense time that we were sharing.

Something shifted that day so that we were no longer carers and patient, but friends. I knew that these people were special and that they would remain a part of my life. Jamie bent down and beamed at me. 'This is all right isn't it?' I nodded. Yes, it was much more than just all right.

July 19, 2005

Dear Folks

All seems to be progressing so well at the hospital that some friends and family have given us donations to hand on to the staff in whatever form is thought best. Joe and Gill's brother Graham suggested that I open an account so that if anyone feels like adding to this fund (and there is certainly no intention that you should feel obliged) they can. We really want to thank the people who saved Gill's life and who will make her future possible. The a/c is called 'Gill@St.Thomas' . It will take a few days to set up but it will mean that we can gather any gifts together to buy something that makes a difference for the staff and the ward – any suggestions?

I'll have more news of Gill soon.

Love to you all

Bella, Lyndon and all the family

Chapter 5

A New 'Normal'

INTENSIVE CARE WAS QUIET. There wasn't the usual bleeping of the life-support machines as all the patients had either been transferred to wards, or unfortunately, had not made it through the night. Nobody stays too long – that's how the ICU works.

Today it was my turn to be transferred to the vascular ward, where I'd be with other patients who had either lost limbs, or who were awaiting amputations. I tried not to think about that – how it would be to see others who looked like me.

I really didn't want to go, to leave the little haven that we had created. We'd had our routine and strangely it had become very 'normal' to be there. I had 'my' bed, with a mattress that had a motorised wave system to alleviate bedsores and any discomfort that may arise from being bed-ridden. I knew the nurses as they gave one-to-one care, so naturally I had become close to them all. And I had begun to look forward to their respective shifts, knowing that if, say, Nurse Stuart was on for the night, we would watch some TV together, drink cups of tea and chat about his new baby niece. The nurses had watched over me day and night, watched every breath I took, monitored every beat of my heart; they come to mean so much more to me than just nurses.

The ICU was the place that marked the beginning of Life Two for me: it was where I woke up and where I had my first memory of feeling safe. Two weeks in Intensive Care felt like a lifetime, which of course in some senses it was, being the only life I had known since losing my legs.

Nurse Karen wanted me to feel good, confident, about facing my new 'home' on Luke Ward. So out of the blue she looked at me and said: 'Right, I'm going to give you a nice shower before you go – what do you think of that?' It wasn't really a question, more a statement of intent. And of course I would want a shower – I had just never even thought of asking. I mean, a shower? I wouldn't even have dreamed it was a possibility; the very idea of that kind of 'normality' seemed like a distant dream to me.

Karen must have known intuitively how much I longed for a 'proper' wash. As good as they were, the sponge baths never left you feeling really clean. I knew that if anyone could make it happen, Karen could. She was that sort of person. When she started a shift you always knew it, as she made her presence felt; she was chatty and happy and her personality filled the room. She always had something funny to tell me, mostly lovely stories about her kids, especially the youngest, baby Jack – or Jack Jack as she called him. I was so at ease in her company and I really loved her for that.

I sat up in 'my' bed and waited. It was late morning and there was a rough target of getting me on my new ward soon after lunch. I could just about make out Karen ringing around various wards looking for an available shower: 'No, I need it big enough to get both me and a wheelchair in ... You do? Uh huh, yeah, great – we'll be there in five.' And with that she reappeared saying, 'Right Madam, your shower awaits!'

'Are you sure? You mean I can actually have a shower?' I was delighted but incredulous. I still wasn't sure how it could be done, given my weak physical state and the heavy wads of surgical dress-ings that replaced my legs, not to mention the weepy, painful wounds on my ribcage. These were the result of the chest drains, and they too were surgically dressed. Oh, and let's not forget my right arm, which was covered in a special dressing to promote healing where the skin had been badly burnt. All these areas had previously been delicately sponged and sanitised with saline solution or something similar, so how on earth could I now have running water flowing all over me?

But then again, who was I to question? I was desperate to wash away the residue of the bomb completely, and with it the haunting memories of being trapped underground. It was as if the dirt and the memories were ingrained, still making me feel filthy. I could smell the acrid aftermath on my skin and my fingernails, despite Steve's brilliant manicuring efforts, were still clogged; the remnants of that scene that clung to my hands almost told a story of their own. I so wanted, so longed to feel like 'me' again – to put myself back together. Could a shower do this, could one shower give me back some of what I thought I had lost?

The bed was lowered and Karen and another nurse who was heavily pregnant helped to manoeuvre my battered little body into the wheelchair. They were so careful not to hurt me, as if I was made of precious porcelain, as if with one slip I could shatter into tiny pieces. Karen whizzed around, getting shampoo, conditioner, body wash, towels – and then we were off, the three of us, on my big washing adventure!

Along the way, Karen pulled over and bent down to talk directly in my ear. She confessed to me that she had never actually showered a patient before – she had done sponge baths yes, but had never actually physically showered anyone. She was trained for intensive-care nursing, so all of this was foreign to her! Her unexpected confession completely put paid to the very few reservations I may have had. Being such a private person, the thought of going off to the showers with someone else had been filling me with dread, but knowing that this truly was a first for us both somehow made the situation bearable. I could even see it as being comical. I knew this would be a moment that I would never forget; I don't know why but I just knew that I would look back on it with a large grin and maybe a tear.

There was a lot of fumbling, laughing and cursing. It was no easy feat getting me close to the shower area and by the time we managed to get the wheelchair into the cubicle we were all in complete fits of laughter. My loud bursts of hysteria were uncontrollable and I worried that this 'side-splitting' entertainment would open up the stitching on the chest-drain wounds!

The commotion and giggling must have alarmed some of the passing nurses and patients. All they knew was that a patient from the ICU had been brought down to use the showering facilities; certainly, no one was expecting a routine that would have sat comfortably in a 'Three Stooges' sketch!

What must it have looked like? I had been transferred onto a plastic chair and was now sitting stark naked with my stumps stuck proudly straight out in front of me. They were wrapped in plastic bin liners and tied tightly around the very top of my thighs to stop any water from getting on the wounds. A catheter bag was plumped up on the side of the chair. What a sight! Karen and her assistant were doubled over, crying with laughter, knowing that the fun had only just begun! What hope was there for us?

The amazing thing is that I was able to let myself go in a situation that just a fortnight before I would have found very difficult and un-dignified. And I was happy – already so happy, and I had barely even reached the promise of warm, rushing water. I was just happy to be there – naked, clothed, in bin liners – it didn't matter, we were all sim-ply 'in the moment'.

I was learning things about myself at such a rapid pace, it was hard to take them all in. And what I learned at that very moment was that I could let my inhibitions go and find dignity from deep within me, through my laughter and my acceptance of a scenario that was potentially very difficult for us all.

We soon realised that the only way we could reach the taps was if Karen was actually *in* the shower area with me! So, without hesitation, she got in right next to me, in her powder-blue uniform 'scrubs', soap in one hand and nozzle in the other. Karen wasn't bothered about get-ting wet – she made it quite clear that all she cared about was me and making me feel 'normal'. I saw this quality in all the nursing staff – they were all so selfless. I felt privileged and blessed to be in their care.

I put the nozzle close up to my face and shut my eyes tight. It was an amazing feeling – in the same league as having my first cup of water or first cup of tea! I didn't want it to end and could have stayed there forever under the stream of warm, running water. We'd stopped laughing by this point and both Karen and I were very quiet for a while. This allowed me to let my mind drift, to believe, for just a moment that I could have been anywhere, that I could have been back at home, standing up in my own shower, raising my face to the flow of water, as I did every day.

But this shower was different. It was monumental in fact: my very first shower without legs and the very first shower I'd had needing someone to assist me. It was yet another one of those moments that would mark the beginning of a new normality.

It was time for the shampoo to be rinsed out. Karen had found a nice conditioning treatment so she put that in and combed it through. It felt like the ultimate spa pampering treatment, only without the champagne on arrival! (Maybe St Thomas' could give this some thought?)

'You'll turn into a prune if you stay there much longer and I am thoroughly saturated, so let's get you dry,' Karen said. And with that she turned off the water and began the process of getting me back into the wheelchair.

Karen and her assistant dried me down, got me into a clean gown and off we went, down the corridor, the squelch, squelch, squelching of Karen's wet shoes leaving a trail behind us. We all got in the lift, trying very hard to look as though everything was perfectly normal – dripping wet intensive care nurses walk around hospitals all the time, don't they? We kept our eyes down and made our cheeky grins as inconspicuous as possible.

Meanwhile, Joe and Debs had been out pounding the London streets to find some suitable pyjamas for my big entrance on Luke Ward. It was time to get out of the backless gowns and what a relief that would be! Life on the ward would be very different. I would be more 'active' and there were also all those who were waiting patiently to visit. Seeing people for the first time ... How would I prepare for that? What would I say? What would they say – what could they say? Just as long as they didn't cry too much, I thought, I would be all right.

I didn't want people to cry for me. I guess I thought of crying as a sign of pity. I was alive and thankful for that and in my mind I was very clear that everything past this point, everything past the moment where we were sure that I would live, was a bonus, whether I walked or not. I was happy just to be there, to have had a shower and to have been able to appreciate it as though I'd been showered with gold dust.

'Hello darling,' Debs said, mouthing the words clearly and directly to my face as she now knew that I couldn't hear a thing and the only way I could understand was by reading people's lips and facial expressions. Debs and Joe were both beaming. 'We have some really great things; hope you like them.' They had several large shopping bags, which was a very good sign, particularly as they'd had to work to a very tight set of criteria: I had to have tops/shirts that buttoned down the front (so that the heart monitor pads and wires were easily accessible and the two chest wounds could be re-dressed every day); they also had to have arm holes wide enough that I could slip my arm through without disturbing the bandaging around the burns. Then the bottoms – the legs had to be three-quarter length and wide enough to ensure there was enough room for the heavily bandaged ends to actually poke through unrestricted. Last, but by no means least, I needed an elasticated waist with enough 'give' for the catheter bag to be pulled through. All that was on the practical side, but they also had to be stylish of course!

Joe left us girls to it. So there we all were, Debs, Karen (who now had dry scrubs on), the nurse who was pregnant and me – going through each of the 'outfits' in turn to see which worked and which didn't. It was funny because it felt so 'normal' – we were discussing amputated limbs as if I had always had them, as if everyone did. A bit like 'Do my stumps look big in these?'

There is nothing like the wonder of women to organise a scene. Whilst I was looking through the purchases, Debs was packing up all the paraphernalia I had accumulated – photographs, cards, statues of angels. I guess it really was high time I went, given the volume of 'stuff' I'd amassed – not what they were used to in Intensive Care! It felt a bit like packing your bag for your first day at school, when the nerves begin to set in and you get that strange nausea stirring in your stomach. 'I don't feel so good,' I said. 'Can't I stay in ICU a little longer? I think I need monitoring,' I went on, only half joking.

Is it really possible to feel so attached to a place that can only be associated with the seriously ill and the dying? I loved them all there, really loved them, and I didn't want to go. This was what I knew – the routine that I now felt comfortable with. I didn't want any more changes. I wanted it to stay just as it was: them and me in our lovely, sterile sanctuary.

I would miss 'my' wonderful medical team: Mairi, Jamie, Anthea, Katie, Jo, David, Perry, Stuart and Helen from Queensland. I would miss them all. I trusted them – they had brought me back and sustained my life. I had so much to thank them for.

'Some things in the safe belong to you,' Karen said. 'I'll go and fetch them and then we can start getting ready for the off, ok my love?'

I wondered what could be in the safe? The police had already returned to me my watch and big silver ring but I hadn't yet opened the 'official' bag they came in, clearly labelled in large, yellow letters 'Evidence'. I just couldn't bring myself to clean them, to wipe the blood away. So every now and then I would just look at them through the clear plastic bag.

I had never taken Mum's wedding band off and had worn it every day since she died. It was inscribed, 'Don and Alison, December 13, 1958' (their wedding day). Her ring – their ring – was a major part of my collection of memories of them. Wearing it had always made me feel close to Mum and I felt bare now without it. It was too painful to think that her ring was gone, lost in the blast, so I just didn't think about it – I couldn't ...

There are three things that Mum left that I have held dear all these years. One is a birthday card, the last she wrote to me, knowing that she wouldn't be with me the following year, or any year after that. The second is her Bible; this was presented to her as a little girl when she completed her Sunday school lessons in the late 1930s. The last and most precious of all was her wedding ring.

'Ok, I need you to sign for these.' Karen was back and she was carrying a bag, similar to the police evidence bag. In it was Mum's ring! I couldn't believe it, but there it was – bloodied and dirty, just a small black circle – no mistaking it. I was overwhelmed with emotion. That ring symbolised so much and I'd thought it was lost forever. I hung my head as I held the bag and sobbed. It was all too much.

Debs, Steve and Joe were there, all ready to take this next step with me – to get me settled onto the ward. Joe wiped away my tears and Steve said something funny which broke the mood. And that was it – Karen pushed me in the wheelchair as I waved goodbye to Carol at the reception desk. 'Bye, thank you, bye ...'

...

A nurse called Comfort was there on the ward to greet me – she had a huge smile and a soft tone of voice. I couldn't hear her very well, so I just smiled back and retreated into my own private world. As she pushed me along the corridor I saw rooms where people were lying on their beds, mostly with one leg bandaged where an amputation had just been performed. I closed my eyes. I didn't want to look at them or to see them looking at me. Joe held my hand and walked beside the chair.

Comfort said something that sounded like, 'Har we rr, thus rum,' to me, and I realised she was telling me this was my room. Everyone sounded the same now – the world was muffled. Somehow I'd adjusted though. I'd adapted to hearing in this way and it was now just another new 'normal'.

Joe and Steve were greatly excited by the view from my new room; we looked out across the Thames, with the Houses of Parliament and Big Ben staring straight at us. They both ran to the window like little boys, Joe eager to impress Steve with his knowledge of London. 'Look, see that building down there, well that was built in 1735, originally for the royal household' (or something along those lines!). I couldn't actually see anything – well, except for Big Ben – as the wheelchair couldn't sit flush against the window due to an air-conditioning system on the ledge. However it was a magnificent view and I felt very grateful to be in my own room. I was also feeling very displaced though and wished I was back 'home' in Intensive Care.

The room was starting to get very hot, as the sun was now streaming in the window. Comfort pulled down the blinds and then started lowering the bed. 'It gets really hot in this room,' she said. 'I might see if I can find a fan for you,' and after getting me into the bed, she left to find one.

I suddenly wanted to be on my own for a while. I wanted to get used to the idea that this would be 'home' for the foreseeable future. I didn't feel like talking and I was too tired to strain to listen, so I asked Joe and Steve to go. Steve said to Joe, 'I know a really great Thai place on Lower Marsh – shall we go there and get something to eat?' and with that they were off. It was good to see them both looking so happy.

I glanced around the room. The walls were pale blue and there was a bathroom – I had an en-suite! I hadn't been to the toilet yet and until I saw the bathroom I hadn't even thought about it. I'd had the catheter all this time – my very own plug-in portable loo! How would I go to the toilet? My mind started racing. Would I always have to have someone help me just to go to the bathroom?

I just didn't know what to expect from life in the future. What can you expect when you are lying in bed, unable to get in or out unless someone comes to help you, unable to turn from side to side, unable to wash? Naturally I didn't know yet what I would or would not ultimately be able to do. I was still too weak to be exploring my boundaries. For now I was content to either just lie on my back or sit up – my only two options. But then at least I had options!

The hours ticked by and Joe and Steve were still out. I was getting more and more distressed. I couldn't reach anything – my books, water, everything was on the window ledge, out of my reach. The television had yet to be connected and so I was there, in silence, with nothing to do, without any distractions.

The tears began to flow and wouldn't stop. I didn't have a tissue, so I had to keep wiping my face with my pillowcase. I was crying because I felt so alone – even though I had asked to be left on my own. I wanted some water, but I couldn't reach it and didn't like to call for a nurse – I didn't want to make a fuss on my first day. I felt awkward, scared. I didn't want this, didn't want to be here. I wanted to have my legs back and to go home. And I wanted to know, to really honestly know that everything would be all right. But this was something that no one could tell me – I was the only one who could face my own future.

Steve and Joe breezed in, laughing about the use of language – the differences between Australian and English – then Joe saw my red face and puffy eyelids. 'Gill, honey, what's wrong?'

'I don't want to be disabled, I don't want to be disabled, I don't want to be ...' I was becoming more and more distraught, trying to explain how distressed I had felt at not being able to 'do' anything, to reach anything, to get out of my bed and into the chair on my own.

Both Joe and Steve felt terrible for leaving me, even though it had been at my suggestion. 'This will never happen again, ok Boo Boo? We will always make sure before anyone leaves you that you have everything you need around you. We are all learning. I'm so sorry.

It's ok my sweet darling, it's ok. Everything will be ok now. I'm here, Steve's here, Graham will be back later. Ssshh, ssshh.' Joe held me as I cried into his chest. I must have drifted off.

July 21, 2005

Hi Everyone

Good news again from St Thomas', where I got to see Gill this morning. She, Graham, Joe and I went and had a coffee in the garden beside Westminster Bridge. Gill's in excellent fettle and the hospital staff are very impressed with her progress and determination to recover. She's out of Intensive Care and now in a room enjoying a good view of the Houses of Parliament.

Yesterday Gill had some rather important visitors: the Australian High Commissioner AND Prime Minister John Howard, who enjoyed a half hour chatting with her. Gill was then mentioned on this morning's 'Today' programme in the review of today's Australian press, where they quoted Howard remarking on Gill's inspirational courage, refusing to allow her injuries to interfere with her and Joe's wedding plans.

So it's all good. With luck Gill should be able to start seeing visitors soon, although each day still involves a good deal of medical procedure, and a couple of hours of physio', all of which is pretty demanding.

Will try to get another e-mail out on Monday.

With best wishes for the weekend.

Lyndon

'Good morning Gill, my name's Emma and I am the ward sister. Welcome to Luke Ward. If there is anything, and I mean anything, you want or need just let me know, ok? There will be a security guard placed permanently by your door, just outside, so that you are not disturbed by the press; I believe there was quite a bit of attention when you were in ICU. Anyhow, we will monitor all post and phone calls, so you don't need to worry – we just need you to get better.'

Emma held my hand all the time she was speaking to me. She had the most magnificent blue eyes, she was firm and in control, but she was also very loving and caring. I trusted her immediately. 'Now, it's ward rounds today, in a moment actually. Every Monday Professor Burnand, your surgeon, and the resident doctors come and see each patient, so we will just get you ready for them. I'll get a nurse to come and take your bandages down.'

This was all so new, a different routine that I had to learn. I was filled with a mixture of anticipation and apprehension. What would they say when they saw the wounds? Would they be pleased? Would there be more surgery?

I sat there, with the now undressed wounds seeming to glare back at me. I didn't want to look at them, so I stared at the door waiting for the doctors to enter. You certainly knew who was in charge when the Prof was in the room; he suffered no fools and was quick to correct a wrong answer or someone who was unprepared. I was terrified of him (in the nicest possible way!). Would he think I was a good patient? Was I healing as I should be? Would I be told off if I wasn't?

I had so much to be grateful to Prof for: his confidence in surgery meant that I had knees. The first time I met him was in Intensive Care. I was quite groggy, but he looked directly at me and said, 'We have managed to save your knees which is very good news; we will have to see how we go – there was so much damage and the right leg will take a considerable time to heal, but for now you have your knees.' I didn't know why this was so good – to me, if I didn't have legs, whether or not I had knees didn't really make much difference. But I was pleased, because he sounded so pleased, and at least there was a bit more of me with knees than there would have been without!

I think I loved Prof from the first conversation I can actually remember. It was back in Intensive Care again, after everyone had learned who I was and knew a little bit more of my background. He was standing there at my bedside and said, 'It all makes complete sense now.' I must have looked puzzled. 'Now I know you are a bloody Australian; my wife's an Aussie and she too is a tough ol' bird!' We both laughed and I knew that we would enjoy having a similar sense of humour from that point on. I think he was just as amazed as everyone that I had pulled through, that I was now in recovery overdrive and not clinging to life by a thread.

I always greeted Prof and the doctors with a big smile – I was still riding on the euphoria of having survived. Prof and Emma warned me that I should expect to 'hit a wall' sometime. They said that what I was experiencing was completely 'normal' but that at some stage the reality and enormity of all that had happened would sink in and it was more than likely I would become a little depressed. They weren't being negative – they were just concerned and trying to prepare me.

I was determined to face each challenge with a positive attitude, drawing on the strength that I knew I had. I made a promise to myself that I will never break, ever – that Life Two would be celebrated at every given opportunity. I would never take anything for granted again, I would strive to be a better person, to make my life count and to make a difference. I simply could not allow myself to indulge in the sadness of the situation. Of course I did miss my legs – both in a practical and abstract way. But I had no idea of what to expect from the future; all I had was the here and now and I had to remain positive. I had arms, I had my mind, I was still me in every sense. I was so lucky to have so much.

The people I loved and who loved me needed me to be strong too. There was so much to come – the challenges of rehabilitation, of learning life again – and every bit of progress I made, they made with me. When Claire threw the bandages at me in that first week in Intensive Care I caught them – to my surprise, but more to Graham's! That one achievement was something we both shared and that was important. That's why I had to stay strong and positive ...

Suddenly it was lunch time. Mila, a nursing assistant, came in with a tray. 'Lunch darling?' she said with a big smile. I didn't want a lot; I still couldn't manage much solid food. But my favourite chocolate nourishment drink was there, so I just sipped on that. Joe went off for a nap. He, Steve and Graham had a routine – a rota – so that they could each spend time with me and also so I would never have to be alone.

Steve was planning his trip to Amsterdam; he had a lecture to give the following week, then he would be flying back home to Australia. His eyes filled with tears every time he tried to tell me that he would have to go soon, so we just didn't talk about it. We had now, and that's what we focused on. And there was so much to look forward to as well – we were all excited as Graham's family would be joining him within the next two weeks and Steve was going to be replaced by my dear friend Stella. So the pain of goodbye would be softened a little by the knowledge of the new arrivals.

I hadn't seen them all in so many years. I couldn't quite believe that they would all be in London! I was worried about Alex and Maddy's (my nephew and niece's) reaction. I didn't want them to be shocked or upset or to feel uncomfortable around me. All I was looking forward to was the idea that I could give them each a huge cuddle, so it was important that they were able to be near me. Neither they nor my sister-in-law Jo had met my Joe. I was hoping that the two Jos would click. I knew they both liked a drink, so hopefully some bonds could be made over a beverage or two!

July 24, 2005

Hello Everyone

Gill seemed very well today and in particularly good spirits because of the arrival from Australia of her sister-in-law Jo and her nephew and niece Alex and Maddy. The Day Room at St Thomas' was the scene of some intensive Adelaide gossip, as well as Gill discussing with Maddy whether she'd be prepared to play the young Gill in the Hollywood film that Gill's already planning!

On the down side Gill's still suffering from severe hearing loss, but the hospital are hoping this should improve in time. She's still managing to keep off the painkillers, hoping that some short-term discomfort will yield dividends in terms of a quicker recovery. She's eating loads of fruit, and seems to be getting better by the day.

Keep Gill in your thoughts, and keep praying, if that's the right thing for you, for her continued progress.

All the best

Lyndon, Bella and family

There was already some mail on the ward for me, addressed just to Gill Hicks at St Thomas' hospital. As Emma had told me when I arrived on Luke Ward, she and the nursing staff had all been briefed to open anything that looked suspicious as no one wanted me to be hounded or upset by the press. Emma had a keen eye and would always manage to intercept any mail that had indeed come from a media source. Joe and Graham had discussed this with me and we'd all agreed that I should be allowed to recover privately. If and when I was ready to speak to anyone it would be for the right reasons, but neither we nor the hospital wanted press intrusion at this moment in time.

My security guard was a devout Christian from Sierra Leone. He was adamant that no one would break through on his watch. He had seen death – we didn't speak about it much, but I could sense his sorrow and I think that's why he became very protective of me. He would always follow behind us – if Graham pushed me outside to get some sun, he would come too, if I went to the Day Room for a change of scenery, he would come too. It was the closest I have ever come to feeling both a celebrity and a criminal all at the same time! I don't know what the other patients must have made of it; they must have wondered who I was. What had I done? Why the security? If anything it was actually drawing more attention to me.

Anyone entering my room was questioned (except Joe, Graham and Steve, whom the guard knew). On one occasion he asked a visiting occupational therapist why she was in my room and what the nature of her visit was. It was not long after this that the hospital management, with our complete agreement, decided that security was no longer needed. Later on though we would see each other in the grounds where he was either assigned to another patient, or on general security for the hospital. He would always stop and ask how we all were.

. . .

On Wednesdays Dr Luff, the rehabilitation consultant, did his ward rounds. He would be joined by the physio' team and my assigned occupational therapist. Dr Luff was the person who first raised the possibility of a future in which I might be able to stand and walk, when

Joe and I had met him in Intensive Care. Up to this point I'd had no idea what losing my legs meant and, without saying as much to each other, Joe and I had both been thinking that I would be confined to a wheelchair. So what Dr Luff had to say was completely unexpected, a stunning revelation. He was confident. He had held my hand and looked me straight in the eye, saying: 'You will walk out of here Gill, I guarantee you that.'

I was mesmerised by the tone of his voice, whilst not quite comprehending what the words meant. His confidence, his unwavering confidence helped me through – because, yes, I did think he was completely mad! I didn't want to be the one to say that I didn't have any legs, so how he thought I would actually walk out of hospital was beyond me! But it was his manner – there was something about him that I trusted, and if Dr Luff said that I would walk out, then that's exactly what I would do. Who was I to argue? Once again, I felt so lucky to have such amazing people caring for me, all being so optimistic.

It was on hearing this extraordinary news that an idea was planted in Joe's mind: maybe our wedding plans wouldn't have to be abandoned after all, and perhaps we might not even have to postpone the date we'd set, now little more than five months away.

'Good morning, how lovely to see you. You know Matt and Nichola, the physios, and Brooke – g'day!' Dr Luff made the introductions. I had already met Brooke the OT in Intensive Care; she was also Australian with that wonderful Aussie friendliness, and we had clicked immediately. Matt gave me a knowing smile and explained that he had already met me. In fact he had seen me a few times whilst I was 'away with the pixies' in Intensive Care. He remembered it vividly as did Joe, but sadly I had no memory of it at all. 'I hope I didn't say anything too embarrassing,' I said, slightly worried that Matt seemed to know me so well. He just smiled again, not answering me directly. Bugger, I thought. That meant I must have done something! Oh God, I knew it. Oh well, what the hell – he looked like he was up for a laugh.

There was a lot of work to be done and the physio' schedule would start almost immediately. There was no messing about, these people were going to get me walking as soon as they could – starting with lessons in how to get from the bed to the wheelchair, then swiftly progressing to how to drive it. You might think all these things were self-explanatory and would come naturally, but there were tricks and techniques that I had to learn and master if I was to know how to turn the chair left or right, or how to stop. (I thought I should listen as carefully as I could to this as it was probably the most useful thing I could learn. I'd have hated to be freewheeling straight across Westminster Bridge, after all!)

Brooke had come prepared with a sliding board, or what is called in the trade, a 'transfer' board. It's a piece of tough plastic, a bit like a very small surfboard, one end of which was placed under my bottom and the other on the wheelchair. Very gingerly (especially as I still had the catheter) I slid over to the chair! 'Nice one,' she said loudly, in a thick Aussie accent. It felt like I was embarking on a journey with friends. We were all similar in age, but I don't think it was that so much – there was just a connection, a thread that bound us all. Impossible to explain.

Dr Luff then proceeded with the team discussion, covering the physio' regime, what I could and couldn't do at this stage and how they were to concentrate on my core stability, teaching me how to balance in preparation for prosthetic legs. Whilst Dr Luff talked to the team, he placed his hands gently on my shoulders, pressing down each time he was making a pertinent point. His manner was extremely reassuring and I had great faith in him.

Matt and Nichola told me they would come and collect me tomorrow to show me the gym area and get started. 'We'll start with just one session a day, then build from there, ok?' Nichola said. 'I'll come and get you and Paul around eleven am.' (Paul was another survivor who had actually been in my carriage but whom I had yet to meet.) Matt gave me a little wink, then both he and Nichola left with Dr Luff to see the remainder of the patients on ward rounds, whilst Brooke stayed behind.

'Are you ok? You'll be fine. It'll be hard but I know you'll be great ... I'll come back a bit later, maybe take you for a stroll around the grounds?' In the meantime, she left me with a wheelchair. This could be dangerous, I thought. I now have transport!

I was so excited about being mobile. Learning how to get into the wheelchair was liberating for me as it meant I was no longer stuck in bed. Joe and I decided to go down to the Day Room at the other end of the ward for a change of scenery. This time as I passed my fellow amputees I smiled and waved, feeling rather pleased with myself because I could now wheel myself along in the chair (most of the time Joe pushed, but sometimes I enjoyed the freedom of doing it myself).

There we were, surrounded by windows on to the most amazing, breathtaking view. We felt so lucky that we were here at St Thomas' looking out onto the Thames, the London Eye, County Hall, the sky a picture-perfect blue. My perspective was only from the wheelchair though and I wondered what Joe was able to see – how different it might be standing rather than sitting. I thought I would test my skills in turning the wheelchair, so I spun around and around and around, giggling and gasping as a deep laugh tried to break through my scratchy, raw throat. Each turn of the chair was followed by another gasp, creating an interesting sequence.

Caroline, who as we later learnt was the senior nurse in charge of the ward that day, burst in: 'Oh my God, is she ok? Is everything all right?' Joe said she looked absolutely horrified. She had obviously panicked on hearing strange gasps coming from the Day Room, and thought that a patient was in cardiac arrest. Instead she had found me, spinning around and around, shrieking like a child at a funfair. I stopped the moment I realised she was standing there. I was mortified – so embarrassed. What must she have thought? What impression had I made? Neither Joe nor I could look her in the eye as we promptly went back to my room!

...

The days seem to evaporate fast. No sooner had they cleared the breakfast tray than I'd be settling down with my evening medication and a cup of tea.

The sunsets were glorious, London was a blaze of summer pinks and oranges, offset by a slight texturing of blue clouds. All this was just outside my window, peaceful, tranquil and beautiful.

In the hospital I was sheltered from the aftermath of July 7. I wasn't exposed to the deserted streets or to the worried, silent, more watchful commuters. My world was in the hospital; my Life Two was all being played out here.

Joe would normally leave me around eleven pm to go back to his quarters. Our ritual goodbye, generally lasting for half an hour or longer, would start with Joe saying that we both needed our rest and that it was time to go. I, on cue, would then respond with a plea, saying that I wasn't tired and wanted to talk to him about 'stuff'. He'd know that I was stalling, or procrastinating, and so the weaning process would begin. We would arrange everything that I could possibly need around me, so I didn't need to worry, then he would walk out and slowly shut the door. Through a small square window in the door Joe would wave and place his hand on the glass, blowing me kisses. I would wave and blow kisses back. He would then press his hand on the glass and leave it there until I turned off my reading light. 'Love you, love you,' I would quietly say.

We did that every night.

...

I would often wake in the night, panicked. I'd be filled with sudden memories of being in the carriage – it was the smell, the smell, that acrid mixture of burning, chemicals, dust, skin, hair burning. The smell stayed, lingering – no matter how clean I was, no matter how many days, weeks later I couldn't get rid of the smell. It was all around me. That smell is still with me to this day, something that has become a part of me, shaping me like everything else from *that* morning has done.

I would sob for hours into my pillow. I was still in disbelief that I was there, that I had witnessed so much destruction, needless, senseless destruction. I hadn't been able to help anyone, to save anyone except myself. I could hear the screams ...

I hated the nights. It was like I was experiencing two separate lives: my daytime life was for the most part filled with laughter, a positive outlook and focus – focus on getting up and getting well. But the nights, once Joe left and I was alone, were overtaken by nightmares, flashbacks and sorrow.

I would cry until I simply didn't have any tears left to spill, then wake up to the smiling face of one of my nurses – and so, a new day would begin. Then I would be happy again – happy that I had survived and that I had this chance.

July 28, 2005

Dear All

Gill is making good progress with the physio' and is sleeping better at night. Having her family here from Australia has kept her in very good spirits but may be tiring her out too!

A gang of us descended on the Design Council on Tuesday and were made very, very welcome. Gill's family wanted to see where she works and to meet some of her colleagues and friends, and we all wanted to bring news to them. Gill was very pleased that this contact had been made and that her family now has an understanding of her work and how well she will be cared for when she returns.

As Gill's physical condition improves she is coming to terms with her injuries - today she met and talked with someone who suffered similarly in a train crash more than ten years ago. There are still ups and downs, as you would expect, but facing some of the big emotional hurdles now will help with coping in the future - the time when a wider circle of friends will be very much needed.

Thanks for all the cards and other things - her room is decorated with them and they give her great pleasure, as have all your e-mails and messages of love and support.

Now please pray for more sun and less rain because Gill likes to get outside each day to drink a latte.

Love to you all

Bella, Lyndon and family

On my second day on the ward Beatrice came in all set to give me a sponge bath and was visibly taken aback when I looked up and said:

'I can have showers. I've had one before – all we need to do is cover my stumps with bin liners. It works, no problems.' This was exactly what Karen had told me to say and it did the job!

Beatrice, who was originally from Africa, was very tall, very strong and so beautiful too. She had a lovely manner – once again I had the perfect person to be with at a time when I felt most vulnerable, when it would be so easy to lose all sense of dignity and pride. Unlike Karen, who had me in hysterics amidst the antics of the first shower, Beatrice was calm and quiet, gently moving the shower nozzle over my back and giving me the control to wash myself. I didn't feel embarrassed or ashamed. It felt natural being in the shower area with her. Of course, I'd have preferred not to be, but there was a beauty in the moment – the nurturing, almost mothering way in which I was being cared for was so special. That morning – that memory of having a second shower – will stay with me always, as will the kindness and tenderness of Beatrice.

Getting my pyjama bottoms on was always the tricky part at the end of the washing process. Initially I had to transfer from the wheelchair to the shower chair, then afterwards when dried sufficiently, we would place a towel on the wheelchair and I would transfer back across. Whoever was washing me would have to untie the two plastic bags that covered my stumps, then gently put one leg at a time into a trouser leg. I would wiggle and wiggle until the trousers came just up to my thigh wound, then, using every ounce of my strength I would hold myself up with my arms whilst the trousers were whooshed up under me – there was a small window of a few seconds in which to do this as I just didn't have the strength to hold myself up for very long. This was why the elasticated waistbands were so important!

One of the greatest inconveniences of daily life was my catheter bag. It got in the way of every action, including climbing in and out of the wheelchair. As per usual we used humour as a means of coping with this. Joe and I adopted a pet name for the catheter – 'Cathy' – and we took 'Cathy' everywhere with us; you might say that we were inseparable. Joe would make jokes about me not having anything to match with my 'Cathy' bag, fearing that it would never catch on as a fashion accessory!

So I was delighted when I was told that the catheter would be coming out soon – this would make life easier in some respects, harder in others. One of two lovely student nurses who had been assigned to my ward one was given the difficult and unpleasant job of removing the catheter. 'Breathe in,' she said. 'It's like a tiny balloon and I'm just deflating it. It should pop out, deep breath. It's coming ... there we are, all done.'

Strange how the body works, but as soon as the catheter was removed I needed to go to the toilet. Negotiating this was going to be a case of trial and error. Firstly the dreaded commode was summoned and my thoughts turned immediately to Mum. She had had a commode installed at home. It was just by her bedside; she was near the end then. I hated that commode. Well, I hated what it represented, and now, here I was waiting to use one myself. How was I going to manage this and retain absolute dignity? Was absolute dignity even an option any more?

I only used the commode that one time, vowing to myself that I would find another way. That other way was Joe! I was reluctant to involve the nurses in any care that was as intimate as going to the loo, showering was about the limit. I needed to gain back some privacy and independence and, of course, to maintain my dignity.

So, when it was time to use the toilet again, Joe picked me up, me in 'koala' position and carried me across the room. He set me down on the loo, held me upright, then cleaned me up and took me back to the bed, my arms locked around his neck the entire time. We were delighted with our new system although we thought it best not to divulge our technique to Emma, the ward sister, or the other nurses for fear that it might not be such a hit in terms of Health and Safety regulations.

The next area of my privacy to reclaim was the shower. I would speak to the nurses in the morning, and just as we had done in Intensive Care, see if they could train Joe to shower me. How brilliant it would be if this worked, if they allowed it – then all I would be reliant on them for would be the administering of the medication and daily injections.

I could never have foreseen a time when Joe would be 'caring' for me in this way. Or that I would share the most private and intimate areas of my life with him. We weren't like that as a couple. We were close, yes, and we had lived together for seven years, but this was different. This was a level, a degree of unity that I could never have imagined possible. Our 'new normal' manual was being co-written – by the two of us, about the two of us, *totally* sharing Life Two. I relied on Joe. I needed him. And he rose to the position – he wanted to be that for me, to be that close to me, to share the entire experience with me and never let me feel that I was facing it on my own. We were in our own impenetrable little bubble, a cocoon that we could retreat into whenever the outside world got a bit too much for us. I never had to doubt Joe's commitment or his love. It was one less piece of the future for me to worry about.

And so, we set about creating our own routine; we were a team and we ran like clockwork. Thanks to our dearest family and friends, who tried – and succeeded – to lift the burdens and pressures of every-day life from our shoulders, Joe and I were able to concentrate fully on each other and on what was needed each day. We could focus exclusively on my recovery and on carving a new life, day by day.

The breakfast trolley would arrive between 7.30 and 8.15am.

It was wonderful when Deborah, a nursing assistant, was on duty. She would spring into my room singing, 'Morning morning mo'orning,' in a way that could have come straight from a West End musical. She was a real extrovert, the absolute life and soul, and I adored her. She would often breeze in for a chat, telling me all about her holiday plans; she loved the sun and warm 'beachy' places and she had the most amazing golden tan. I felt extremely close to her. She was great with all the patients and as she went from room to room she would leave a trail of laughter behind her. She was larger than life and had a pres-ence that made her seem part of the very fabric of the place.

At 8.30am Joe would arrive with coffee: one cappuccino, one café latte. He would often enter the room to find Deborah and I in fits of laughter over something and would not say a word, just sit down, open his paper and begin to read – hoping that the moment would pass without incident. Deborah and I would exchange a wink and a smile – Joe wasn't a morning person, well at least not before his sec-ond or even third cup of coffee.

By 9am we would be ready for the shower. Joe would run through the checklist: two bin liners, tape, three towels, body wash, antiseptic wash, shampoo, conditioner, wash cloths and a clean outfit for the day (the choice of which normally changed three times before we'd even left my room!).

. . .

Now that I'd be going to the physio' gym, I would need an outfit that was flexible enough for all that lay in store for me. Thinking about this new stage made me nervous. For me there was a strange comfort in familiar routine. I was getting used to being institutionalised, even beginning to enjoy it. I felt like I had been there for years – as if I was becoming part of the essence of St Thomas'. But it seemed that just as I'd reach a point where I was getting used to daily life, easing into my environment, something would change, crank up a gear.

As Graham had pointed out in ICU, I've never been very sporty. In fact, I remember saying to the staff behind the front desk when I opened a gym membership through my work, 'Hello, it's so nice to meet you. This is probably the first and the last time you will see me.' We'd all laughed, but it was true – I never did go into that gym again. To think, if only I had known that one day I wouldn't have legs, boy, would I have tried everything going – cycling, climbing, running, swimming. But that's life isn't it? You never know what is just around the corner! I did just love having the plastic membership card in my wallet though – you know, flashing it now and again so that people would think I was dedicated to my fitness. Ah, the things we do ...

Matt was going to come and collect me. The physio' area wasn't on our floor; actually it was in a different building. I was wearing loose tracksuit bottoms – black of course – and hoped that was the right choice. Joe was going to be handing me over to Graham; sports and physiotherapy felt like a natural area for Graham to be 'in charge' of. And this way Joe could have a break and Graham and I could spend some time just together – it was a good system; everyone was happy.

This would also be the first time that I would meet Paul and I felt quite apprehensive about this. One of the nurses had told me a little bit about him when I was leaving Intensive Care – that he had lost a leg in the blast.

The only other survivor that I had met at that point was Emma, who was involved in the bus bombing; our meeting had been brief but powerful. She was in bed in an intensive care ward on the floor below mine; I went in to see her with Joe and Graham and Jamie pushing me along in a chair. Both Emma and I were suffering profoundly from the effects of partial deafness and whilst we tried to talk to each other, all we could really manage was a smile – a knowing smile. I held her hand and we just looked at one another as Joe, Graham and Emma's parents chatted away. I think it was a relief for both Graham and Joe to meet others who were feeling just as they were. For me it was all surreal: not only trying to understand that I had been involved in a bomb attack, but that there were others too who, like Emma and Paul, were alive but terribly injured.

What would meeting Paul be like? All I knew was that Paul and I had something in common – both of us having lost part of our body and having to adjust to a different life. What would I say to him? Did he know that I had lost both legs? Would the very sight of me upset him? Had he seen me in the carriage? Was he also suffering from hearing loss? I was running through every eventuality in my mind, trying to prepare myself. I was sure that this would be a difficult meeting for us both, so the only way to get through it was just to be myself; to be happy – happy to be alive and grateful.

We had arranged to meet Graham at the fountain, our special meeting place in the grounds – we would stop and get his coffee too most days, that way we would have more time to spend together. Joe had developed a special relationship with the people in the coffee shop, especially with a wonderful woman, Florence, who had got to know our routine so well that she would have the coffees ready every morning, as soon as she saw Joe walk in the main entrance.

Florence would always ask after me. She had seen Joe wheeling me around the grounds and he had explained what had happened. Joe told me how shocked she had been and that she had promised that she would pray for me every day.

'Gill, we've been looking for you everywhere!' One of my nurses came sprinting over to us, having run all the way down from the tenth floor. (The staff knew by now that I spent most of my time outside, in my wheelchair by the fountain.) 'There is an appointment available with the cardiac department, so no physio' today. We will have to rush you back up to the ward and then to your exam.' And with that I was swivelled around and taken back inside. Worrying about meeting Paul and anticipating physio' would have to wait.

We pushed the elevator button, waiting for the doors to open – some people were getting out on my floor ... hang on ... it was them – my family. I hadn't expected them so soon – how wonderful, how absolutely wonderful. I had only a moment to give them each a hug before being whisked away for the heart examination (my heartbeat was still irregular and this was just one of many appointments with the specialists – no one was taking any chances). I shouted out to the kids as the elevator doors shut, 'Wait for me on the ward; I won't be long, I won't be long!'

An hour or so later, I was back, and there they all were sitting in the Day Room taking in the amazing views of London. Alex and Maddy had grown so much – they looked like real little people, not children. Maddy looked just like me, even her mannerisms were like mine.

It was just brilliant to have so many Hickses in the one place and they too began to fall in with the routine. They spent their days on Luke Ward with me, or at the fountain for lunch. And as I progressed in the gym, they participated in my rehab. It was a family effort. With a family that I had turned away from and thought I had lost. Yet there they were, with me every minute that they could be, putting their own lives on hold to be here with me in London.

'There's Big Ben, and the Millennium Wheel' – the hospital couldn't have been in a better location for 'visitors' to the capital! The kids and Jo could get a feel for the city without necessarily travelling around; neither Graham nor I were happy for them to use public transport, the events of both the July 7 attack and the failed July 21 attack being still too fresh.

Just having the family there somehow made me feel that life was going to be ok – we had the perfect world, right here in the hospital, our utopia – we were safe, we were fed, we were all cared for and became fast friends with many of the staff. It was our little home away from home.

The kids would push me around and we would 'gang' up on Joe, who was always up for being teased and did a fair bit of teasing back.

I would often sit and watch them all race around, laughing in the sunshine and running around the fountain, the water rotating on a rather magnificent structure. And I would feel so blessed, so lucky. After all, my family and Joe hadn't even known one another a month earlier, yet here they all were now – all as one. This really was a gift. Soon Stella would be arriving and the circle would be complete – or as complete as I could hope for.

I spent as much time as I could out in the grounds, by the fountain – it became the centrepiece for our lives and was the backdrop to many scenes that shaped my time at St Thomas' Hospital.

I remember pointing out to Brooke that the fountain rotated and she hadn't believed me until I showed her. She had sat with her lunch by that fountain for months and never realised. We laughed together. I said that I must obviously have been spending far too long out here if I knew those sorts of details. Brooke was fast becoming much more than my occupational therapist – she was a friend. She had that sunny Aussie nature, always smiling and bubbly – but she was also there to hold my hand and just be with me when I needed someone.

We always knew when it was Thursday as that was the day that the army helicopters would fly over, every week, around the same time. They made it look and sound as though we were at war and rather than instilling me with a sense of confidence and security, they filled me with despair and fear. Fridays were the best day of the week, bringing with them a much-needed and welcome break in the form of lunchtime jazz concerts in the grounds. Every week a different jazz band featured, always helping to ease Thursday's tension away.

We would meet up at the fountain in the mornings. Plans would then be made with the two Jos and the kids, whilst Graham took me off to physio'. Then we would all meet back there to eat our lunch together – Alex would always have ham and mustard sandwiches and I would have a hummous and salad pitta bread wrap every day for lunch. Then we'd discuss the evening plans – maybe take a trip out to a restaurant on the South Bank, or to a particular favourite spot – a Turkish restaurant called Troia. Alex always voted to eat there because he loved their lamb burgers – he missed the barbecued meat he was used to eating at home. We expanded and contracted as a group until eventually, when the family left, it would be just me and Joe at a table for two. I would be always be given a complimentary glass of champagne. This was a little tradition that started when they found out what had happened to me and that all the new regular diners were my family over from Australia. (Joe and I still eat there to this day and, in keeping with tradition, they still place a single complimentary glass of champagne on my table.)

Alex and Maddy would take turns at pushing me in the chair, taking me back to the fountain and positioning me so that I could watch them play as they chased each other and ran around and around on the grass. Joe, a big kid himself, would relish the chance to muck in. If it hadn't been for the fact that I was in a wheelchair, if I hadn't been wearing a hospital arm bracelet and if I didn't have both legs amputated, it could have been just a normal family scene at the park!

Because Maddy was so much like me we called her 'mini me' or 'min' for short. The two of us quickly developed a routine in which I was big 'me' and she was mini 'me' only with legs. Then we would do 'take offs' of TV commercials: '... but wait, for only $20 more you can get a Gill doll, that's right, she talks, she sings ...' then the voice-over would cut in: 'Legs sold separately, batteries not included.' We laughed so much – we'd laugh until we cried.

It was great having the time, the concentrated time to spend with the family, especially the kids. They handled everything with such maturity even though Alex was just twelve and Maddy nine at the time. I asked them if they were ok about their Aunty Gill being disabled and not having legs – naturally I was worried about their feelings – but they weren't repulsed or frightened of my new form. Rather they were inquisitive and concerned. My weight dropped considerably whilst I was in hospital and, if anything, this seemed to bother them more than the injuries. Alex in particular was concerned that I looked ill, not strong enough to cope with all that lay ahead. But they both took my physical state in their stride, accepting it immediately and not making anything of it. This was their Aunty Gill – she'd been involved in a bomb attack and now had no legs and was in a wheelchair. That was it.

I managed to have some snatched time with the kids, just on our own, and I was able to talk both openly and honestly with them. They wanted to know how I felt about the bomber – did I see him; did I hate him? I explained that I did not hate the bomber but that I wished

I understood the reasons why he had done this, why he would have wanted to hurt so many people and lives including those of his own family. Being with them, talking with them at such a level made me realise how much of their young lives I had missed. To them, I had been the aunty whose picture on the wall was not taken at a family barbecue or any other such gathering; it was for the cover of one of my promotional records and showed me in a feather boa, looking like a 1920s film star.

But at least I had this time now – a second chance to share my life with them. We were all together now and nothing could break us. Life was everywhere. I was back and everything was to be celebrated as often and as heartily as we could.

Seize the day.

August 1, 2005

Dear All

No major news except to say that Gill is well and continues to improve but gets very tired.

Gill is now asking for fundraising ideas – I think she really wants to thank the hospital but maybe also needs a project to focus on. This is what Gill loves to do and does best, so all thoughts gratefully accepted.

Love to you all

Bella, Lyndon, Gill, Joe and families

Chapter 6

On My 'Own' Two Feet

'TOUCH, RUN, RUN, RUN, RUN, TOUCH, run, run, run – drag, drag ... touch.' These are my memories of learning to walk *the first time*, memories largely influenced, I think, by stories told to me by Mum. It was Graham who had taught me to walk. As he tells it, he was eager to have me up and about. Strangely, I apparently never crawled and instead scooted along on my bottom, in a sitting position, bobbing along the ground. I must have looked like an overgrown caterpillar.

Graham was nearing his eighth birthday so I can see why he urgently needed a more energetic playmate. There were so many outdoor games we would be able to 'enjoy' together, like soldiers, or cowboys and Indians, or his favourite – not mine – which was climbing up a frame and pushing his little sister off!

He would grab my tiny hand and whisk me from one side of our living room to the other, making my legs keep pace with his. It was a combination of quick marching and gentle dragging. No sooner had we 'taken off' than there would be a wall in front of me; Graham would hold my hand out to the wall and say 'touch' – as if I were an Olympic swimmer having completed a length – then march me back in the other direction. This was his technique for teaching me to walk – and it worked! By the end of my millionth 'touch' I was upright, standing on my own, taking steps without holding onto him. His teaching method may have been crude, a little heavy-handed even, but he got results – he did it! We did it! I could walk!

I never would have thought that some thirty-six years later, my brother would play a leading role in teaching me how to walk again.

. . .

'Right – now let's get you up on this bed and start with the stretching and strengthening exercises.' Matt led me – pushed by Graham – through the gym, ushering us over to a physio' bed. Well, they called it a bed but it was more like a padded table; it didn't have all the things I associate with a bed, like sheets, a pillow or blankets. But then I certainly wasn't there for a nap! This was all about hard work and pushing personal limits.

'We need to strengthen your core muscles,' he said. 'So, lie down, flat and I want you to breathe in deep ... in and hold ... and out. Slowly out. Pelvis straight, flat, feel your pelvis touch the ground, flat to the bed and slowly raise one stump – control, slow, hold and down, slow, control. Are you all right with them being called stumps? Would you prefer them to be called legs?'

Now, there was a question; what *did* I want to call them? Were they still legs? Did they qualify as legs? I didn't need to think for too long though; I blurted it out as if this had been something that I had been considering for some time: 'Let's call them "Stumpingtons". That can be their English name.' And then, even to my own astonishment, I went further still, saying: 'I also think that they are twins, boys. Definitely boys. Not identical – I mean, it is hard to tell them apart. But to the trained eye, like their "father" the surgeon Professor Burnand's and to mine – well, we can tell the difference.'

This set the tone, not only for that session, but for the rest of my rehabilitation. Matt immediately shared in the 'game', recognising that this would be no ordinary rehab' process, but then I think that both he and Nichola had already guessed as much. Carol, Matt, Nichola and Rich all adopted the 'ington' suffix – so I became known as Gillington – and most names and words were translated into our new language. This may sound a touch juvenile, but it worked for us. It was a difficult time for them and naturally for me, so our games lifted the sessions – we laughed together and that's what's important. I know the difference between people laughing at you and with you and I am one hundred per cent sure that they were all laughing with me. There is no doubt in my mind of this and I'm sure they enjoyed this time as much as I did.

Matt encouraged me to 'bond' with my new physical form, showing me techniques to rub and touch the delicate tissue that was forming a scar, and the outer skin that had been sewn together to form a shape: the more I touched and rubbed them the more desensitised they would become. It was important to prepare them for spending most of their time tucked inside an artificial limb. At times I felt it hard to acknowledge 'them' – somehow if I didn't look down, then I didn't have to engage. This is how I had always coped with hardship or trauma – with every situation in my life that I'd found too difficult to face. I would just pretend that it wasn't happening and if I did that well enough, if I ran far enough away, I could convince myself. Living in denial allowed me to smile, to laugh and to create a sense of happiness with 'my lot'.

But this time it was different. My legs were gone. I couldn't run. I couldn't hide. I couldn't cover this up. I couldn't pretend that I had just fallen and broken my ankle – I didn't even have an ankle! And I couldn't pretend that these 'stumps', these poor, wee, hurt parts covered in bandaging, had nothing to do with me. This was not happening to someone else; this was right here, right now and the stumps belonged to me – they were a part of me and needed me to heal them, to cherish them, to accept them.

So ultimately, my maternal instinct, the natural force within me that wanted to 'make them better', to hold them and promise that everything would be all right, took over. I guess I compromised with myself. I allowed my preconditioned coping strategies of the past to co-exist with my body's new, immediate needs, the result being that I named my 'stumps' and treated them as two separate 'beings'. Two small twins that needed my care, my attention and most importantly, my love. I could do that. This meant that I could heal and accept them without having to admit that they were actually my legs and that this was how it would be for the rest of my life. And so, they were born – two boys, poorly, but with a prognosis that was optimistic.

By now, there was nothing more medically speaking to be done for me, except for keeping an eye on the wounds and ensuring that they were healing as best they could. Both my ears were severely damaged and had not healed of their own accord, as had been hoped, so I would need to have replacement eardrums fitted. I put this off though as I couldn't face another operation just yet. I was good at compensating with lip-reading and hearing conversations through my neck. (Well, technically it was the inner ear, but to the untrained eye, it looked like I was craning my neck to listen, so everyone just started to talk to my neck.)

It was all about learning to walk now, with physio' the focus and the gym at the centre of our lives. Everything revolved around my two daily sessions: one in the morning and one in the afternoon. Nichola and Matt who ran the sessions, would often play 'good cop' and 'bad cop' routines; just when you thought it was all getting cosy, they'd switch roles. It certainly kept me on my toes – so to speak.

Often, I would conveniently forget that I was a patient and feel comfortable enough to launch into my imaginary stage persona, Gigi Fontaine. As Gigi, I was happy to suggest a stage show theme for our sessions like *Physio: the Musical* or *Physios On Ice*. For my favourite, *Evita*, I would sing the very well-known 'Don't Cry for me Professor Burnand, the truth is my legs never left me', completely oblivious to my surroundings and laughing so much that it hurt (which was a problem as I still had to be careful of my chest wounds).

It was fantastic. A little bit of 'old Gill' would sneak in and reveal herself at all of my physio' sessions. I didn't want this to be a horrible experience, for me, for my physio' team or for Paul either. We were all in this together; every achievement that Paul or I made our physios made with us. Sharing the experience somehow made it all bearable. Like when we watched Paul stand in the parallel bars for the first time; it was amazing – he was so tall! The physios' dedication, hard work and preparation time – the hours, days and weeks spent building us up, making us stronger and stronger, pushing, encouraging and praising us – it would all pay off, eventually.

But it wasn't easy. Every detail, every muscle was under scrutiny. It was intense and rapid rehabilitation – the aim was to get me up and walking as soon as possible. Time and space took on another dimension whilst I was in hospital but I know that these gym sessions started at the end of July – less than a month after the bombings! When I was in the thick of it, balancing on one ball whilst another was being thrown at me, it was sometimes hard to see how it all would come together, how there was a grand plan. But I had to trust in their instincts. All roads led to walking, it was just that when I hadn't walked – hadn't even stood up – however much I wanted to believe it, and however much I trusted them, I still didn't think in my heart that I would ever walk again.

'Can you do push-ups Gillington?' I could tell by Matt's tone of voice and wry smile that this wasn't really a question, more of a hint of what was coming next. 'We need to start building those muscles. Let's try something easy to start with.' And so I slowly lowered my body down until my nose touched the bed, then pulled myself up again, finishing with a 'Phew' of relief.

'Now I want you to do five of those. I know you can do that, nice and slow.' But Graham quickly interrupted: 'Five? That's nothing Matt. She's Australian – she can do twenty-five! Don't let me down now Gill, I know you can do twenty-five. Come on – your country depends on you. There's a lot at stake here. C'mon.' And instantly I was transported back to when we were little kids and I'd wanted to do everything that Graham told me to do. And I'd wanted to do it all well so that he would be impressed with me, proud even ... Who knows where the strength came from but there I was, shaking on twenty-one, wobbling on twenty-two and twenty-three, close to tears on twenty-four. But I did it! I did twenty-five push-ups. I don't really know who I did them for: for myself? Graham? Matt? But it didn't matter. I was igniting a side of me that I never knew was there – maybe I was going to be good at this physical rehab' business after all! I was experiencing so many 'firsts' that I certainly couldn't rule out the possibility.

That day, Graham earned himself the title 'Captain' and this is what he was known as from then on. It was a title that embodied both his training ability and his status – I was Team Australia and he was my coach. He would spur me on – 'C'mon, c'mon, one more, two more, c'mon; looking good Gill, good, now five more ...' – day after day, week after week. I would learn something new in the morning session, discuss it with Graham over lunch, and often, I'd have just about mastered it by the end of the same afternoon. It was phenomenal. We were unbeatable. We were Team Hicks.

I didn't always grasp a task though. Some things were too difficult to excel at first off, and it was then that I needed to find the greatest personal strength, to believe. It was balancing that proved the most challenging goal, but for me as a double amputee, it was also the most important. I needed to learn to balance, something that one normally took for granted and I found the concept of being taught – trained – just to be steady, upright, to not topple over, completely bizarre. There were sessions where I would leave feeling deflated, unable to face another setback. Who would think that so many 'everyday' movements would ever need to be re-learnt? And it wasn't as simple as remembering how to ride a bike either.

'It's all about the core muscles,' Matt said, as he so often did. 'We need your core to be strong so that when you get your legs you will be able to stand and hold yourself up. Ok, now,' he said, as he rolled over a huge Swiss ball towards me. 'I want to see if you can sit on this ball and balance.' He wedged the ball tightly between himself and the bed so that I could slide onto it – my midriff was rolling as if there was a hoola hoop swinging around and around it.

'Whooooo, Matt, Matt, Matt ...' I was trying to stay on the ball and stabilise myself. 'It's ok. I'm right here, right behind you. I won't let you fall off,' he said, his hand steadying me. I controlled my middle, straightened up my back, and positioned my Stumpingtons either side. 'I, I, I ...' I fixed my eyes onto an object – the parallel bars that were straight in front of me. My head was perfectly centred. I was doing it, I ... whoa ... I was balancing on a giant ball ... with no legs! With nothing to root me to the floor! Graham nearly cried with joy: not only could I catch, but now, now I could balance as well! I think I made an impression. This was no easy task, and by showing them so early on in my rehab' that I had this unique determination to perform, I think I paved the way for some creative thinking in the planning of my future routines!

Gradually, Matt and Nichola started raising the stakes, each session getting a little harder than the last. No two days were the same. I felt like an athlete, and in many ways I was. I would work out in the morning, break for a protein-packed lunch – a full-fat yoghurt with fruit, for example – discuss tactics with my personal trainer, oh, I mean brother, and then head back for the afternoon session, hoping to perfect whatever I had been taught that morning. I had never had this intense relationship with myself, with my body, before. It had all just worked in Life One without me noticing – I got mad at it when it put weight on or when it didn't look good in an outfit, but I had never pushed it before. But my body had been strong when I needed it the most – it hadn't let me down – and now it continued, showing me how resourceful it could be.

It was like witnessing a thousand miracles each and every day. I was in awe of my body; I was in awe of the human spirit. It was the first time that I listened to my body, and just followed its lead – and it worked. Every day I got the hang of something new and I impressed myself. Not in a self-loving, self-important way – I was just impressed by all the things I was able to do, things that I hadn't even done *with* legs.

I was dedicated and I made a promise, a vow, that I would look after myself, love myself every day. I would feed my body good food and never do anything to harm it. I wanted to repay it for not letting me down, for continuing the fight, not just for life itself, but for quality of life. I watched my body adapt and repair. I watched my skin as the burns healed and I watched my wounds as they too healed: these were my own miracles.

...

It was early August, just about a month after the bombings, and Paul and I were ready to have our stumps cast for prosthetic legs. This was what all the exercise and co-ordination techniques had been about. Everything up to this point had been leading up to me getting prosthetic legs. It was like waiting for Christmas: getting excited and knowing that it will come, that the day will come, but then experiencing a moment of doubt – what if, when the day comes, I don't like my presents?

Because I would be relying on two prosthetic legs (that is, without even one of my own legs with which to navigate and negotiate the ground) there was a little more pressure on both me and on the team to ensure that I would have the ability to walk. Indeed, to fulfil Dr Luff's original prediction that I would walk out of hospital!

Lynsey, our prosthetist, was coming in especially to cast our stumps, using a process that was a bit like papier mâché. A mould or impression was to be made of the stumps in order to make sockets in the artificial limbs that would fit the stumps perfectly. This would allow for better comfort which, in turn, would mean easier mobility. Simple!

Dr Luff was overseeing the procedure, discussing intently with Lynsey the various solutions, the mechanisms and the foot type that he was considering. (The foot type? I didn't know there was more than one foot, but oh yes, there was quite a range to choose from!) Dr Luff had difficult decisions to make as to what system would be best for me, what would suit my needs and what I would be most comfortable with. Of course I had no idea. I was just so pleased that I was being treated by someone who cared and was dedicated to finding the appropriate 'bits' to make the 'new' me.

I was going to have something called 'Elite Feet', often referred to as 'sports feet'. As the reading material given to me suggested, they were designed to offer the user a better 'sports–life/balance'. Well, as you can imagine, I found this particularly funny. Here I was – Gill Hicks, ex-ten-cigar-a-day-smoking, coffee-drinking, workaholic – sitting in a gym reading all about a new sporting life with my new feet and legs. It just didn't get any funnier. Who would have ever thought! 'I don't want to be a para-Olympian. I don't want to be sporty just because I'm disabled,' I said. 'I just want to be able to brave the January sales with the best of them – and still be standing!'

The foot was pronged, streamlined and fast-looking. There was a distinct Star Wars look to it – very futuristic. I didn't quite understand how it would work – it didn't look very stable – but apparently once the foot covering went on (a synthetic cover with toes!) you wouldn't be able to see the mechanics or the shape of the prongs.

I was fast becoming part of a new world with a new language. Being disabled, being an amputee was like joining a new club. One that I had joined overnight and, without wanting to, and I had got life membership! There was so much information to take in, so much on offer! Dr Luff's words still ring in my ears, saying, 'You will never have a set of legs better than your first pair.' And I remember thinking that was strange because I only ever expected to get one pair – how many legs would I have?

. . .

By mid-August my left leg was ready. Let me just say that again, because it sounds so strange – my left leg was ready! And I was going to see it, to wear it; my new left leg. Paul and I were to have our first fittings together, for even though he was a little more advanced than me, our legs were ready at the same time. The limbs were made at a specialist centre in South London, a little way from the hospital. It was an amputee rehabilitation facility and both Dr Luff and Lynsey, the prosthetist, were based there.

It was an early morning pick-up. We were going in a special transport ambulance/van especially assigned to the ferrying of patients. Both Paul and I were given blue NHS lunchboxes (mine was marked 'VEG', as I am a vegetarian) so it felt a bit like setting off on a school outing. The driver pushed us up the ramp to the vehicle in our wheelchairs and the chairs were then chained to the floor to ensure that they wouldn't move around whilst we were travelling. I swallowed. A big gulp. This journey was yet another new experience and I hated every minute of it. I felt trapped, I missed my legs and I didn't want this any more. I wanted to be like everyone else. People looked at us from the street as we drove by and I knew what they were thinking – 'Poor them, they're in one of those buses. Poor things.' I wanted to open the window and yell out, 'I was like you, just weeks ago. Just four weeks ago, I was like you, so don't look at me with pity.' But I couldn't. I couldn't reach the window; I couldn't say a word.

I was disabled. Stuck. I was at the mercy of the driver, chained and restricted. This wasn't me. Nothing about this felt right. I wanted to scream, but I couldn't. I wouldn't do that. I wouldn't lose sense of where I was. Paul was there and he needed me as much as I needed him. No, I had to think of something witty to say, something that would make us laugh. But nothing came to mind. This journey was one of the most significant that I have ever made. I knew – I vowed – that from that day on I would never again be chained down. Never again would I put myself in that situation or allow myself to feel so helpless and trapped.

It was a long journey – one that should have been filled with anticipation. However, by the time we arrived I felt deflated, demoralised and dehumanised. I just didn't want this – to be arriving at an amputee centre that was full of ... well, amputees. I didn't want to be part of this world. I wanted my legs back, to wake up and realise that this was all one long nightmare. But it wasn't. This was my 'new' normal and all the people I could see whose limbs were missing were just like me. In fact, on that day, I was the only bilateral amputee in the centre, so they were all looking at me, trying not to be noticed as they stared at my legless body.

'What happened to you then?' asked an elderly man in a wheelchair as I waited for Lynsey in reception. 'Diabetes? Gosh, you're young.'

'No, I was in the tube bomb,' I replied. And that was all I needed to say. He looked at me, said how sorry he was, then wheeled away. That was a conversation stopper!

Lynsey was just like Matt and Nichola – part of our 'gang' – and her cheer soon brightened me up: 'How're the boys today?' she asked. And scruffing them both as a mother would the head of a small boy, I said, 'They're ok, aren't you darlings?' (Clearly, I should have had children by now, but if the Stumpingtons could act as some sort of surrogate family, it was only right that I should go along with my feelings, wasn't it?)

I was fascinated by what Lynsey did and intrigued as to what led her into this profession. I hadn't known previously what a prosthetist was, never having even known anyone who had lost a limb. She wheeled me over to the parallel bars, then out it came: my left leg!

Getting my first leg was a monumental moment and Joe was with me to witness it, to be on hand with the camera so that Graham and the family could see me standing – that was the plan: that I would be standing up! After this session, Joe or Graham, and later Stella or Jo and Maddy and Alex would always be there, with me for every step, so I never had to face anything completely on my own. We all shared the whole thing, every step of the way. That made a huge difference to me because although they could never know how I felt – what it was like to have your legs gone, to have been involved so directly in a terrorist attack – they could share my day-to-day experience; things like having a strict routine of physio', travelling in this van and going to an amputee centre.

I had brought along a shoe, it was one of my 'Rebel without a Cause' shoes, like the white patent ones I was wearing on the tube that morning, only these were black and white striped and pointed. Lynsey put my shoe on the foot, and suddenly the whole leg was transformed. It carried my identity, as if the shoe was a part of my DNA. I pulled the liner on – it had a large pin that stuck out of the end and this went into the leg. Then click, click, click, click, click (there were ten clicks in total) ... click and I was 'in'.

Slowly I rose from my chair. This would be the first time that I had been upright since July 7 and we were now in early August. 'Joe, Joe, look, look at me – I'm standing, I'm standing.' I couldn't hold back the tears as they fell down my cheeks. I think even Lynsey had moist eyes. I was like a newborn foal taking its first steps: wobbly and with a look of terror on my face – but at the same time totally elated. It was like sky-diving, flying a plane, being on top of a mountain. I felt like a person, that I could look the world in the eye again.

I needed to hug Joe. It's different when you are confined to a wheel-chair or a bed; the hugs are different. You can't get your arms around someone properly. It's just not the same as standing and nestling your face in their neck. We both took a moment. It felt like we were the only two people in the room – but we weren't.

'Let's try some steps shall we?' Lynsey had to improvise: as I didn't have a right leg, I couldn't walk forward, so she propped my right Stumpington up on a stool on casters, so that I was able to move along the bars, dragging my stool along. My knuckles must have been a brilliant white as I held on so tightly. I looked down to see my left leg, complete with black-and-white striped shoe, take a step – a giant leap – forward.

'How does it feel? Any pain anywhere?' I didn't feel any pain; I didn't feel anything. I didn't feel the ground – it was bizarre. I was walk-ing (-ish) without knowing where the ground was. Other amputees sat the length of the room, watching, silently as I took those first steps. They had all been there before, so they knew how I felt. 'Looking good girl, that's the way,' a voice from the sidelines yelled. 'I'm not too sure about that stool though, I don't think it will catch on.' We all laughed and I replied, 'Don't you be so sure. This is state-of-the-art. Once they see me, they will all want one!' Then I turned and slowly perfected a technique of stepping on my left leg, dragging my right and holding myself up through my arms. What a day!

I was taller now than my natural height. I remembered Dr Luff measuring my arm span to gauge my original height; I had stretched my fingers as far as I could, trying to distort the measurements! 'Will I be able to return to my career as a supermodel? I was nearing five foot nine or something around there,' I had told him. But Joe had intervened: 'Now Gill, tell the truth, you weren't much over five foot were you? You can't fool Dr Luff!' I had tried to ignore that comment, thinking, 'Thanks for the support Joe,' and leant over to Dr Luff saying quietly, 'Actually I was hoping to be a little taller, maybe two inches or so?'

But this was not recommended; if anything, the plan was to start me a little shorter than I had been, as that way I would be closer to the ground, able to gain a better sense of gravity to help me balance and learn how to walk. 'I have been through enough trauma,' I said then. 'I really don't want to be any shorter, please. I'll learn how to walk just as well being taller, please, please.' And so, against his better judgement Dr Luff had nodded and Lynsey smiled. She was the one who would be making the legs, so if she *accidentally* on purpose made them a little taller, well who would know?

'You can take your leg back with you,' said Lynsey, 'then Matt and Nic can get you up on the bars. That's so exciting isn't it? It's been so lovely seeing you stand up today. So wonderful.'

I didn't want to start crying again – it had been wonderful. It was a day, a moment that will forever be etched in my mind and in my heart. Joe carried my leg and together we waited for the van to come and take us back to the hospital. I didn't notice being chained in so much on the way back; I couldn't get the sensation of standing out of my mind. It was like a drug: I wanted to know when I would stand again, get my next fix. Could I stand up every day? I didn't want to race ahead too much, but this was an amazing triumph – I had a leg, and I could stand!

...

It was so amazing to be able to give Graham, Jo and the kids proper hugs – to be able to wrap my arms around them and they me. I never wanted to let go but I had to – there was work to be done, after all, and 'Captain' would not let things be held up by sentimental huggings. He wanted me to walk.

It would be another few weeks until I had my right leg as the wound was healing very slowly and I wasn't able to put any pressure on the end of the stump. So whilst we waited for the right leg to heal enough for a fitting, I was 'doing the bars' with one prosthetic left leg and a large grey blow-up structure called a PPAM Aid (pneumatic post-amputation mobility aid) on my right. I didn't mind what I walked on though, just as long as I was upright.

'Weight over to your right and step, weight over to your left and step. I'm here. It's ok. Again, weight over ...' Matt sat on a stool in front of me holding my middle as I took my first steps in the parallel bars. 'This is harder because of the PPAM Aid, but doing good little Gillington. The boys are doing very well.'

It's hard to describe the sensation of walking. Well, I call it walking but it was like nothing I had ever experienced before. It wasn't anything like the walking I knew of old – it was like balancing on air, only the air was tough and tangible. It was like wearing twenty-inch stilettos whilst balancing on stilts. It was terrifying and exhilarating all at the same time – moving along the bars, a step at a time was better, far better than just standing.

'Look at you – look at you walking, this is fantastic!' Claire, my intensive care physio' often popped in to check on my progress. She too was part of the family. I loved showing all those people who had played such a crucial role in my miraculous recovery, how well I was doing. I wanted them to feel proud – I was a product of their hard work, dedication and love.

Not every day was like a musical though or like a stage for comedy routines. There were tears too, lots of them, and we all shared those moments. I didn't feel sorry for myself – I didn't ever ask 'Why me?' – but I did often feel overwhelmed by the journey ahead, by the unknown, uncertain of what and how different my life would be now.

Everything was an enormous challenge and some days I was tired, unable to achieve what was being asked of me. That would leave me doubting myself and my capabilities. Matt, Nichola and Carol never wavered though – their faith in my ability to overcome any obstacle was unshakable. They would go off, get a tissue or two, then sit with me and talk me around, saying that everyone has off days, even the best sportspeople. They would explain that I – and my body – had been through extreme trauma. I needed to be kind to myself, not beat myself up if I couldn't do something. All would come in time.

. . .

Meanwhile, Graham, Jo and the kids had to leave. Their lives were calling. Graham had been with me for six weeks, Jo and the kids for four. Their flight was scheduled in a matter of days, before my right leg would be ready. We didn't talk about it. The only thing that kept us all going was knowing that they would be back in a few months' time for the wedding, so we wouldn't have to be apart for too long. But it didn't really make it any easier; goodbyes are always tough.

The flight back to Adelaide was at six pm, so we decided that we would all have lunch together, then they would go back to Richmond, get their bags and head off.

I found myself slipping back into my old ways, pretending that this wasn't happening. The greatest feeling that the hospital gave me was the sense that we'd created this perfect environment where we all lived, where there was no distance and where we were all together every day, supporting each other. The real world seemed insignificant and small – nothing outside the hospital walls mattered. But my family's imminent departure was breaking that fantasy down. Cracks were appearing and my utopia was being altered. My idea of a perfect world had them in it. My heart was breaking. A chapter was ending.

They felt the same. As much as they knew that they had to get back, they had all accepted this new world that they belonged to, quickly falling into a routine, supporting me every moment, sharing everything with me. I could barely see them through my tears as they walked away, further and further into the distance, still turning around and waving. They kept waving until I couldn't see them any more, the trees at the edge of the hospital grounds blocking my view.

'We'll see them soon, darling. They'll be back for the wedding. It's not long.' Joe tried to comfort me, but he too was crying, saying goodbye to people he had quickly grown to love, especially Graham – they had had each other to turn to in those early, fragile and dark days.

When Joe said that I would be seeing them soon, even he hadn't known quite how soon. In fact it was the very next day and through no intervention on my part – I mean it, I didn't do a thing! There were strikes of essential workers at Heathrow and whilst initial predictions were only that there would be severe delays, it soon became obvious that the problem could take days to resolve.

So that evening I received a call to say that they'd be back to see me the following day! Jo was laughing and crying at the same time, trying to tell me the exact details of what was happening. Apparently, she'd had a call from the Australian Government representative saying there was no way of knowing how long the strike would last and that the best plan would be to reschedule their flights for the following week and she would call them with updates.

Now you can guess what Jo had thought – she'd thought it was me calling, playing a joke, so her response must have sounded a little strange, to say the least: 'Sure, sure, no worries, yeah, whatever, sure.' Then she'd laughed, 'Ha, ha. Yep, oh dear, staff striking, who'd have thought? Ha, ha, ha.' It wasn't until the woman gave Jo her personal number that she suddenly realised that it wasn't me playing a joke at all – it was for real! A seed of doubt still lurked though and Jo said to me, on the phone, 'What have you done? Who have you called to arrange these strikes?'

So, courtesy of striking airport workers, we stole back another four days together. And even though we'd already had a 'practice' run of saying goodbye, the second time – the real and final time – it wasn't any easier. 'The next time you see me I'll have legs and I'll be walking!' I yelled out to them – much to the amusement of everyone in the grounds who heard me.

The most special thing for me was that Graham, Jo and the kids had all got to share the total experience with me. They'd got to know everyone, from the doctors, nurses and physios, to the man who ran the newsagent, the woman who ran the coffee shop, and the people who ran the local restaurants. They had been embraced, and they, in turn, embraced all.

Every inch of our daily routine, our daily life had their imprint on it. I couldn't pass anything without being reminded of something funny that we had done. Like the 'talking sign' in the reception area at the entrance of the hospital that gave people directions with various translation options. Naturally this had appealed to our Hicks humour, and, one day, as Graham and I found ourselves at the talking sign, me in my wheelchair and him beside me, we amused ourselves by selecting a language option and then pretending to understand it. We chose Chinese and sat nodding at each other, pointing and smiling as the sign directed us to the place we had requested. Well, just as we were settling into long peals of laughter, a Chinese family came along to use the sign – or worse, ask us for directions. We were about to be found out! Graham spun the chair around and we quickly went out to the garden area. We had a lucky escape. We knew we were being silly, but that was why it was so much fun! We were both determined to fill every day with as much fun and joy as we could. I was alive and everything was different now. Nothing else mattered any more – just laughing, being together and enjoying the time that we had.

I was so pleased that we had built up so many happy memories within the hospital. It could easily have been so very different. These precious moments would keep me smiling until I was discharged, although there were still many more memories to be made.

. . .

My right leg was here! I was complete. I had the set!

It's funny that I immediately called them 'my' legs. I did feel an immediate emotional bond with them; they were, after all, going to be a part of me. And as soon as my shoes were on either foot, well, that was it – it was like looking down at two familiar friends.

Claire, my intensive care physio', popped in to see the new arrival. To celebrate she'd brought the new legs a small present – a pair of fishnet stockings! How well she knew me. I immediately put them on and they transformed very standard, plastic-looking prosthetic legs into stylish 'Gill' legs.

It was a shame that the family missed all of this, but now Stella was here, having been handed the reins by Graham. She stepped naturally into the role of personal trainer/head coach, being dubbed 'Captina' by Matt, Nichola and Carol. And yes, she was every bit as tough as Graham, Jo and the kids!

'Now, today, we are going to try something new – let's step out of the bars. Don't worry, I'm here – Captina is going to throw balls at you whilst you stand. You need to catch them and throw them back. Captina, whenever you are ready ...' Matt signalled to Stella to start. I was wedged between two beds, so I wasn't going to fall and if I did lose my balance, I would fall onto the bed. Matt stayed close, whilst Nichola, Carol and Stella all started throwing balls at me – 'Faster, faster, c'mon.' Matt would encourage them, pushing me, knowing I could do this.

I couldn't stand on the legs for long as my wounds were still heal-ing and it was quite painful and awkward after a while. So we would do one task a day in legs and the rest of the session would be devoted to muscle-building, mostly my favourite exercise – push-ups.

Day after day the work was focused and the progress rapid. Matt worked by instinct: whenever he felt that I was ready for the next leap, without warning, we'd be off. We dubbed him 'the Horse Whisperer' because he just knew; he was in tune with me, he could 'tame' me, and would get me to jump through hoops, if that's what it took! To get me walking outside of the bars I was given a walking frame. I was on it for just two days before Nichola and Matt agreed that it was time I went onto crutches and started to learn how to walk up and down stairs!

'What?' I thought. I was secure in the frame. I could do that. I had walked around the ward to practise and the nurses had been amazed! I remember what it was like the first time I saw the nurses when I was standing. All those wonderful people who had lovingly cared for me – they'd all looked so big when I was either in my chair or in bed. But they weren't – I couldn't believe it. We so enjoyed 'meeting' each other whilst standing. It was really only then, even though I was hold-ing onto my walking frame for dear life, that I started to feel like I was their equal, just one of the girls. Just Gill. A few of them cried – it was a big moment for us all.

But crutches? I wasn't sure I was ready. I don't know why I was suddenly filled with such fear as up until this point I had been willing to take on new challenges with open arms. But this was different. I knew that if I didn't master the crutches, I wouldn't be able to walk. I was scared of trying and failing, then leaving myself with no options. I had to have my independence back – I had to learn to walk.

Nichola began a daily mantra, realising that I was building up an unwarranted fear of the crutches. 'Now Gill, the crutches are your friends. They will help you to walk and go outside; that will be nice. Frame is bad. He isn't your friend; he wants to hold you back. Bad frame!' The game continued until the day came when there was no frame, just a pair of crutches in the gym.

Matt pushed me to the end of the parallel bars and helped me stand. 'Ok, now instead of holding onto the bars, support yourself with the crutches. That's it, nice and steady.' I collapsed back into the wheelchair. I was wobbly. I couldn't hold myself up. I couldn't support myself on the crutches. The tears rolled down my face.

Nichola sat in front of me on her stool – she understood, but she also needed me to get over this. The crutches were a crucial part of the next stage. 'I can't do it,' I said. 'I can't do this. I miss my legs. I want my legs back. I just want my legs back.' We ended that day's session. There were no jokes. There was no laughter.

· · ·

When I saw Treena and Adrian, our Family Liaison Officers, I asked them about my legs – my real legs. I wanted all the details. I felt that I was able to deal with facts, to put emotions aside, and just deal with the cold, hard facts. I wanted to know what happened.

My legs had been held for forensic examination purposes and were being kept in the hospital morgue, awaiting a decision from me as to how to dispose of them – cremation, burial, all the options you are given for a loved one who has passed away. Treena got the all-clear so that if I wanted to, I could see my legs, or what remained of them. But Joe was not in agreement. 'I don't think this is such a good idea. You don't know what state they will be in and it might haunt you. It might be just too much.' I explained that I had seen them in the carriage that day, and that it couldn't be any worse than what I had already dealt with. And besides, they were a part of me. I needed to say goodbye. I needed to know how they looked; what had happened. I just needed to know.

So it was arranged. We went down to the basement, to the morgue. There to meet us was a nurse. She was very softly spoken and I had to strain to hear her, but I knew by her body language and facial expressions what she was saying. I had been here before. It was exactly like seeing Mum in her coffin before her funeral. The same feelings, the same sweating palms, fast-beating heart. I was going to be seeing myself dead. This was my body, a corpse, yet it was me.

Joe wheeled me into a room and there, on a large cushion, delicately lit by a down light, were my limbs. The legs were completely blown apart. There was no skin holding them together. I couldn't recognise them – they didn't look like legs. But there were the feet – and they were perfect, protected by the shoes I had been wearing I guess. They were just as I remembered them, wearing my favourite nail polish, each toe lovingly painted. That had been my Sunday night ritual – hands in a neutral tone and toes in a bright red, or something more daring.

Up until that point I had mostly been longing for the *use* of my limbs. I had missed being able to walk, to move without thinking, to do everything that you normally do in life, with legs. But when I saw them, lying on a cushion, it all came flooding back. I missed *them* – I missed having a relationship with them every day. I missed noticing how the toes were shaped, where the pressure areas were, the callous spots, the wrinkles on the skin. I used to nestle them into Joe's thigh when we got into bed on a winter's night when they were cold and I wanted to get them warm. I leant over and touched them, as they lay on the cushion. They were ice cold, detached. Different from any cold I had felt before.

I tried to remember every event, every moment that involved my legs, my feet. I wanted to let them know that I would never forget, to reassure myself that I would never forget. I remembered having reflexology, zipping up knee-high boots, queuing for silver Birkenstock sandals – they had to be silver – I remembered enjoying a foot spa, Joe tickling the soles and me squirming, begging him to stop. I remembered how wonderful it was to come home after a long day and take my shoes off, wiggling each toe and then walking around barefoot on our wooden floorboards – we have under-floor heating. I remembered. I remembered carpet, feeling carpet, thick, woollen carpet, and wearing woolly socks. I remembered Mum telling me not to put my feet too close to the heater when I was trying to get warm in winter because I would get chilblains.

All the memories were there, all the sensations recorded deep in my subconscious. And they were all surfacing, one thought, one memory triggering another. I asked Joe for a moment alone. He too was overwhelmed by emotion.

'Hello my legs and my dear, dear feet. I am so sorry. I miss you so much.' The tears were distorting my vision and I wanted to see, to soak up every minute of being united with them. I wanted to stare at them, so I did my best to dry my eyes and, gently, I touched each toe, memorising every last detail, etching them into my mind so that I would never forget. I was mourning my dead self. It was me in that room, a part of me that was dead.

I didn't want to leave them, but it was time – time to say goodbye. Joe came back in to get me. We said goodbye together. I signed the papers for them to later be cremated. I would never see them again, but I felt so lucky that I had had the chance to see them one last time. They were dignified. It was a respectful and beautiful way to say goodbye. I had got over the immediate horror of seeing them so obviously the victims of a bomb blast, and seen beyond the wounds. They had looked strangely peaceful and at rest. That's how I like to remember them.

This was an important part of my recovery – to be able to process the fact that my limbs were gone, that my amputations were permanent and that my new prosthetic legs were my future. Joe and I sat in the garden area in silence, watching the spray of water turn slowly around as the fountain rotated. It was a very calming place. We both needed to gather ourselves after what we had just shared.

I realised I would never leave another footprint.

. . .

'Morning Gillington. Crutches were asking after you; they so want to be your friends, you know.' Matt was trying be light-hearted, making jokes about the crutches, in an attempt to put the disaster of our last session behind us and in the knowledge that we had to tackle and overcome my fear.

I struggled up, wobbling, rocking backward and forward. 'Matt, Matt, Matt, I'm falling. I'm falling.'

'No, you're not. You, my girl, are standing. You are standing up with crutches. I'm here, I'm right here. Now, just like we did before: weight over to the right, take a step – I'm here, I'm here – take a step, and crutch forward, weight over and step, again, again. Brilliant, again, take another step.' Nichola walked alongside the bars as Matt stood in the bars with me – both of them encouraging me to keep moving forward.

Within days of going up and down the length of the bars, I was out, holding myself up with crutches alone. I was staring down at the ground, watching every step, the placement of my foot, the leg swinging forward. I couldn't feel the ground, so I had to look down to know that I was even on the flat gym floor. I was concentrating so hard that I didn't realise that the bars were far behind us. I had cleared the bars! There was no way I could reach over and touch them. I said to Matt, 'Is this walking? Am I walking? Is this what it's like?' 'Yes,' he said. 'This is walking. YOU are walking. This is it; you're doing it.'

But it was what Matt said next that amazed me: 'Gillington, I'm back here. I'm not holding you. You are on your own, you are walking on your own.' 'Whoo, wh – ooo' – I couldn't respond. I thought I would fall at that very moment. I was doing it all on my own. I was walking. Matt wasn't there, Nichola or Carol weren't there. It was just the crutches and me – those dreaded crutches that I now loved, that were indeed my very new friends. My best friends in fact.

I kept staring down, I couldn't look up, I had to just keep moving forward, crutch, leg, crutch, leg, balance. This was the breakthrough that Matt and Nichola had been wanting. Now they could reflect on the same style of regime that I had experienced when I was first in their care; showing them that I could walk with crutches opened up all sorts of possibilities. All they needed was for me to be mobile – then they would get creative!

It wasn't long before they had me going up stairs. 'Good leg, bad leg, crutch, and again, good leg, bad leg, crutch' – this was the climbing-the-stairs mantra. Going up was ok. I just concentrated on the stair above; I didn't look up further than that and I certainly didn't look down! It was the going down that I was absolutely petrified of.

There was one occasion when I was with Nichola and we were working with the false set of stairs that were in the gym. I climbed the stairs, just as I had been taught, holding tightly onto the handrail, but when I reached the top I just froze. Now when I say top, it was only twelve or so steps off floor level, but to me, well this was a dizzy and extremely dangerous height to be standing at.

'I can't get down. I can't do that. I can't even look down – sorry Nic, I'm so sorry, what do I do?' I was in a complete panic. Nichola had to think through every possibility, including coming up and carrying me down herself – but that wasn't really a safe option. I couldn't sit and take my legs off to crawl down. I was just frozen to the spot. The tears were welling up. I hated being stuck; I hated everything about the predicament that I was in. I wanted to be back on the ground. Why did I have to go up stairs anyway? Couldn't I live on ground level? The world was a cruel, cruel place – I hated those stairs.

After a half-hour or so, I managed to get back down – with the help of Nichola at my side. We left the stairs alone for a few days after that; it took me a while to recover mentally.

When you have all your limbs it must be hard to visualise and fully appreciate just how difficult it was, how difficult it *is* to just stand, to balance – let alone move, walk or even climb stairs.

Everything was new. Everything was a 'first'. The old behaviours, the patterns that had been carved out over time, had to be re-taught and re-learnt. Every action that was previously taken for granted, such as bending down to pick something up from the floor, had now to be thought through and taken very slowly, if at all. Being able to carry a cup of tea, for example, is something that I have only mastered very recently!

I had to form a new code, a new language with my body. I had to introduce it to its new artificial limbs, broker a relationship, build trust and dependency. This had to work. I needed my body to accept that this was our 'new normal' – this was how it now felt to walk, to stand, to shower, to be mobile. I – and my body – had to forget about before, the old life. Life One was gone; this was how it was now.

It was funny how my brain seemed to simulate a computer. Often it would bring my body to a complete halt, not letting me take another step; it had obviously assessed the situation, scanned the environment that I was in and deemed it too harmful, too much of a risk, for me to proceed. I would then have to try and 'override' these judgements by trying to explain to myself (in my head – I wouldn't have wanted to alarm anyone by talking to myself out loud!) that whilst what I was attempting to do was risky, it would benefit 'us' in the long run.

. . .

The hot summer days were giving way to the winds of early autumn and it was getting cooler. Matt, Nichola and Carol took me outside. The wheelchair was there on hand but the object of this particular lesson was to learn how to walk across different surfaces. I had to try and negotiate balance and form – staying upright on different types of concrete and slopes, learning what to do if there is a pothole, or if the path is blocked and so on. All real-life scenarios and a completely different ball game for me. The stakes were now being raised very high.

I would hear Matt and Nichola's voices inside my head and this helped me to manage each step – 'Squeeze, squeeze, tummy in, head up, head up, squeeze, squeeze bum, tight, weight over, step'. They were always there, watching every movement, their supporting hand or arm never far from me, ready to catch me if I fell – I would joke with Matt that he had magic hands. I would dare to try the seemingly impossible if he was holding my hand, if I could hold onto him. He would take all my fear away the moment he held my hand; I trusted him implicitly.

We tried my theory on several occasions and sure enough, the moment I let go of his hand, my inner computer would bring my body to a halt. It was that simple – I clearly couldn't do anything unless Matt was there.

It was as if I was a toddler, with Matt and Nichola the proud parents and Carol, the young, cool aunt. Like a toddler, I wanted to do things by myself, for myself and, as most parents, their aim or goal for me was to see me 'grown-up' enough that I would be able to leave the 'nest' and make my own way in life – independent of them.

But we were also friends. Our relationship was very intense as we spent every day together, sharing every smile, every tear, every laugh. We were similar in age and in our views. They were central to all I did, to my whole world and it felt like I had known them all my life.

Matt gave me so many 'firsts', like the time he helped me onto a patch of freshly cut grass where I sank my nose right down into the earth. What a smell – amazing! He watched me as I indulged in the moment, crawling around in the grass cuttings – little knowing that I was creating some interesting grass stains on the white bandaging that covered my 'boys'. This would be hard to explain to the nurses when I went back up to the ward!

Perhaps our most special day was when we made an impromptu visit to a local adventure playground – a double amputee's dream as you can imagine! There were dirt ditches and rocks to walk over, pebbles – every uneven and unstable surface imaginable. Suddenly Matt ran off to inspect a piece of play equipment at closer range.

'Right Gillington, see this?' he said, pointing to a large structure with a series of rope ladders that led to a slide at the end. 'Now, I think you can do this – up you go.'

My first thoughts were, you must be crazy, out of your mind to think that I could ever do that. But then my fear was replaced by bravado. 'Ok, you're on, I can do it – but you are going to have to give me your finger to hold – I can't do it without you.' And so Matt was there, at the end of the slide, ready to catch me as I came hurtling down, and we were all amazed by what we had just achieved. I say 'we' because I felt that way about everything I conquered – it was all a team effort. Yes, I had to do the physical work, but they were all there with me, supporting and encouraging me all the way.

. . .

I have one particular memory of a time that says a great deal about all those people who make up the whole community of the hospital – not just the doctors and nurses.

Matt had taken me down in the lift (in itself a scary adventure), through the doors, along the outside pavement and then back through the main reception area. I looked down all the way, staring at each foot, placing them in turn, as I had been taught, onto the ground. As we walked through the main reception, from the corner of my eye I could see the man behind the counter at the newsagent, clapping his hands and smiling. Then as we walked on I saw Florence from the coffee shop. She stood there in total disbelief as I walked past her – she hadn't even seen me stand before, let alone walk. She was clasping her hands together, open-mouthed, with tears rolling down her face.

We went back up in the lift and into the third-floor gym where Joe was waiting for us, wheeling himself around in my chair, having a great time. Matt looked at him, then said to me, 'Let's go down again only with Joe in the wheelchair and you pushing him?' He thought this would be a good idea as I would get another walk in and I would be stabilised by holding onto the chair.

So, off we went again, but this time, as we paraded through reception the earlier tears of joy and amazement at seeing me walk were replaced with screams of laughter. The picture here was all wrong: someone (me) with no legs – well, wearing prosthetic legs – was pushing Joe, who was perfectly fine, around the hospital in a wheelchair.

I never expected a profound outcome from this exercise, but by me pushing Joe, and him experiencing what it is like to be confined to a wheelchair, charging through crowds of people and not feeling any control changed his view of the world. He was able to gain a small but very significant insight into what it was like for me – how vulnerable I felt. It was a very interesting swap – we both took a lot from the experience.

. . .

'Looks like I'll be going home at the end of the week – just a home visit to see if I can cope ok. Then if all goes well that's it – I'll be released!' I was thrilled for Paul that he would soon be going home, although I felt a little sad too. He was my 'buddy' – we had shared our whole rehabilitation, never needing to say very much about the bomb, the carriage, or our injuries. Just knowing how it felt to be us was very comforting. I remembered watching as Paul took his first steps and thinking about the day when I would do the same – he was always just that little bit ahead of me as he had one prosthetic leg and was a young, fit, sporty guy. He had mastered using his new leg very quickly.

'Let's have a dance,' I said. 'Can you waltz?' I don't know why I said this – like I could dance! – but before Paul could answer, I had taken hold of his hands and we had started to move gently in a circle. Joe, Matt, Nichola and Carol all looked on. Joe couldn't help himself and just had to say, 'Well that's a first, I've never seen a couple dancing who only have one leg between them!' We all laughed.

It was a perfect ending and a memorable way to say so long to Paul.

August 5, 2005

Dear All

Lots of things have happened this week. The physiotherapist and the occupational therapist have visited Joe and Gill's place and given it the thumbs-up with a few minor additions. They are talking about the end of September as a possible time for Gill to go home. This is far earlier than the original plan of December, so fingers crossed. There are still some problems with Gill's ears - not healing as quickly as expected - but there will be more news on that soon.

Gill has seen a few visitors but wants to spend most of her time with Jo, Graham, Alex and Maddy before they go home to Australia next week. She is looking so much better and is getting stronger both physically and emotionally, but there are still some very low times.

Joe and Graham went to visit Russell Square tube station at the invitation of the police and London Underground staff. For Graham it was a first and last visit underground, but they both found it helpful and were touched by the care and thought put into the event.

The police have organised a surprise visit for Gill to a swish spa (across the road at the Marriott Hotel - hair, nails, facial?), so we await news of how that went.

Love to you all

Bella, Lyndon, Gill, Joe and family

August 30, 2005

Dear Everyone

Hope you've had an enjoyable August. We had a long chat with Joe today, and there's a fair bit to report.

First of all, and with apologies for any coyness you might have detected up to now, Gill has said that she now feels comfortable with everyone knowing the full extent of her injuries. In case you don't yet know, Gill was very close indeed to the blast on the Russell Square train, and has lost both her legs below the knee. She also has significant perforations to both eardrums.

The good news with which to temper this is that she is setting about her physio' and rehab' with intimidating determination, and is now up and about on crutches. She's still learning to balance on her new legs, but Joe says that when she stands on her own it's impossible to tell that anything is different from before. The physio' team is confident that she'll be able to walk again, on her new legs, unaided. As far as her ears are concerned the ENT specialist reckons there's no damage to her inner ears, and is discussing a skin graft and new ear-drums in a couple of months' time, so that should yield a significant improvement.

The whole story of Gill's survival defies belief, as she was very close to death for a very long time; and it seems implausible that so many miracles have occurred in sequence to keep her with us. Doubtless you'll get the full story from Gill; but suffice it for now to say that on Saturday Gill and Joe will be meeting two of the four policemen who carried her down the tunnel. This week Gill also met the nurse and doctor who disregarded police orders to evacuate the area outside the tube station for fear of a suspected second device, and who kept her alive on the pavement when she suffered her first cardiac arrest.

She's also met the A&E team who tended her in St Thomas', most of whom still can't believe she made it through such an appalling ordeal.

But she has, and the hope is still that Gill should be able to walk back into her home around the end of September. This does throw up the fascinating scenario of whether or not Joe can get it finished on time. Anyone with close contacts to the 'Changing Rooms' production team might do well to alert them to a potentially interesting edition.

The other good news is that Gill's now recovered sufficiently to begin to see visitors. She is actually very busy — nothing new there (!) as she's doing, and recovering from, about three hours of physio' each day. She's receiving ward rounds from several consultants, enjoying hospital food etc., but there are now opportunities to see her, particularly as her Australian relatives have returned home and Joe has a new term starting.

So if you'd like to call on Gill, drop us an e-mail here, ideally with some times that could work for you, and we'll talk to Joe about when. PLEASE be patient, as we're anticipating quite a few folk to fit in!

With best wishes to everyone

Lyndon and Bella

Chapter 7

Leaving the 'Bubble'

'How much stuff can one little Boo Boo accumulate? There's enough here to fill twenty bags!' Joe was amused, amazed even at the number of bags piling up in the doorway – and there was still so much more to go. I had 'checked' in with nothing, not even an identity, and here I was, nearly three months later with bags and bags of 'stuff'.

I hadn't expected to feel so nostalgic yet at the same time optimistic. It was a little like the feeling you get when you leave the family home, going out to face the world on your own; it's a rite of passage, a natural progression, yet it is filled with uncertainty. And that's what was happening to me. It was time for me to stop being a patient; I was as mended as I could be. I now had to leave the warmth and security of the hospital's womb-like environment. It was time to be born – to be released out into the world and to 'stand on my own two *prosthetic* feet'!

I folded the last of my pyjamas. I knew I would never wear them again. They belonged to this time and place; they were about me being here in hospital, about the good and the bad nights. I pushed my face into them, breathing in deeply, trying to inhale that one last bit of scent before they were packed away.

There were only a few items left, mainly all the tablets and creams and lotions. But there was one other very precious item – standing upright and proud on its own. It was my powder – the talcum powder that I had been given when I was taken to Intensive Care – and it still carried the label that served as a last, stark reminder of who I was when I arrived here just months earlier, stripped of my identity and fighting for my life. The label read very clearly, 'One Unknown – estimated female, 1960'. Then there was a long hospital/patient number and a bar code – that was it. That's who I was – no one. The same label was on my wristband and anything that 'belonged' to me.

It was very powerful and symbolic: nobody knew who I was, yet still they fought to save me. It was a positive reminder for me of how wonderful humanity is, how outstanding the people who rescued me were and are, as well as the doctors, surgeons and nurses. Mine was a precious life that they all wanted to save, without knowing who I was.

It didn't matter – I could have been rich or poor, I could have been of any faith, I could have been from any background. None of that mattered. One Unknown had to be saved. One Unknown – I – had to be loved and cared for because mine was a human life, because I could have been any one of them. I was somebody's daughter, maybe someone's mother, a girlfriend, a wife, a sister, an aunt? One Unknown belonged somewhere and they were all determined to get me back to that place.

After receiving such devastating, life-changing injuries at the hands of one human being, and after witnessing the destruction and hurt to so many that just that one person – that one act – caused, I was then shown the purest of all love: the love and devotion of strangers, all desperate to save life, no matter what, no matter who.

Some would say that I was incredibly unfortunate to have been in that carriage, on that day, at that time and, yes, I was. But equally I have been shown the depth of what makes us human. I have had the opportunity to know individuals who risked their lives to save mine; individuals who made decisions – difficult decisions – based on instinct and, in so doing, saved my life. I feel blessed to have been so loved and I am just one of many; just one more unknown that they treat and deal with every day.

I found my label both profound and eye-opening. It has forced me to think about 'us', individuals – each of us holding such power to make a difference. Never more so than now have I believed in the power of one.

One Unknown person can change many lives.

I read all the cards again as they were being packed, much to Joe's annoyance. There were so many – from dear friends, from work colleagues and family. Looking at them displayed every day had made such a difference – they had transformed my room. 'Hey Joe, do you love me more than Kylie?' He had no idea what I was on about. I was looking at one of my favourite cards that said: 'I love you more than Kylie'. The person who sent it must have loved me an awful lot!

But for every humorous card, there were others that touched me very deeply and still bring a tear to my eye to this day. Words of encouragement, support, hope and love flooded in from people all over the world. It really had given me that little bit of extra strength when I'd needed a boost; just knowing that so many people cared enough to send me a letter or a card was incredible. The hospital was the only world I had known since the bomb and these strangers, these members of the public were cushioning my re-entry into the 'real' world. I was overwhelmed by the fact that so many people had reached out, that they felt so strongly and so sad for all of us who were involved.

This was yet another strong example of the wonder of the human spirit – its capacity to show such empathy. It made me feel very guilty as although I may often have been very touched by a story – a tragedy that someone faced or a triumph they made – not once had I sent a card to say how much I admired or supported that person. I had always considered myself a good person, someone who cared passionately about the world, but I had never sent a card to a complete stranger. I do now. All those cards, all the letters, the good wishes and prayers – they all made such a difference to me.

I was nearly done, when I saw one more envelope waiting to be packed. It contained a letter written by a bilateral amputee. He was an Australian, a Member of Parliament who had lost both legs fighting in Vietnam. The letter had arrived when I was feeling quite low. Whilst everyone around me was being encouraging and supportive, they didn't know – how could they know? – how I was feeling. I was desperate to talk about life in the future – what to expect, how I would cope, general practicalities – with someone who was just like me, someone who'd been through it all and come out the other side.

I had pored over each word in that letter when I'd received it and did so again now. He had experienced everything I was feeling. I wasn't alone; this was one of the most precious gifts given to me. He alleviated my concerns – I was 'normal', my fears were 'normal' and immediately I was put at ease. He was honest and I appreciated that. He said that life wouldn't be easy, that he was sorry, deeply sorry that this had happened and that I had been involved. But, he wrote – and this is the most crucial part of the message – I had survived against all the odds and I had what it took to get through this ('this' being the double amputations). Life, he said, would throw a multitude of obstacles in my way and a lot of the time it would be a real uphill struggle. It would be completely natural for me to feel extreme levels of anger, frustration and sadness at times, even mourning for my limbs. I would experience every conceivable emotion – but I would find my 'new normal', I would get through and I would enjoy life again.

'Boo Boo, don't cry. This is positive, we are starting our new lives.' Joe was right, this wasn't a time to feel melancholy. I would be ok out there. And the letter was right: I had survived the unimaginable – I knew I could face any challenge head-on, I knew I could win (or, at the very least, reach a compromise).

So the bags were packed and I was ready. My room was now bare. It was no longer my home.

'Knock knock – are you ready young Gillington? It's time for ... it's time for your big surprise!' Matt was rubbing his hands together eagerly, as both he and Nic stood in the doorway of my room. 'It's bus time! We are going to take you on a bus!' Nichola was greatly enjoying the look of shock on my face. When this had been mentioned in one of our physio' sessions, I had thought it was all a bit 'tongue in cheek' – it was bad enough learning to get across the main road, let alone getting onto a bus! I was beginning to sweat. Surely they weren't really going to go through with this?

Joe wasn't any help. He was giggling as he continued sorting out the bags. 'Yes, that's a great idea,' he said. 'A red bus, a double-decker; it's just such a shame there isn't a Routemaster that passes the hospital. Well, that would be the number 159; it was first on the roads in 1958. No, sorry, it was much earlier than that – could even have been 1920 – '

'Ok, ok Joe. I don't want to hear any more. Well I can't really hear – ok, I don't want to barely hear or read your lips about buses. I don't want to get on a bus. Today is my leaving day, can't I just have a nice time? Huh?' Matt, Nic and Carol could see that I was apprehensive, so together they came up with a compromise: 'Right Gill, we are going to go on a bus, yes, *but*, it's just the hopper bus – the little bus that travels between the hospital buildings. That's all right isn't it?'

What could I say? I would look pathetic if I went all cowardly over that. I mean – a hopper bus? How scary could that be? Right?

The tension built. Joe was pushing the wheelchair – empty – behind me; I had to walk out. It was like slow marching: crutches in co-ordination, 'left leg – right crutch, right leg, left crutch'. My mind was filled with the sound of Nic's voice – like when I was climbing the stairs, 'Good leg, bad leg, crutch,' in that order; oh, or was it left leg matched with left crutch ...' These thoughts occupied me all the way down and out of the building – 'Left leg, right crutch, right leg, left crutch,' then, 'Look, look up, it's the bus stop just there; now, what do you do when you get to a kerb?'

I climbed the platform of the bus, managed to stagger down the aisle, find a seat and plonk myself down – with all the grace of a wildebeest performing in *Swan Lake*. I could already tell that I would need to practise my sitting technique in public places!

Just then, one of my special nurses from the ward got on the bus and, not having noticed me, said to Matt, 'Hello. Where are you going? Aren't you going to Gill's surprise party? I've come in especially for it.'

I cut in: 'Hello Sinead, it's me, Gill!' to which she replied, in her wonderful Irish accent, 'Aaaaargh. Well I suppose it's not a surprise party any more! What are you doing on the bus?' She was devastated that she'd let the cat out of the bag, so I reassured her: 'It's ok. I can still look surprised, see –' and I made as wide-eyed and wide-mouthed an expression as I could.

Matt insisted that I *walked* into the Day Room. I wonder why?

'Hoorah!' was the shout that greeted me. Everyone was there – well everyone that could be. Caroline, Louise and, of course, Sinead had all come in on their day off; it was a real honour for me. There was also a great spread of cakes, sandwiches and drinks (non-alcoholic, this was a hospital ward after all!).

I stood and gave a speech, thanking them all not only for the level of care that I had received, but for making me feel that I was a part of their 'family'. I said how much I would miss them and the world that we had created there. Emma then spoke for all, saying how proud they were of my progress and what a pleasure it had been to know and care for me.

We all drank a toast with our lemonade and orange juice, 'To life and to happy endings, or beginnings!' Everyone was very emotional and it was so lovely to feel that saying goodbye was equally as hard for them as it was for me. I stressed, as I was leaving, that 'a Gill is for Life, not just for July 7 – I'll be back!'

Then Kat, a very close friend to both Joe and I, arrived in her car – I thought it was more likely I would need a small van to take everything that I had accumulated! – and everyone grabbed a bag or two and headed down with us.

The car was so stuffed with all my hospital memorabilia that there was barely enough room for us all to get in. There was just about time for a final round of hugs – I didn't want to let go, as the tears turned to sobs – before Joe extracted me and I got in the car. I rolled down the window and began to wave. We were all crying and waving and shouting out, 'Bye, bye, love you, miss you already, bye,' when I was suddenly overcome by an urge of 'Gillness'. I pulled my left leg off and stuck it out the window, waving it about for all to see; then we opened the sunroof and the right leg popped through it. Everyone was laughing hysterically, including the innocent bystanders who happened to be in the car park. I wanted to leave on a high. I wanted to leave them laughing, not crying. And I wanted to be remembered with a smile ...

I then put my legs back on, with some difficulty I must admit and howled all the way to our destination, namely Joe's sister Rose's cottage in the tranquil, idyllic setting of Richmond.

September 25, 2005

Dear All

Sorry not to have been in touch for a while.

Gill (and Joe) have now been discharged from hospital and, though not back at home in Tufnell Park as building work is ongoing, are very comfortably housed in our sister's place in Richmond.

The fund - Gill@St Thomas' and the account ... the account
has finally been set up and we were sent details on the day
Gill left hospital! We hope that people are still interested
in contributing or fundraising — anything, however small.
(My hairdresser has offered to do a raffle — she was the first
person to give me some money - when she heard about Gill she
gave me £10 and in a way that's where the idea came from.) We
hear that the Design Council has been doing some fantastic
fundraising — their (presumably design-aware!) Hawaiian
night must have been a thing to behold — all this is so we
can give something good back to the hospital — so whatever
you can do will be very much appreciated.

The benefit concert is still an ongoing idea and Joe and Gill
are thinking about the six-month/one-year anniversary as
possible dates. This gives us a time span for fundraising and
will allow them to concentrate on getting better and making
wedding plans in the meantime.

Any ideas for a venue or music acts for the show? It's not
only about money but also about putting on an event where
we can all meet, celebrate, and thank the hospital staff.

Thank you for all your support, kindness, and all the love
that has been shown and offered through the last difficult
months.

With all best wishes

Bella, Lyndon, Joe, Gill, and all the family

Richmond is the area where Joe was born, in a street just around the
corner from where we would be staying. It must have been odd for him.
Our new start, Life Two, was a bit like coming full circle, back to where
he began life over forty years before. This was also where Graham had
stayed during those first dark days when my life still hung in the balance,
and then with Jo and the kids when things were a little more optimistic.

We turned into a narrow street, lined with the most charming, tiny
cottages. It was like being on a film set – or what I imagined a film set
to be like.

We were so grateful to have been given the opportunity to live there, to be somewhere so beautiful whilst waiting for our own home in north London to be finished. Our dear friends Chris and Fernando, the architects, were working on it against the clock with Simon, an expert builder who had also become a friend over the years. The wedding date was getting closer – just two and a half months away – and there was still a substantial amount of work to be done for there to be any hope of me ever living there. Everything had had to be rethought with my needs at the centre of the design: heights, space, safety and accessibility all had to be taken into consideration. Our home is spread over four floors with our bedroom up in the loft, so to say that this presented a challenge is an understatement. But once again, I was very determined that I would not be forced from my home. I would make the decision to stay or to move once I had the chance to be back there and, until such time, all plans would go ahead. We were also concerned that the family would be back in London a week before the wedding and I was desperate for us all to be together, under one roof.

But this was no time for stress. That was something that belonged to Life One. This was a new beginning for Joe and I, a chance to continue the 'bubble' experience by not fully engaging or integrating with our old lives. We could create our own little nest in Richmond and experience all the many 'firsts' in the relative safety of this cosy environment. It was our 'trainer' home – a place where we could learn to adapt and adjust to the new life, to gain enough strength and confidence to eventually return to our home.

Routine. We still adhered to routine, even though we didn't have to *do* anything. We could have just stayed in bed all day if we'd wished, but we were happy to continue with what we had become accustomed to whilst living in hospital. The cottage was already adapted appropriately as Joe's elderly aunt had lived there up until her death a few years earlier. This provided me with options, which was brilliant. I could brave the slatted, winding staircase to use the bedroom and bathroom upstairs or I could live entirely on the ground floor (there was a sofa-bed and a shower/toilet area just off the lounge). I could either move around the ground floor, from kitchen to lounge in the wheelchair, I could crawl, or use my legs! The floor span was bijou, with just enough space for a wheelchair to turn in. It was perfect!

Before I was 'allowed' to leave the hospital, Matt and an occupational therapist had brought me to the Richmond cottage to check that it would be suitable. The staircase was the only potential obstacle as far as Matt could tell, but he was eager for me to at least try it – he was never prepared to admit defeat! We practised it together, 'Next leg, that's it, up, crutch and lift, that's it, just don't look down'.

I had managed to get up – but I couldn't get down. It was always the coming down that terrified me – yet another thing to add to the list of 'fears I must conquer'.

During the 'home visit' Matt had also spotted the kettle, which prompted some useful kitchen tips; like never to fill the kettle up completely as it would be too heavy for me to lift and pour. And, before doing anything like cooking, making tea or washing up, to practise both in my wheelchair and with legs whilst Joe or someone was with me. It was all about repetition: trying something, then doing it over and over again until I was confident.

I had smiled at Matt as he'd talked about re-learning things like making tea or doing the washing up, but really I'd just wanted to cry. It took all my strength to stay positive. I had to understand that I couldn't take anything for granted; life 'on the outside' would be completely different. I kept drawing on the fight that I knew I had within me, the inner strength that had got me through the carriage. I was tough and kept saying it over and over and over: 'I am strong, I am tough, I can cope. I am strong, I am tough, I can cope.' It's an amazing trick – when you say something enough you actually start to believe it! I was counting on this theory to get me through.

I tried to have my legs on as much as possible as I needed to get used to wearing them for longer periods each day. The 'boys' hated being trapped in the legs, being much happier when I spent the day crawling or in the wheelchair. They wanted to be free.

The right stump/boy was still healing and had to be dressed on a daily basis; I was becoming a dab hand at sterilising the area and applying the surgical pads. The wound was still weeping, having borne the brunt of the blast, and although Prof was optimistic about its complete recovery there was no telling when it would finally be healed. Twice a week a district nurse would come and check the wound. It was as if an umbilical cord still connected me to the system so that

I didn't feel abandoned or alone. They were still there, still caring for me. And I, in return, loved to show off my miraculous progress by making them cups of tea!

Matt had photocopied images of his hands for me, the idea being that I could pin them up around the house and reach out to touch them whenever I needed that extra burst of confidence.

So, Life Two was beginning. It was under way and this was the first chapter in our 'new normal' manual. At ten am we would turn on our television to watch our daily dose of *City Hospital* – a live programme on the BBC, filmed entirely at both Guy's and St Thomas' hospitals. It was our vicarious hospital life: Joe and I would watch, waiting to catch a glimpse of a corridor or a nurse we recognised, then we'd both yell at the same time, 'Hey, that's the x-ray nurse. Do you remember him?' It would be fair to say that watching the programme did help to stave off all the withdrawal symptoms we were both experiencing.

I looked forward to my daily walk. This was a chance for me to practise living in my legs. I gained more and more confidence with every step – which was exactly what I needed to do – amazed that I was still standing, that I hadn't fallen over. I chose to do most of my walking on the road as the footpaths presented too many unexpected bumps and different surfaces, like cracked paving stones, or the roots of a tree poking up through the concrete. These obstacles were intimidating and I didn't yet have the skills to deal with them. I was scared of tripping or falling over, so my strategy was simply to avoid them all together. The only danger the road presented, apart from a slight gradient that tipped me forward, was the traffic. I still found it difficult hearing noises that did not come from directly in front of me, so Joe would wave to warn me if a car was coming, and I would 'pull over' and let it pass.

Like a toddler seeking adult approval, I would take a few steps with my crutches, then stop and look around to see if Joe was watching. He always was, of course, and he would automatically praise me – 'Well done Boo Boo, that's fantastic' – and I would go on. We did that every day, Joe on hand with the wheelchair. I wonder what the neighbours must have made of us: 'There's that poor girl who obviously has difficulty walking and that terrible man just pushing an empty chair alongside her. Why on earth doesn't she just get in and use the wheelchair?'

We set the goals together. On the first day Joe suggested that I try walking to the end of our tiny little street. That became my target and by the end of that week I had done it! And so we would set a new goal, trying to get a little further each day, both physically and metaphorically.

I was relentless, determined not to let my physio' slip now that I wasn't in the gym every day. Joe would spur me on and I needed it, especially when we approached an uphill road where my legs would come to a complete standstill. 'Come on, you can do that. It's nothing. You can walk up there.'

One evening we made a breakthrough that became the catalyst for walking longer distances than either of us would have thought possible at that stage. Our dear friends, Berni and Si, came over for a visit and we had planned to have dinner. Food was something we were all passionate about – Berni and Si were famous for their Sunday evening picnic hampers at the hospital. Si would lovingly make a huge feast, wrap it all up and the four of us would sit on the grass, by the fountain on a lovely summer's eve, toasting life and eating roasted peppers with couscous, bean salads and crusty French bread. I would always look forward to our special hospital picnics. But this was their first visit outside of the hospital grounds and this time I was able to entertain them!

There was an interesting-looking pub about half a mile away at the very far end of our main road and we all decided that this might be a nice place to eat; the cottage was so small that four people really did feel like a crowd in it. So, to demonstrate my new walking abilities, I set off, whilst Joe explained that our current goal was for me to walk to the end of the main road by the end of the month. He dutifully followed with the wheelchair, calling out for me to let him know when I was ready to get in. Distracted by my conversation with Berni – we had a lot of catching up to do – I just kept on walking down the road. I didn't notice that everyone had gone quiet. I stopped. I looked up and there was the entrance to the pub. I had just walked all the way from the front door of the cottage to the entrance of the pub!

Berni and Si were shocked, amazed, delighted and scared all at the same time. They had never expected to see me do this; well, they hadn't really had any expectations at all. They were just happy that I was alive; it didn't matter if I was walking, standing or sitting. They were speechless. 'Say something. Someone say something, or I will,' and I let out a great scream of utter delight. 'Yes, yes, yes! I walked all the way; I walked all the way. He he, look at me, I'm a walker!'

Berni felt that this called for a celebration – it was champagne all round! My triumph was sadly short lived though. The moment we got into the pub I couldn't hear a thing, our conversation being completely absorbed by the chatter of everyone around us. But we drank our champagne and I was still euphoric at my achievement. Joe had to push me back as I was a little 'shaky' from all the celebrating – ok, I was drunk!

So the stakes were raised once again and coach Joe set new, more challenging goals the next day. The joy! Eventually I did make it into the main high street, where all the shops, coffee bars and restaurants were. I would arrive soaked in perspiration – it was hard work, bearing in mind that I was using 200 per cent more energy than an able-bodied person. Joe still followed with the wheelchair just in case.

Every street held a special memory for Joe and as we ventured around the area it was lovely to hear stories that I'd never heard before about his antics as a little boy. We visited the church where he was christened and places he would go to with his mum. It was a very special time. Joe could never have thought that one day he would be seeing these streets again, as a man supporting his bride-to-be, helping her as she learned to walk again on prosthetic legs. An unimaginable scenario.

. . .

I was being introduced to real life, the real world – a world that wasn't built for people in wheelchairs, or with no legs. The wheelchair became a definer of life for us as it would decide which shops I could go into, which restaurants we could eat in, and which direction we could take. I was still very dependent on it – it was more an extension of me than the prosthetic legs were. I hated having to face the public in my new disabled state, having to move amongst them in a wheelchair. I never expected to resent it so much, but I couldn't retreat back now into the protective arms of the hospital.

If I'd thought that the barriers had long-been eroded, that there was a greater understanding now of the needs of disabled people, I was wrong; I was in a minority and that's how it felt. Both Joe and I come from the fields of architecture and design and I had been exposed to many enlightened professionals whose designs were all user-centred, so I – perhaps naively – had assumed that everyone and everything would be like that: naturally, entrances would be accessible, paths would be smoothed, disabled toilets would be available. But that wasn't the case.

I now had an entirely different relationship with architecture and design – what had worked perfectly well for me before, now seemed laughable. I had to be aware of every surface, whether I was walking or in the chair. I was living Life Two with my head down, not out of shyness or embarrassment, but because I had to scour every inch of every surface for potential obstacles. This was life on the outside.

Joe loves to cook – actually it's one of the things that he is most passionate about – and being back at the helm in the kitchen was something he'd dreamed of when he was staying in the hospital with me. He is a man who finds as much pleasure in the preparation as he does in the eating. Completely the opposite of me – I just enjoy eating the finished product!

Our trips down to the high street were partly aimed at shopping for ingredients. Joe would usually have a special recipe in mind, something that he could spend the afternoon preparing. These outings stirred mixed feelings in me: on the one hand I was excited that I was going to walk, aiming to reach a goal, but on the other hand I would be in public, in my chair, feeling awkward. For the most part, I couldn't get into the shops that Joe needed to go to, so he would park me outside and I would wait – a bit like a pet dog, except I wasn't chained to a post. He didn't mean any offence by it – we just couldn't get the chair in, so I had to stay outside.

I remember one particular day when, for some reason, every passer-by wanted to 'help'. I was in my chair, waiting for Joe and the sun was peeping through a cloud to shine on my face, just brightly enough to warrant me closing my eyes. 'Hello dear,' said a man's strong voice, startling me. 'Are you waiting to be pushed somewhere? Can I push you down the road?' I must have looked completely puzzled and for a moment I couldn't say a word. 'Dear, are you ok?' He started to talk louder and slower, almost spelling the words out to me, 'D-o y-o-u w-a-n-t s-o-m-e h-e-l-p?'

'No, I'm fine, thank you,' I said. 'I'm just waiting for my partner. He's in the shop. He won't be long. Thank you anyway, thank you.' I tried to respond in my best English accent, although I don't know why. I guess I wanted him to think that I was posh and therefore fine.

I got a little anxious and it must have shown on my face. I was wishing Joe would hurry, when suddenly another voice came booming down at me. 'Hello there, are you ok? Would you like a push?' I tried not to make my reply sound grumpy, 'I'm fine, honestly. Thank you. I'm just waiting for my partner. He's in there buying some fish for tonight. Thank you though.' And the man walked off. He was smiling – the sort of smile you smile when you feel you have done a good deed. I was his good deed. I never thought I would be that. I don't mean to sound ungrateful as these gestures were wonderful and thoughtful – just not what I needed.

I felt vulnerable. I could have easily become a recluse. To Joe, to my friends and my family, I was still Gill, legs or no legs. This was still me. But I had to face the fact that the world didn't see me as Gill first. How could they? They didn't know who I was. What they saw was someone who they thought needed help, a disabled person; someone not like them.

Then again, I didn't really mind, it was nice that people bothered to ask if I needed help. Really, nothing mattered. I was just happy to be alive, in a chair or not. I valued every moment, good or bad. Everything I was experiencing felt like a bonus.

...

The wedding was now a little over a month away and we still seemed to exist in a strange zone where there was no time – only moments.

We couldn't get panicked. What was the point? The main concern was getting our home ready. I wanted to sleep in my own bed, see all my things. I was missing my old surroundings – I had gone to work on July 7, never made it in, and hadn't been home since. That was nearly four months ago.

Everything would be different there now – not how I had left it. So much had happened. We were approving designs, schemes and colours by proxy, trusting that it would all be brilliant. Joe's daughter, Lily, was still there, sleeping amongst the rubble; she couldn't bear the idea of being extracted from north London and all her friends. Richmond was over the River Thames – for her it was a world away from home.

...

I didn't have an engagement ring yet – well, not a proper one, with real diamonds anyway! The cobble-paved labyrinth of streets off the main stretch of Richmond was filled with exclusive shops, all one-off designers spanning fashion, food, and ... jewellery.

On one of our many expeditions Berni and I wandered slowly, keeping an eye out for something that sparkled. 'Look, what about this one? This is lovely – very you!' Berni had spotted something promising, and to see it, I would have to prop myself against the shop frontage, forehead pressed against the glass, crutches either side of me, thinking, 'balance, balance, balance'. Once stable, I could concentrate on the ring! Berni had a good eye for fashion and knew what I liked. She had been responsible for buying many of my hospital outfits: she would burst through the door with an armful of shopping bags and whatever didn't fit, she would take back. I had got down to a size 6–8 then, so luckily most things did fit!

The ring was perfect. I wanted something simple – just a single diamond but in a thick, brushed platinum band. I couldn't see the price though and there's always a catch isn't there – whilst the ring may have been perfect the price probably wasn't.

There was a very steep step up into the jeweller's. It was far bigger than any step I had tackled before and my nerves got the better of me. So I waited outside whilst Berni went in to investigate. She was in there for a while, looking at other designs, bringing them up to the glass panel in the door for me to see. I would smile and nod, or screw my face up to indicate what worked and what didn't. For me, the one in the window was it. After a year or more of searching, that was what I wanted. I knew it in an instant.

. . .

The nights were drawing in and there was a real nip in the air – it was late October after all. Joe and I decided to take a late-afternoon walk and, given my pace, it was early evening before we reached Richmond town. All the cobbled paths led to Richmond Green. (We have a painting of the park that Antony, Joe's dad, painted when they lived in the area; it was a place that had many sentimental associations.)

'Let's walk to the centre of the park. It's so beautiful with all the leaves on the ground and we can look back to the lights of the shops and the street,' Joe said.

I was wary, I hadn't actually walked on grass before, and because the ground was covered in leaves I couldn't judge the terrain. 'I can't Joe. It's too dark, I can't see where I'm walking, what I'm stepping on.'

'Please,' he said. 'It's important. Take my hand and I'll guide you through.' I must have looked like an ice-skater, balancing on thin blades whilst crossing smooth ice – only this was a park.

'Can we stop here? I don't want to go any further. Please.'

We stopped and Joe put his arms around me and hugged me tight. 'You know how much I love you, don't you?' He knelt down on one knee, 'Give me your hand my precious Boo Boo.' I couldn't believe that he was proposing right there in the park, in full view of everyone! 'Will you do me the greatest honour of becoming my wife?' Then he opened a box, and in it was the ring that I loved.

'Yes, of course I will!'

Joe put the ring on the fourth finger on my left hand. We just stood and hugged each other as tears of joy fell from our eyes. 'We are so blessed and so lucky. I am so lucky to have all this, to be here, to be loved.'

I was grateful to be alive, and so thankful to have had this moment.

Chapter 8

Piecing It All Together

WHAT'S STRANGE ABOUT BEING INVOLVED in such a public event, one that shocked and horrified many around the world, is that you can never really remain anonymous. I had started as 'One Unknown' but couldn't stay that way. I was now on a list; on one of two main lists, in fact. They were: the dead and the seriously injured. I was also on another, smaller list: Australian citizens injured.

I was news and the press were eager, wanting to know if I was going to recover or become another fatality. I was one of the most seriously injured Australian nationals, so naturally the press there took great interest in my 'case' too. There were two Australians on the critical list: myself, and a man who had been on the number 30 bus when it exploded. Sadly, he died of his injuries whilst in hospital. I was 'next in line', so to speak and there was increasing pressure from the media on close family and friends, each paper vying to be first with any breaking news.

They wanted all the details and the prognosis. There were rumours that both my legs had been amputated, so they wanted either to dismiss or qualify these. I was mostly in a coma, unable to speak for myself or indicate which, if any, details of my injuries should be released. So Joe, Graham and Joe's family, the Kerrs, all agreed that it was best to say nothing in order to protect me and leave any decisions to me, as and when I was able to understand. Remember that at this time, neither the medical teams nor my family were expecting me even to survive, so they were reluctant to release any information at all until everyone had a clearer idea of what the following week would bring.

This was a harrowing time not only for all who were gathered around me in London, but also for Jo and the kids on their own on the other side of the world in Adelaide. Graham had left for London and Jo had to hold the fort, and remain positive and optimistic whilst simultaneously being bombarded by journalists, some calling as early as 6am, desperate to get the scoop. I can only imagine how upsetting it was for her, Alex and Maddy. They'd had no warning. Their lives had been 'normal' one day and thrown into complete chaos the next. They were trying to cope with the situation themselves, trying to deal with the news that I had been involved in an explosion – a suicide bomb attack! They certainly didn't expect to be chased to their front door, followed down the street, or called repeatedly day and night.

Jo recounts one particularly upsetting phone call she received from a well-known Sydney paper. The reporter wasted no time with pleasantries and went straight in, saying: 'We have just had a report that Gillian passed away overnight. Can you comment?' Jo began shaking uncontrollably, her immediate thoughts being for Graham who hadn't landed in London yet. She couldn't bear to think that he might be too late, that he might not get the chance to say goodbye. Rage coursed through her veins. She was furious at this reporter's insensitivity, furious with the whole situation. She felt so far away, unable to do anything, to see for herself if I was alive or not. She slammed the phone down and tried all the numbers she had for Joe or Steve in London. She couldn't get through on any of them so she called Stella at home in Queensland. The frantic calling went on, Jo to Stella, Stella to Steve, Steve back to Stella, and finally Stella to Jo. I was alive – critical, but alive.

Jo didn't know how much more of this she could take. No one knew if I would live; if anything they were preparing for quite the opposite – but she knew she needed to stay strong for the kids and Graham. All the Minears, Jo's family, rallied around, shielding, advising and doing all they could to protect her and the kids. In the meantime a press statement was released in the hope that this would satisfy the media.

...

Once I was out of danger, after those first few crucial days, the press attention eased a little, but as I grew stronger, especially when I was released to the ward, the press wanted exclusive interviews, with me and/or my family. The hospital had a strict security system in place, not only for me, but for all patients who could be subjected to press intrusion.

This protective wall did not prevent us from being inundated by enquiries, though and whilst I couldn't deal with all of these, I didn't want to be rude and not respond. I felt a bit like a 'Big Brother' contestant, trapped in the house, not really knowing much about what is going on outside but with the rest of the world all knowing about me. So, following discussion with our friends and family, Joe's sister Rose suggested we talk to a media specialist, someone whom she knew and respected. Claire Sawford worked mainly with art and design clients, which chimed perfectly with us. During many a coffee and chat by the hospital fountain, Claire gained a deep understanding of my concerns and my wishes: I didn't want to be called a 'victim' – I saw myself as a survivor – and didn't, therefore, want to be portrayed as someone whom the public would pity. I was eager to make my survival, my second chance, mean something. There was so much that I wanted to say – above all, I wanted my message to be positive, well as positive as it could be. It was just finding the words to express it all and waiting for the clarity that time alone could bring. But whilst I was in hospital I just wanted to concentrate on getting well enough and fit enough to cope with whatever life had in store for me.

. . .

My experience with the media was certainly not all bad. In fact coverage of my story actually led to many powerful and emotional encounters with people who were key players in my rescue and survival.

The first meeting I had with someone who was 'there', someone who had contributed to my survival, was with a woman called Angie. (Mum had wanted to call me Angela – she always said I was her angel – but Dad had insisted that Gillian was a much stronger name. Apparently, so I have always been told, Gillian means 'child of God', and by giving me this name Dad thought I would always be protected and watched over.)

Angie had written a piece in a newspaper about a woman whom

she'd accompanied in the back of an ambulance to St Thomas' hospital. The woman had had dark hair, blue eyes and suffered severe lower-leg injuries. It could only have been me she was describing. We arranged to meet her.

I sat in the Day Room, waiting for Angie to arrive. I kept moving from my wheelchair to the sofa, then back to my wheelchair, finally deciding that I looked more relaxed on the sofa. I was worn out by the time she walked in!

'Oh, it *is* you, it is you.' She looked so shocked to see me, I guess, as a 'proper' person for the first time.

I wanted to know every detail. I was hungry for everything she could remember, desperate for my scrambled memory to make some sense. Every day I would remember something new, but had no way of knowing where or how it slotted into the bigger picture.

Angie said she had rushed to Russell Square station (she is a specialist nurse at a children's hospital near the station) to be met by a scene that was almost indescribable. She said it was like a war zone. Badly wounded people were lying on the floor of the ticket hall. Emergency workers were everywhere. Everyone, she said, was just in shock. She explained that after arresting for a second time (she thought the first arrest had been just as I was brought out of the tunnel) I needed to be stabilised enough to be put in an ambulance.

As Angie was talking my jaw was dropping. I was listening to someone talk about me, but taking in the information as though I were a third person. I was nodding, sighing at all the 'right' moments, indicating in every way that I was absorbing it all, every detail. But I wasn't. I was watching her mouth move, even heard some of the words fall out, but I simply could not digest them.

Angie then pointed to Waterloo Bridge from the window: 'Then you arrested in the ambulance as we were going over the bridge,' she said. It had been a long time, she went on, since she had dealt with an adult, so she had spoken to me as if I were a small child, saying, 'Come on my girl, come on my little one, please angel.'

She remembered the line of A&E staff all waiting as they pulled into the hospital and how she had never seen anyone whipped so fast out of an ambulance before. Then, just like that, she said, I was gone. I was theirs now. Angie said she had prayed and prayed that I would survive. She thought it was a miracle that I had, and that I was sitting there with her now.

This meeting with Angie was the first of many. There were still so many details, so many things I needed and wanted to know.

Above all though, I wanted to meet everyone who'd had any involvement with me and with my rescue. I desperately wanted to thank them and show them how well I was doing; how grateful I was for everything they had all done. I thought about my rescue a lot – I could hear the conversations, I could feel the awkward manoeuvres. I had a strong sense that many people had put in a superhuman effort and I just wanted to thank them all. To hold them.

The Day Room was once again the venue for a meeting, this time with two of the Metropolitan Police officers who had been involved in carrying me down the tunnel. I had met some visiting officers at the hospital who told me that two of their colleagues had helped with my rescue. I expressed my wish to thank them and happily they agreed to meet me and Joe.

I was so nervous. These men would know; these men had been there, down there in the dark. I was worried for them. What if meeting me would upset them? What if they didn't want any reminders of that day? It was nearly three months now since the bomb ...

Then in they walked. In full uniform. They looked amazing – the most handsome policemen I had ever seen! I was in my chair, both prosthetic legs on but resting on the footplates. At least I was 'dressed' as I like to call it. I didn't want them to meet me with just my bare Stumpingtons! They took their hats off and bent down in turn to hug me.

'I want to get up,' I said. 'I can get up. I want to do this properly!' So they supported me under my arms and gently raised me into a standing position. We then threw our arms around each other. 'That's better,' I said, sinking into their grasp. I felt like a small precious gem: each of them held me with such care and tenderness, yet at the same time I could feel the strength of their arms wrapped around me. 'Thank you, thank you so much for all you did. Thank you, thank you.'

'So, do you remember me? Do I look familiar?' I asked. Andy and Jon both looked long and hard at me, and said, in unison: 'The eyes, it's the eyes.' I then fluttered my eyelids at them flirtatiously as a joke, and we sat, the four of us, over tea and biscuits. (I would have loved something stronger, but we were in the hospital!)

I didn't know where to start, what to ask, so I just blurted out: 'Do you want to see how my legs attach?' What had I said? This wasn't 'show and tell' at school. I couldn't believe I'd said it – but then it got worse, as rather than waiting for them to answer, I swiftly began taking one of my legs off!

I gave a running commentary to go with the actions: 'To attach the legs, I first put on a liner that has a ratchet on the end. The ratchet then clicks into the leg.' Well, as the stump came out, revealing said ratchet, Jon jumped, nearly spilling his tea: 'What's that? You could have warned me!' Clearly he wasn't comfortable with me revealing the hidden injuries. I then started talking at a hundred miles an hour, obviously nervous and embarrassed that my demonstration had gone wrong.

'Let's get some pictures!' Joe said, coming to the rescue. He took some photos of all of us standing together; and I didn't mention the legs again after that!

At one point Jo, one of the nurses, came in to check on us. She knew that this would be an emotional meeting for me and wanted to ensure that I was all right. She brought in a tray of fresh tea and, being very attractive, distracted the boys from our intense conversation. 'Where were we?' Jon asked politely. 'I do love coming to St Thomas' – they have the best-looking nurses!'

Andy and Jon had not entered the actual carriage that day. They were part of the team that helped to carry me along and eventually out of the tunnel. They told me of how I was slipping in and out of consciousness, that I had lost a lot of blood and that my pulse was getting weaker and weaker. It had been a difficult rescue – they explained the problems they had encountered with trying to carry me, mainly because of my obvious injuries.

Jon then paused for a moment and quietly asked me if I wanted them to continue, if I really did want to know. I held his hand and nodded, explaining that I had seen for myself when I was in the carriage waiting to be rescued. It couldn't be any worse than what I already knew.

Jon went on. He said that one leg had already come off; the other was so fragile that they were all scared to move me too much. The greatest concern was for the amount of blood that I was losing; they needed to get me out as fast as they could. Jon said that at one point he had tried carrying me by my belt (my jeans were still on) – a bit like a suitcase – but they could only get a few yards at a time before they would have to put me down and check if I was still alive.

He said that they all knew my name. I had told everyone that my name was Gill. The only thing that gave them hope later when they were looking in the obituary notices for me was that there was no Gill listed.

We sat chatting for over three hours and both Joe and I felt that we had made two new, important friends. We swapped numbers and I stood to hug them again. I looked them straight in the eye and said, 'Thank you,' then looked over at Joe who had tears rolling down each cheek and added: 'We are getting married in December. Nothing would give us greater honour than to have both of you there ... please, will you come?' They both accepted immediately.

As they walked out of the Day Room the humour kicked in as Joe and I said, 'Sorry, officers, we won't do that again. Thanks for the warning.' Andy and Jon latched on instantly, responding in character with: '... and let that be a lesson to you both.' As the two men put their hats back on and walked with an air of authority out of the ward, the nurses laughed. But their facial expressions gave away the fact that they were not entirely sure if this really was a joke – nothing would surprise them where I was concerned!

Andy and Jon were the warmest, most caring and dedicated men. It was with them that Joe and I first heard the phrase, 'I was just doing my job' used; but this was an expression that did no justice to the be-yond-human efforts that these people made that day. It was a phrase that would come to anger us, and we would always quickly correct anyone who used it. They were not just doing their jobs; what they did was nothing short of heroic!

It was Treena, Jon and Andy who accompanied Joe and I to the Memorial Service held at St Paul's Cathedral on November 1, 2005. They were in their best-dress uniforms and I felt so proud to walk in with them – with my three men (and my two boys!). I remember that Jon in particular was very protective of me, ensuring that I was sitting in a chair that was comfortable and even helping me to stand at the points in the service that required all to stand in respect.

. . .

So what made me speak out eventually? Why allow myself to be interviewed? I believed then, as I do now, that it is important to talk about experiences, good and bad. It was imperative to me that the public had an insight into just one of the people affected by this terrorist action. It changed my views on life completely and I wanted to share that. I wanted to tell the world how happy and how grateful I was to be alive. 'Remember to live' – that's really what I wanted to say. Remember what is *truly* important to you and never forget it; make the most of every day, because you just never know what lies ahead. I was still filled with the euphoria of being here; even though there were dark days, I was thrilled to be alive and wanted to shout about it!

The most truly wonderful part of losing my anonymity has been becoming known to many of the people who did so much not only to ensure my survival, but also to enhance my life ever since. These people have left their mark; they are an intrinsic part of the foundations of Life Two and I am sure they will be central to its structure.

Perhaps most telling, in a way, is the address book on my mobile phone – now filled with the names of people whom I certainly didn't know before and would probably never even have met were it not for July 7. Theirs are my most frequently called numbers. The bomb may have given us an initial reason to be 'introduced', but it is a deep friendship and mutual respect that will ensure a lifelong bond.

The first interviews I did, once I was out of hospital, were for very different publications. One was with an Australian magazine, *Woman's Weekly* and the other with a respected broadsheet newspaper, the *Telegraph*, here in London. With my background in publishing and my experience of conducting many interviews myself, with all sorts of people, I thought I would know what to expect – how it would feel. But there is a difference, as I quickly learned: I was used to interviewing from a trade perspective – discussions about architecture, design, graphics, art and culture. Intimate, emotional, life-changing events were another story.

Being interviewed, in depth, was really very tough. Both journalists/writers were very professional and sensitive. Both sat quietly and listened as I recounted my movements, going through the motions of what led me to be in that carriage on that day at that time ...

The headline in the *Telegraph* article read, 'I wasn't dancing in the face of death, I was just on my way to work.' It was true. It captured my sentiment exactly – I hadn't put myself in danger, I wasn't flirting with death in any way. I was simply trying to get to a meeting, I was just on my way to work. Reading the articles triggered unexpected tears. I was reading my own story and it was making me cry as if I were taking this information in for the first time.

The *Telegraph* article was reproduced by a major daily London paper – they printed an edited version of the interview along with a large picture of me. Thousands of Londoners read this paper and the first I heard of it was when I received a distraught telephone call from someone I used to work with. She hadn't even known that I had been involved in the bombings, so she certainly wouldn't have known the extent of my injuries. She was in shock. It was strange because I had already been through these emotions and felt like I was starting to come through the other side, but her reaction – which I completely understood – took me straight back. I felt a need to console her and many others who were contacting me at the time. The article was also seen by many who were uplifted by reading it, including people who had been directly involved with me that day but thought I had died. Suddenly, there I was, staring at them from a page in a newspaper.

One of these people was a doctor. She was given Joe's mobile number by the paper that carried the original interview. Joe and I were out; he was pushing me in my wheelchair, down a sloping street, when he let go of the handles and stopped in the middle of the road. I had rolled a little way down the road before I realised he wasn't there, applied the brakes and attempted a sharp turn in order to see what had happened. Joe was on the phone, waving his arms around, crying and laughing, whilst I, puzzled, was mouthing, 'Who is it? Who are you talking to?' It was the doctor who had worked on me when I had been brought up from the tunnel and placed in the ticket hall of the station. She'd thought I had died! She wanted to meet me and we agreed to meet at the cottage in Richmond within days of the call.

She arrived holding a bunch of flowers, looking like she could so easily have been one of my friends – same style, same age. I stood; I wanted to be standing, upright for every meeting like this one. It was important to me to be seen as 'whole' – strong, alive. I was eager for her to be left with a powerful impression of me, and with the feeling that what she had done that day had not been in vain. We held each other for a while, stopping only to take a long look at one another's faces. 'Thank you, thank you, thank you,' I whispered.

Then Joe and I settled down to hear her story.

That morning she had been commuting with her husband, an anaesthetist – they are both based at a hospital near the station. They arrived and volunteered themselves to help with an unimaginable array of severely injured people, all of whom had been placed in the ticket hall. A chief paramedic at the scene placed both hands on her shoulders, having been told she was a doctor and turned her around to face me. He told her that I was her first priority. As she and her husband worked tirelessly to resuscitate me they heard another explosion. We now know this to have been the bus bomb. Everyone was told to evacuate, to leave immediately. What is so remarkable, however, is that no one did – they all carried on tending to the injured, regardless of their own safety.

She described me exhaling as she held me, taking my last breath in her arms. She looked at my face, looked into my eyes and saw herself. She felt connected to me; felt that it could so easily have been her lying there. She said it was my eyes – they'd haunted her. So when she saw my picture, she had immediately covered everything else on the page apart from my eyes and said to her husband, 'Who's that?' He'd replied: 'It's her!' They both knew in an instant.

...

Now that I had spoken out, other branches of the media – radio, television, news and current affairs programmes – were all interested in talking to me and especially in knowing more about my wedding plans. It was a story that captivated and inspired many – that a woman who had lost both legs in a terrorist attack would 'walk' down the aisle just five months later. It was viewed as nothing short of miraculous.

The BBC contacted me, through the *Evening Standard*, through the *Telegraph* and finally through Claire. They were filming a documentary about the emergency services, focusing on key individuals and what they had done that morning of July 7, 2005. One of the men being interviewed, PC Aaron Debnam, from the British Transport Police (or BTP) had consistently mentioned my name. He'd explained how he was primarily involved in my rescue, confessing to her that he'd been haunted by my face. He described how he'd tried so hard to get me out but that unfortunately I had died and he'd been unable to trace who I was. My 'death' had affected him very badly. He told Louise, the producer, that he'd combed the pictures in every paper, every obituary notice, but I wasn't there – no Gill or Jill was mentioned as dead. Louise was determined to find me, to answer the mystery of 'Gill'. Surely someone would know who I was and what had happened to me?

At around the same time, by coincidence, Ray, a BTP officer, saw the article in the *Evening Standard*. Clutching a copy of the paper, he shouted to Aaron, 'She's alive, she's alive! Look, here she is. This is her, it's our Gill.' It was the same piece that had caught the doctor's eye. Aaron looked at the picture and, like the doctor, he knew in an instant that this was his Gill. I was alive. They were all euphoric – having spent months not knowing what had happened to me.

Louise at the BBC had also by now put two and two together and realised that this was the 'Gill' that Aaron had been speaking about. She wanted to unite us and also to include me in the documentary. Naturally I agreed. I wanted to praise the emergency services' efforts as often, as loudly and as publicly as I could. I also felt a great need to meet everyone who'd had a crucial role to play in my survival.

The interview was to take place at a beautiful eighteenth-century house in Richmond. I would be meeting Aaron and Steve Bryan, two of the BTP team who were there that day. They would be able to provide some of the missing pieces of the jigsaw for me, but most importantly, I would be able to hold them and say, 'Thank you'.

I had to do the interview first. I described that day, what happened, what I could remember, how I had felt – then the cameras kept rolling. Louise wanted to capture the moment we met, but to do so with integrity and consideration. So she carefully explained that the cameras would be turned off the moment we said, that there was no pressure, and that what was important was just for the three of us to meet and talk. Claire Sawford and Joe were never far away, but this was about me. This was something I wanted to do on my own.

Any minute now. They had just arrived and any minute now I would meet them. I stood in anticipation. I didn't want them to meet me in a wheelchair – I wanted them to see me as a vision of what I was before, what I might have been like had we met under other circumstances. I was shaking. My crutches were wobbling, I wanted to be strong, not to break down. I wanted them to be proud of me – to look at me and feel that all their efforts had been worthwhile.

The door opened and in they walked. Steve introduced himself first. We hugged and the tears started instantly. I spoke through my tears, saying softly into his ear, 'Thank you so much, thank you so much.' Aaron was next. I held out my arms, the tears now pouring down my cheeks, but grinning at the same time. 'Look at me, I'm standing,' and I fell into his arms.

The most wonderful warmth went right through me during our embrace. I'd felt this before. I knew this person. It was him. He was the man who had held my hand in the tunnel, who never let go. I could feel him, I could feel his soul, and when he spoke, I remembered his voice, calling out to me, 'Stay with us Gill; stay with me'. I remembered. I didn't want to let go of him. I owed him so much. He had kept me alive.

Eventually we sat down, but I grabbed Aaron's hand and held on to it tightly. We were all very emotional, me, Aaron and Steve. Aaron asked for the cameras to stop filming. This was our moment. This was private. There are no words to describe how we all felt – we just sat staring at each other for a while, I think in disbelief: they couldn't believe that I was alive and I couldn't believe that I was sitting with them.

There was a bond. Meeting Aaron was as I would imagine it would be for an adopted child to meet their birth mother, or for long-lost siblings to be reunited. It was that deep love. That feeling of being complete in someone else's presence. I needed him to know that I had felt his life force, that he had 'given' me some of his life, his energy, when he had held my hand during the rescue. It's incredibly difficult to explain and maybe it's just one of those special mysteries or miracles in life that simply can't be explained. I don't know. All I do know is that when I was being carried out of that tunnel I could feel how much he loved me, how much he cared and how much he was willing me to live – intensely willing me to stay alive. I had sensed all of those things even though I was in and out of consciousness.

Aaron had saved me by holding my hand. I wanted to tell him that but I couldn't. I thought I would break down and I did not want to do that in front of them. This was the only thing that stopped me from telling Aaron that my greatest fear that day was of dying alone without someone to hold my hand, without feeling loved – he gave me that.

To lighten the mood, I joked with both Aaron and Steve that 'A Gill is for life, by the way, not just July 7; you have been warned!' I wanted them to feel relaxed in my company and happy to be with me. Then I went on to ask them if it made a difference to them now that they knew I was an Australian – would they still have rescued me had they known then? We all laughed. I never let go of Aaron's hand.

Joe knocked at the door. We had been alone for over twenty minutes and he was desperate to meet them both, to shake their hands and give them an enormous 'man' hug. Without hesitation we asked them if they would do us the great honour of attending our wedding. They agreed, and we swapped numbers, promising to keep in touch.

Aaron wanted me to meet the rest of the 'guys' on B-shift. I meant something to each of them, including Inspector Glen McMunn, the head of the unit and the person in charge of them that day. After weeks of preparation, we finally agreed on a meeting in their local pub. It was a Friday night; perfect timing as Graham and Jo were back in London for the wedding and they were able to come with me, although Joe was in Italy on his 'bucks night' so he couldn't make it.

My dear friend Helen, fellow Aussie and baker of fine banana cakes, had arranged a special pre-wedding treat for me that day. I spent the day at the spa of a top London Hotel – the Dorchester! I had a luxurious facial and then had my hair done. It was amazing; I was so relaxed that I fell asleep there in the deepest sleep I'd had since July 6, 2005. Helen also planned a fun evening for Alex and Maddy (Graham and Jo's kids), helping them to make all their favourites like chocolate milkshakes and pavlova, giving Graham and Jo the opportunity to have a drink or two with me and the 'B-shift boys'.

Thanks to all the lotions and potions I'd been pampered with all day I looked no older than twenty! I was thrilled as this was exactly how I'd wanted them to see me: all cleaned up, all together, complete. I walked into the pub, followed by Graham and Jo. There was Aaron, smiling from ear to ear. 'This is Chris, this is Gary, this is Ray and Inspector Glen,' he said. I hugged each one of them in turn, as tightly as I could. I knew what they had been through, what extraordinary people they all were.

Gary and Jo quickly settled into matching drinks, whilst Graham and the Inspector talked in depth about July 7, the rescue and how miraculous my recovery was. They told me that they had never met a survivor before, not just from the bombings of that day but in general. It wasn't something that tended to happen. This made our meeting even more significant.

We laughed, cried and laughed some more and all of us had the most special evening. Meeting all of these men was incredible. They filled in many gaps for me, and told me things that I needed to hear, to know. They told me how difficult it had been to get me out, how thick the air had been and how hard it was to breathe. They told me of the deep pain they had felt for the ones they couldn't save. And they confirmed for me everything I had *thought* was happening when I was being taken down the tunnel.

...

A big part of the puzzle that was still missing was the paramedics and the ambulance crew. I had made some enquiries to find them, but to no avail. I tried to let it rest, but the need to find them was still there. The 'family' felt incomplete.

In the meantime, I had been asked to be on the BBC's live daily programme *City Hospital* at the centre of which are St Thomas' and its affiliate, Guy's. I was an obvious choice to have on the programme, not only because I had been involved in the bombings, but also because I was making such amazing progress. My segment was filmed entirely in the physio' gym with Matt on hand to discuss the more technical aspects of what I was demonstrating. We had a great time! I loved the crew – the presenter (Nadia), the features editor (Halina) – they were all brilliant at capturing 'me' and the positives of my story.

Brian's mum (Brian was one of the crew from the ambulance) was watching the programme and called him straight away to tell him to switch his TV on. She said she thought the woman they were featuring could be the same one that he'd been with in his ambulance on July 7; the one he had thought had died. Reluctantly he turned it on, never expecting to see me, never believing that I could indeed be very much alive and walking up and down, showing off in my new prosthetics and laughing with Matt and Nadia. Brian couldn't believe his eyes.

London Ambulance Service contacted me through Claire in a very considered letter, saying that the crew who were with me on the day would like to meet, if I wanted to, but that they would completely understand if I chose not to do so. If I chose not to do so? Were they crazy? I contacted them immediately to say, 'Yes – please!' And so it was arranged.

In a swish hotel in central London, the two ambulance crew, Brian and Lisa, accompanied by the Silver Command officer, Paul, met both me and Joe. The tears are coming back now, even as I write.

Lisa was beautiful, tiny in size, but with an amazingly big heart. I couldn't stop smiling at her. Brian wore an expression that just looked like Christmas! I wanted to bury my face in their chests and not come up for air.

Then the wine was poured and I prepared myself for what I was about to hear.

Lisa had been driving. The roads were blocked; all of London was in a state of organised chaos. She put the call through to the nearest hospital, describing my injuries and condition but they were full to capacity and unable to take me. Paul had intervened, suggesting St Thomas', which was quite a distance from the scene, but a police escort helped get the ambulance through the gridlock.

As she was telling me this, I interrupted and said that taking me to St Thomas' was such a blessing – I told her how brilliant they had been, how much I had loved being there and, most importantly, how this crucial decision really had saved my life.

Brian held my hand and explained to me just how close to death I had actually been. I had lost an enormous amount of blood – they estimated at least 75 to 80 per cent – and I arrested again in the ambulance. Brian did all he could to bring me back.

We all paused. I had no memory of the ambulance. This was very hard. We were all reliving those moments together.

Brian continued. He said that my eyes were wide open and I was staring at him, and even though there was a tube down my throat, and virtually no output, no pulse, I was trying to say something. I was trying to talk. On arrival at St Thomas' I was whisked, like lightning, out of the ambulance and that was the last he saw of me. He had presumed I was dead. There was no way I would have survived given my condition – or so he thought. Brian told me how he had thought about me often and wondered what it was I had been trying to tell him. Was it important? Maybe the name of a loved one? He didn't know, but my face had haunted him.

An official photographer was there, snapping away as we drank more and more wine. We spent nearly five hours together, just getting to know one another. We all swapped numbers, and I texted madly all the way home: 'Love you Paul', 'Love you Lisa', 'Love you Brian'! I also warned them, as I had the others, that a 'Gill was for life' not just July 7, so this was only the beginning.

The London Ambulance Service (LAS) invited me to give awards at a ceremony dedicated to those involved events on July 7. It was there that I met David, the paramedic who had taken charge of me at the scene in the ticket hall at Russell Square station, and who had played a vital role in my rescue. He was the one who had directed the doctor to me telling her I was her first priority.

Both David and I were emotional. It had been his experience and quick thinking that saved me from brain damage that day: he had insisted that I be kept cold, in spite of the more traditional approach using blankets and warming a casualty. He also kept on believing in me – he was not prepared to give up. He described a conversation that had taken place about me, as to whether to replace my Priority One tag with a black one (the tag attached to those who have died). David wouldn't allow it; he still held out hope. He looked at me when we met and said that I had renewed his faith in life, his belief that where there is life, even the faintest pulse, there is hope. These words will stay with me for ever. How lucky I was to have been given David to watch over me and take charge of my survival.

I stood up on the stage at the awards and gave a short speech. What could I say? The word 'thank you' seemed ridiculously inadequate. I said that I wished I could invent a new word that embodied all the praise, all the gratitude and all the love that it is possible for one person to feel for another. Praise. Gratitude. Love ... Maybe by taking the first letter of each of these I could create a word that was all-encompassing: 'pagle' – a new word to say so much more than just 'thank you'. Pagle, pagle, pagle!

The ambulance service really took me to their hearts. The LAS magazine cover after the awards featured Joe and me (or rather drunk versions of us!) with Brian, Lisa and Paul. Within a short period of time I felt that I had many 'friends' there. I loved them all and appreciated everything they had done. I think they knew that, which is why I became a 'friend'.

There were still two important people for me to meet from the LAS: Liam and Tracey who had entered the carriage and tagged me as a 'Priority One'. They had been there with Aaron and Gary, checking all those who were left, assessing and re-assessing their condition and labelling or tagging them accordingly. They were in there for hours; they had to be thorough in their search for life.

The setting for our meeting with Liam and Tracey was a large boardroom at the LAS headquarters. As I looked around the room I saw large screens displaying very clear labels – Gold or Silver to reflect the varying levels of control; we were in the very command room that was put into place on that morning. It was odd to be sitting there, waiting for Liam and Tracey in absolute silence – imagining how different the scene would have been on July 7.

Liam is based in Scotland. He is currently studying medicine and works with the LAS on his summer breaks. Tracey is the same age as me and, like me, was married in 2005.

They somehow felt so familiar to me, although I had surrendered after I was tagged, so I didn't actually *remember* them at all. But I didn't feel like their 'patient' when we met; it felt more like we were all mates, maybe old school friends, catching up because we hadn't seen each other in a while. It was strange. There were no awkward pauses in our conversation, no silences that needed to be filled with babble.

They remembered *me* vividly – where I had been sitting and how what remained of my legs was hanging over the armrest of the seat. They said they had made a stretcher for me out of coats that were lying around. It was lucky for me that there were coats around to put me in, July 7 being a drizzly, overcast day, after a long spell of hot weather. They described it all exactly as I had remembered it.

Beyond this, though, I didn't really need to discuss the details, I just wanted to look at them, laugh with them and bask in their company.

. . .

I have mentioned that since July 7 there are a lot of new numbers in my mobile phone; many of these belong to fellow carriage-1 survivors – Richard, Hannah, Susan, Rachel and others. Each has their own horrific story and each has their own perspective, but I have yet to know a survivor who harbours hatred for the bomber. Maybe it's just that I am naturally drawn to those people, but I do find that this seems to be a powerful and commonly held sentiment. What I am most aware of in each of the survivors whom I have come to know and call a friend is a deep desire to 'make life count'. We have all gone on to do something and/or become involved in projects that will, it is hoped, make a difference to many.

It was through an interview with the BBC's Security Correspondent, Frank Gardner, that I met Richard. Frank featured both our stories on a programme for Broadcasting House on Radio 4. As I listened to the programme, I heard Richard describing the smoke in the carriage from where he landed after the explosion – the acrid, wretched smell; and as I sat there, staring at the radio, I could smell it all over again. I had to meet Richard. That was all that was going through my mind.

After weeks of trying to arrange a mutually suitable time, we agreed that he and his now fiancé, Poppy, would come to our home for dinner. As soon as they walked in that evening, we held each other in a 'knowing' embrace. We said very little at first; just that it was good to meet and how very lucky we were to have survived. Then we sat down at the table and ate, drank and chatted away like old friends.

We had so much in common – not just that we both happened to have been in the same carriage when a bomb went off. It was clear that we share a passion for life and a desire to get as much as we can from it. This was the sentiment that shaped not only that evening, but every occasion we have shared since. It's what has prevented us from becoming 'supportive' train buddies; our relationship is not based on helping each other get through the day, or the night – it's based on the future, on how we can make a difference and, most importantly, what we can both do to stop further terrorist attacks.

It's not that I don't think support groups are a good thing – they are fantastic. It's just that I am fortunate, as is Richard, in that we did not need such a group. Richard and Poppy have become permanent fixtures in our lives and the ties that bind us are now far more than just the events of July 7. Neither Joe nor I could imagine life without Richard and Poppy.

It was a similar scenario when I met Hannah. She got in contact through Joe, calling him on the morning of our wedding to wish us both much love and joy. She introduced herself as someone who had been in the carriage with me and said how thrilled she was that I had survived. Once again, we invited her and her partner Gus to join us for dinner. There was always something about that first hug, that first embrace. It's so difficult to convey the impact of wrapping your arms around someone and feeling that you are touching their soul, feeling their pain and their joy. The emotions of just being with another who really understands are impossible to describe. Gus, or 'Gusington', as I now call him was animated, full of personality and verve. The four of us sat eating and drinking until the early hours of the morning!

Joe first met Susan at a commendation ceremony for Jon, one of the Metropolitan Police officers who had helped to carry us both down the tunnel. Joe felt straight away that I would get along very well with Sue and he was right. She is strong, dedicated and, most important of all, has a brilliant sense of humour. We both share the view that the emergency and medical services responded magnificently on July 7 and we have nothing but absolute praise for them and for the National Health Service. Sue and I both know that not everyone in the world is lucky enough to receive the expert treatment that we did. We also share a physiotherapist, Jennifer, who works us hard. Sue has inspired me to use a treadmill and even to try an exercise bike, although I'm always a little behind her with my rehabilitation.

I contacted Rachel through her blog site. She and Richard initially set up Kings Cross United for everyone who was on the Piccadilly Line that day and wanted to meet others, swap stories, experiences, or just have a drink. Whilst I did not feel that this group was for me, I was keen to meet Rachel. Miraculously, she had managed to walk out of the carriage that day, fully conscious, so I was eager to listen to her story and hear what she saw and knew.

Rachel and I met up at a pizza place. She had with her a diagram of the carriage, showing where people had been placed at the moment of impact. I showed her where I had been standing, just near Germaine Lindsay, by the double doors where the bomb was detonated.

Rachel has now turned to writing about her experiences as a way to gain greater understanding, not only of the bombing itself but also of her own feelings and emotions. Her website has become one of the most widely read sources of information about the London bombings and their aftermath.

I had many other meetings with survivors from all the sites; each was different from the last, each at different stages of recovery. Amongst these was an emotional and moving encounter with Gary and Alison who had been sitting directly opposite me in the bombed carriage and one with Philip, whom I first met when we went to view the wreckage along with others who were seriously injured.

There are many, like the the tube train driver, Tom – a quiet and retiring person, not someone to 'blow his own trumpet' – whose heroic efforts that morning saved lives, including mine, without a doubt. These are people who have made an impression on me and on how I live my life now.

Together, we all represent a sample of society, a cross-section, thrown together in an event that shook the UK.

. . .

I was asked to give Andy his medal of honour at a commendation ceremony to which, of course, I gladly agreed.

The arrangements for that day were all carefully handled by Sergeant Bignold and I was treated like a VIP. They made me feel as though it was *their* honour to have me there, which puzzled me, as I was thrilled at even the suggestion that I should be there.

Deputy Commissioner, Paul Stephenson QPM came to collect me. Naturally I was a little nervous to meet such a very senior police officer. What would I say? What would we talk about? But my nerves quickly vanished the moment I entered the car and my very own brand of 'Gill' black humour took over. I must say, I don't think I have ever enjoyed a car journey more than I did this one, with Paul, his assistant Laura and their driver. When we arrived, an exhausted Deputy Commissioner said to Andy, who was there to greet us: 'Have you been dealing with her all this time? You really do deserve a medal!'

I had a very moving exchange with a senior forensic squad officer who was part of the team dealing with Russell Square station. He shook my hand, but I 'broke ranks' and pulled him close enough to wrap my arms around him. His eyes filled with tears as he said how sorry he was that this had happened and that neither he, nor the force had been able to stop it. I looked him square in the eyes and said that he had nothing to apologise for. I told him I knew what he and his team had had to deal with down in that tunnel – something that no human being should have to go through – and thanked him, not only for doing what he does, but for doing it with such dignity and care.

Many high-ranking officers were present at the commendation ceremony. Jon came as a surprise for me but also as a support for Andy. The BBC news crews were filming the day and interviewed all three of us after Andy received his medal. Andy said that for him to have been given this award by me was the greatest honour of all. He was just pleased that I was alive and able to share this day with him.

When the interviews and farewells were all over I climbed back into the Deputy Commissioner's car and gathered myself for the journey home. I felt that I had forged some significant new friendships that day.

...

So everyone was now accounted for. I had as full a picture as I could ever have of what happened to me on July 7, especially what had taken place during the 'missing' moments when I was unconscious. But, somehow, piecing together the details didn't seem to matter as much any more. For now, without actually setting out to do so, I had built a new 'family' – a family of special people for whom I felt absolute and unconditional love.

Chapter 9

Becoming Known

BECOMING KNOWN WAS STRANGE, extraordinary and, of course, unantici-
pated. People would come up to me in the street, in a department
store or in the supermarket and hug me, telling me how inspirational
I was. The first time this happened I stood there and cried with the
woman who was holding me, I was so overwhelmed. Then there were
taxi drivers, many of whom wouldn't accept a fare, offering me words
of encouragement and saying how proud they were of me and of my
progress.

After appearing on *City Hospital* I received a letter from a young
girl who was facing surgery to amputate an arm. She said that she
had been dreading the day, feeling that she wouldn't be able to cope
without an arm but that when she had seen me on TV, her fears were
replaced by determination. This reaffirmed to me that being in the
media was a good thing. It was right for me to continue to show how
I was rebuilding a life that was going to be remarkable, and that if I
could achieve walking, or carrying a cup of tea, or doing the house-
work, then anyone could achieve anything they set their mind to!

It was wonderful to feel so loved, yet by strangers. I could feel
them all willing me on, wanting me to triumph. Every smile, every nod,
every unexpected hug made all the difference; just knowing that every
time I took a step, many took a step with me. My heart was filled to
overflowing.

Once again, the true nature of humanity prevailed. I never felt
alone.

...

Aside from all the meetings and 'reunions' with people involved in events on July 7 in one way or another, there were other, more formal introductions. Having survived the ordeal that I had, there was little now that affected me in terms of nerves prior to an official meeting. This meant that invariably these became warm, humorous and very personable occasions. My view on life had become (and remains) so different from what it was before the bomb. My new state of mind was liberating and allowed me the personal freedom to be natural, to be myself, when meeting such figures as Her Majesty the Queen.

Life Two was certainly surreal. Many dignitaries and prominent figures were a part of it; people whom I would never have met had I not been so severely injured and it got to the point where these out-of-the-ordinary encounters no longer surprised me. It was all part of the experience and I was just thrilled to be alive and able to enjoy so many memorable moments.

I remember vividly meeting the Prime Minister of Australia, John Howard and his wife, Janette, when I had been on Luke Ward for just a week. There was a flurry of pre-visit activity: first, the security chiefs scanned the ward, then everything was buffed and polished, including me! Other patients must have been wondering what was going on and, more to the point, who was in room 29 to warrant all this fuss!

Graham was with me. It was extraordinary for him to have travelled from Australia, to meet the Prime Minister of Australia in London, at St Thomas' Hospital, at my bedside!

There was no press. This was to be a private visit, which is just how we wanted it. I kept thinking about what we would talk about. I didn't want to talk politics – I didn't feel the need to ask him his position on, say, the War on Terror. What could he say?

When he walked in I felt I knew him, his face being so familiar to me. We started chatting instantly and he and his wife were amazed by my story and my miraculous recovery. Richard Alston, the High Commissioner, also accompanied the Prime Minister. It was Mr Alston who had been instrumental in making the arrangements for Graham's trip over to London. Although he had seen me in intensive care, I had never met him, so this was a chance for me to thank him personally for all he had done to help my family and me in such a time of crisis.

This was also an ideal opportunity for both Graham and I to express our gratitude to the Government for all they had done. I felt that Australia had opened her arms and embraced us, showing ongoing support and attention in a way that made me proud to be Australian. I confessed to the Prime Minister some feelings of guilt that they may have thought I was an unfortunate Australian who was here on holiday and who happened to get caught up in the bombings, when, in actual fact, I had been living in London for thirteen years and considered London my adopted home. To all intents and purposes, I was a Londoner. The Prime Minister turned to me and said words to the effect of: 'Gillian, I am the Government. I know exactly how long you have been gone.' Then, with a smile on his face, he continued, 'And I also know that one day you will come back, won't you? They always come back.' We all laughed and I think I may have responded by promising that my children would be born in Australia – or something along those lines.

It was time for Mr Howard to leave. Both he and his wife had been charming, compassionate and sincere and Graham and I were thrilled that they had taken the time to meet us both.

Another great honour was meeting the Agent General for South Australia, Maurice de Rohan AO OBE, to whom this book is dedicated. Sadly he died in 2006. Maurice was a remarkable person and meeting him left a lasting impression on me; undoubtedly, he was a strong role model and an advocate for making a difference.

My first contact with Maurice was when the most beautiful, delicate, white orchids arrived, along with a hamper filled with South Australian delicacies. A personal hand-written note from Maurice was enclosed, expressing sympathy and sadness that I had been involved in the bombings, but also a sense of pride in that I was a tough South Australian of whom the South Australian Government and all at its office here in London were very proud indeed.

I was overwhelmed and wanted to thank him immediately for his generosity and kindness. Joe managed the calls for me (hearing on the telephone was still very difficult) and made arrangements for us to meet Maurice.

It was a very warm late August afternoon when we met. I noticed Maurice straight away; he was the only man in the hospital's reception area who was impeccably dressed and he also sported the unmistakable emblem of South Australia on a bag. We sat in the grounds, near the fountain, making the most of the late-afternoon sunshine.

Maurice was very moved by my story. I explained to him how important I felt it was to have a positive attitude, how special life is and how grateful I was to be alive. He agreed. He knew only too well the feelings I was describing, having lost his daughter and son-in-law in the Zebrugge ferry disaster. We found we were able to speak to each other with great ease and depth about our experiences, but soon agreed that if we continued we would both end up sobbing! So we turned to lighter topics, like my favourite South Australian red wines!

Suddenly Maurice's mobile phone rang and he apologised profusely, explaining that he had to take the call. He was an important man and I completely understood. When the phone call was over Maurice seemed excited but equally anxious and Joe and I couldn't help but ask if everything was all right? It transpired that Maurice was trying to arrange a live transmission in central London of an Adelaide football team playing in a cup final. A near impossible feat, but apparently all that was now needed was for the last bit of the connection to get to Australia House.

Joe and I sat there taking it all in, watching a great man in action. And he did pull the screening off – hundreds of South Australians gathered in Australia House to watch the match live, all thanks to him.

It was an unforgettable first encounter with a remarkable man and I am honoured to say that both Maurice and his wife Margaret became friends. Although we met only a few times each of those occasions was rich in what it gave, I hope, to us all.

It was through Maurice that my love for Adelaide and South Australia was re-ignited. He orchestrated and shared some of our most memorable events.

The first time that I ventured back into central London after July 7 was by invitation to the annual gathering on October 1 of all South Australians in London at the Eros statue in Piccadilly. Maurice sent his driver, Orhan, to collect us in his car and take us back home afterwards – we were still in Richmond at the time.

A large crowd gathered around the statue. Maurice spoke, then, without warning, he announced to the crowd that I was there, adding what an inspirational person I was. Everyone applauded and, as the first lines of the Australian national anthem rang out, I was too choked with emotion to sing. I had just been celebrated and was overcome with pride, joy and a strong sense of solidarity. Joe was squeezing my hand tightly; he too was crying. And then I caught a glimpse of our dear friend Debs – her eyes were moist, but she looked happy – happy, I think, to be there, sharing all this with us.

We all went back to Australia House where I drank my first ever sparkling burgundy wine!

...

An invitation came from Buckingham Palace to a reception to be held in February 2006 for prominent Australians living or working in London. A separate card was enclosed with the main invitation, saying that Her Majesty the Queen along with Prince Philip requested the company of both Joe and I at a private, smaller gathering. This was to be an exclusive audience with Her Majesty! I couldn't believe it. But then again, I could, as nothing so far in Life Two had been anything like 'normal'!

Maurice was to be there, as would His Excellency Mr Richard Alston, High Commissioner, and his wife Megs. Maurice wanted the day to be an extra special one for me, so, once again, Orhan collected us and we drove to Buckingham Palace with Maurice in the specially marked car – 'ADE1' – with South Australian flags on the front. We were directly behind the High Commissioner's car, also bearing Australian flags and the apt number plate of AUS1.

I can't begin to describe the sensation of sitting in a car that represents your 'home' as it drives in all its glory through the gates of Buckingham Palace. It is the perfect, if not the only, way to pass through those golden gates – in true state style! Maurice had given me a lifetime of Christmas gifts in that one gesture. I had to keep looking up, rolling my eyes to the back of my head, then thinking of something stupid or ridiculous – anything to stop me crying. I did not want to enter the Palace in tears. But I just felt so damned proud!

The car pulled up alongside red-carpeted stairs. I felt like a celebrity – a celebrated Australian. Her Majesty's Equerry greeted us and briefed us to ensure that we knew the correct procedures and protocols. The Queen and Prince Philip would spend a moment chatting with us and then we would move on to the larger gathering that would be held in the opulence of the Throne Room.

The Queen entered the room. She was small in height but grand in stature and filled the room with her grace and presence. She knew who I was, beyond the briefing, and commented on how miraculous my recovery had been. I was quick to praise the level of care that I had received at St Thomas' and to assert how brilliant our National Health Service is. We then spoke about my rescue; she had already met and honoured some of the men and women involved on July 7, in particular those who were involved with my rescue. I told her that many of those brave people were now my friends and how blessed I felt to know them. Then, with a look of real concern on her face she urged me to sit down, worried that I had been standing for too long. Being the stubborn person I am, though, I naturally declined. In fact, I insisted on standing for the entire reception, which lasted just over two hours. Then, just like Cinderella, it was time for me to leave the ball. The car returned for us, state flags still standing proud, and we were driven back home, through the streets of London.

It wasn't long before another royal invitation arrived! Before opening it I noticed that the crest on the envelope was different this time. This one was not from the Queen but from Prince Charles; he was opening his house at Highgrove in June to all those who were either bereaved or left terribly injured by the terrorist bombings. Prior to this I had met only one person who had actually lost a loved one on July 7 and it would also be an opportunity for me to meet many survivors from the other sites. Whilst I didn't expect it to be a wholly enjoyable reception – in fact, I was filled with trepidation, wondering what I would say, how I would even look at the families of those who had died, particularly in my carriage – the invitation was a generous and greatly valued one.

In the event, the day was organised exceptionally well, the pressure of how to approach people greatly alleviated by guided tours around the enchanting gardens, the guide pausing intermittently to share a story of a treasured seat that was tucked behind a tree here, or the thinking behind a particular plant choice there.

The gardens provided the ideal setting to start conversations – they offered a talking point, other than the obvious. I met two women, both of whom I now know on a much more personal basis; one had lost her daughter, the other her husband. Any fears I had had ended the moment we put our arms around each other. I needn't have worried about the right words – there were no words. They knew, I knew; we shared a common pain.

Prince Charles spent time both listening and talking to as many people as he could. He made his way round to where Joe and I were sitting and sat with us. We discussed everything from the horrors of terrorist attacks to the latest technology in prosthetic legs. He, like the Queen, seemed genuinely concerned about my welfare and that of my fellow survivors and marvelled at how far I had come in my rehabilitation.

. . .

I wish I knew why, but I was now being asked to appear on TV to present awards at all sorts of high-profile ceremonies!

The first of these – filmed in late November and aired at Christmas time – was hosted by Jonathan Ross and recognised the 'best' moments on TV in 2005. The documentary in which I had met Aaron and Steve – *7/7 The Day the Bombs Came* – was nominated.

I was ushered through the side door of the studio, down a corridor and into my very own dressing room, with 'Gill Hicks' on the door. Inside were a bathroom, a shower, a dressing table and sofas. There were also fresh flowers, chocolates and water. It was all so surreal! Jo and my dear friend Helen were with me. As we walked in and closed the door behind us we jumped up and down and screamed. (Or, at least, they jumped up and down – I just did the arm motions!)

I had mixed feelings about the event. Whilst I was thrilled to be there because I was so proud of the documentary, I was not a celebrity and did not feel that I belonged. Familiar faces from my favourite TV shows were everywhere – this was their world, not mine – and I just smiled and nodded as we passed them in the corridors.

The celebrated British actor, Denis Lawson, was my partner for the evening. He would be the one to help me on and off the stage and we would do the double act of running through the nominations, then revealing the winner. I made it safely through the mass of lighting and camera cables on the ground, to my spot, ready to go on with Denis by my side.

They first ran some clips of various scenes from the documentary, news footage from the day itself, and myself speaking. Then Jonathan Ross introduced us and that was our cue to walk out onto the stage. What I wasn't expecting was a standing ovation from the audience! It brought me to tears. I was staggered. I could not believe that all these people were standing and applauding me – it was completely overwhelming.

I struggled to regain my composure. Then I got to say the good bit:: '... and the winner is ...'. I was slightly unsteady on my feet as I opened the envelope but I did it and was more than a little relieved when we were back in my dressing room, relaxing with a glass of champagne!

My second televised appearance was at the BAFTAs, when I presented the award for the best documentary. This was a black-tie, sparkly-dress affair. I wore a female tuxedo as I would not have felt comfortable in a glittering dress. I sat next to Jesse Metcalfe who, at the time, was most famous for his role as the gardener in *Desperate Housewives*. Every woman who passed our table whispered to me, 'How much did you pay to sit there?' But even though Jesse is a very good-looking guy, I only had eyes for my adoring husband who just happened to be sitting right next to me on the other side! Also at our table were actors from *ER* and senior commissioning people. Joe and I squeezed each other's hands under the table. It was a squeeze that said, 'How much more bizarre can Life Two actually get?'

No one at our table knew who I was. Why would they? Most of them were based in Los Angeles and everyone was too polite to ask. I imagined what must have been going through their minds as they racked their brains, trying to think what film I was in, or what behind-the-scenes role I played.

I was to present the award accompanied by Andrew Marr, a respected political journalist and presenter. Davina McCall, famed for presenting *Big Brother* in the UK, was the host. She realised that this was not what I was used to and that I needed a little extra reassurance. She was caring and sensitive and immediately put me at ease. I walked out to my mark on the stage with Andrew and took the opportunity to say to the millions of people who were watching, 'Remember to live! Make a difference,' and, once again to thank those who risked their lives to save mine. The adrenaline was pumping through me and I was on a high because I did it – I did it without falling over and without fluffing a line.

When I got back to our table Joe was standing there with the cricket legend, Richie Benaud. Of course I was very excited and honoured to meet him, but at the same time he was a reminder of the voice that I had grown to resent so much as a kid. Maybe this was my chance to make peace with cricket? Anyhow, he signed my programme and I, in turn, gave it to Graham for his collection of sporting memorabilia.

. . .

The producers of *City Hospital* now wanted to create a documentary that followed my progress and the challenges that I faced in Life Two. The programme was called *Surviving 2005, My Story* and was to be part of a series featuring personal stories of survival and overcoming tragedy.

Having already appeared on *City Hospital* I knew the crew so I felt very relaxed in their company, as did Joe. They captured many important moments, including my first journey on an overground train post-July 7 (I still will not travel on any train that has to go through a tunnel), crossing a main road and, the greatest triumph of all, going home – going back to our home in north London.

The crew filmed me as I 'stepped' back into my home for the very first time after being away for five months. I struggled up the stairs, determined not to let them beat me and just made it to the first level – our dining and living area. Joe put his arms around me and said, 'Welcome home, Boo Boo,' at which point I broke down. I couldn't believe that I was 'home', that I had made it back. Yet the saddest part was that this was no longer my home, my haven or nest – it was a place that presented challenges at every turn. Our bedroom – the room that we had lovingly watched being created, even felt a little smug about as no one had ever lived in that space before – now seemed like the top of Mount Everest to me.

The camera crew slipped out, so that we could grieve in private. I felt heartbroken and displaced. I didn't know where I should really be – what and where home was. But I knew I would just have to get on with it and convince myself that every day it would be a little easier. I could beat this. Besides, I had the family coming from Australia and a wedding to organise!

The documentary ended on a positive note, with me coming out of church, a married woman. It was aired on the BBC during a lunchtime slot and, in keeping with the surreal nature of Life Two, this book came about as a direct result of it because Liz, Senior Editor at Rodale Books International, happened to see it when she was off sick. Once she was back in the office, Liz did some research into my story and felt confident not only that it had the makings of a great book, but also that it bought into the Rodale philosophy: 'Live your Whole Life'. I liked Liz very much, and, of course, was delighted at having been approached by a publisher whose beliefs and sentiments echoed my own.

...

Around the time of the first anniversary of July 7 I was interviewed by renowned journalist Tara Brown for *60 Minutes* – Australia's most successful current affairs programme, reaching over 5 million viewers a week across the country. It was a very open and honest exchange in which I was able to reveal my deepest thoughts, hopes and feelings. Filmed over a few days, it gave me a chance to see just how far I had come in the months since the BBC film, and to show *myself* as much as anyone else that, as I put it to Tara, whilst there is less of me now physically than there was before, my experience has made me far greater in spirit.

...

Perhaps my finest moment and the truest indication of my new-found recognition was being asked to be a guest at the St Thomas' Open

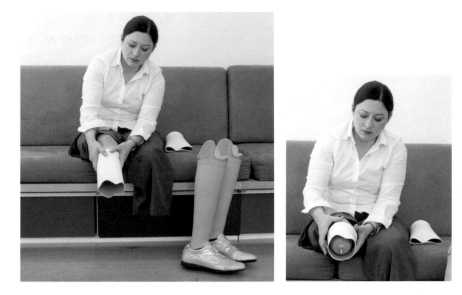

Don't try this at home! This is the ritual of putting my legs on, something I might do up to four times a day. The prosthetic legs are held in place with a ratchet attached to the rubber liner that rolls on over the stump, which then slots into the leg socket.
(© Mike Prior)

BELOW: Honoured to be there.
I'm standing in-between Police
Constables Andy (left) and
Jon, after I'd presented Andy
with his Commendation for
bravery. Jon had received his
at an earlier ceremony.

ABOVE: Never give up on life. This is David, in
charge of Triage at Russell Square, who took
the decision to continue resuscitating me,
even though I was showing little sign of life.
How do you say thank you for that?
(Courtesy of LAS)

LEFT: A special bond. Laughing with the
wonderful Tracey, who with Liam was part of
the first ambulance crew to enter my carriage.
(Courtesy of LAS)

ABOVE: Laughter after the tears. A truly emotional first meeting
with Brian (second left) and Lisa, the ambulance crew who
rushed me to St Thomas', and Paul, London Ambulance Silver
Officer at Russell Square on the day. (Courtesy of LAS)

BELOW: **Very much alive.** Reunited with British Transport Police (BTP) officers Steve (left) and Aaron, who after their heroic efforts to save me, thought that I had died. I'm holding the hand that held mine during my rescue. (Tim Anderson © BBC)

ABOVE: **Some of the finest.** Presenting awards at the London Ambulance Service July 7, 2006 Commemorative Event. (Courtesy of LAS)

RIGHT: **Better than words alone.** A huge hug with Ray, another valiant BTP officer, who helped to carry me off the train and down the tunnel. There was a standing ovation at our wedding reception for all who saved me and this image captured the moments following that. (© Richard Eiserman)

ABOVE: Last minute adjustments.
Bridesmaid Maddy ensuring
my gold glitter tights are
smoothed over my prosthetic
legs. (© Nicholas Bowman/
The Sunday Mirror)

ABOVE RIGHT: A proud moment.
Posing with Lily and Maddy
outside the enchanting and
ancient St Etheldreda's
Church, Holborn, London.
(© Nicholas Bowman/
The Sunday Mirror)

ABOVE: The Hicks' clan,
surrounding its newest recruit!
(From left: Maddy, Joe, Jo,
me, Graham, Alex). (© Nicky
Willcock, *www.nickyclaire.co.uk*)

LEFT: The newly weds! Moments
after walking down the aisle
together. (© Nicky Willcock)

ABOVE: **Two families united.** Kerrs and Hickses together at the reception. (From left: Antony, Elizabeth, Lily, Joe, Jo, me, Alex, Maddy, Bill, Rose, Graham, Julian, Bella). (© Nicky Willcock)

LEFT: **All aboard!** One of the vintage Routemaster buses to take our guests to the reception, a gift from Arriva. (© Nicky Willcock)

ABOVE: **Sharing a private joke.** Christmas Day with Graham, Adelaide 2005.

RIGHT: **It's safe for me to cross.** On honeymoon, Barossa Valley, South Australia.

ABOVE: **At the Palace.** Meeting Her Majesty the Queen at a reception for Australians in London, February 2006. (© Stephen Butler/Rex Features)

BELOW LEFT: **Fair play.** Opening the St Thomas' Open Day in June 2006, with Ainsley Harriott and Nadia Sawalha, presenters on BBC's *City Hospital*. (© Piers Allardyce)

BELOW RIGHT: **And the winner is ...** Presenting a BAFTA award, London, May 2006. (© ITV)

ABOVE: **One of us is fast!** Presenting an award with Dame Kelly Holmes, Olympic Double Gold Medallist, at the Charity Awards in June 2006. (© Tabatha Fireman, *www.tabathafireman.com*)

ABOVE: **Behind the scenes.** Shooting my short film for Peace Direct, in our North London home, September 2006. (© Chris Jamieson)

LEFT: **Mutual support.** A quiet moment for Joe and I at home together. (© Mike Prior)

OVERLEAF: **A year on.** Marking the two minutes' silence, 12pm, July 7, 2006. One of many such scenes across London, which came to a complete standstill in a moving act of remembrance. (Simon Dawson © PA/EMPICS)

Day opening ceremony. I can't even begin to describe what that meant to me: for me to be honoured by a place that I so revered.

I was asked to give an opening speech along with the two main presenters of *City Hospital*, I would then accompany the Chief Executive, Sir Jonathan Michael, to judge each stall and to select a winner at the end of the day.

I couldn't believe it when I was there, back at my beloved fountain area, only this time I was standing behind a microphone, speaking to an audience who had gathered to listen to and be a part of the celebrations. St Thomas' is an extremely enlightened hospital – one in which culture is highly valued and which has people at the centre of its thinking. And it shows. Just the very idea of opening your doors to the general public is brave, let alone actually doing it.

I held back the tears as I started my speech. 'Hello, my name is Gill Hicks and I think I am this hospital's number one fan! Nearly a year ago I was brought here, to A&E, very near death. I was labelled as "One Unknown" – an unknown patient: no identification, nothing to say who I was. But that didn't matter because to the people here I was a life that was in desperate need of their help. They worked tirelessly to bring me back and to keep me alive.'

I had to pause here; my throat was dry and my voice was beginning to wobble. It doesn't seem to matter how many times I tell the story, I am still affected by just how close I came to dying and what they all did for me.

 'Nearly a year ago I was put back together by the people here and because of them I am able to stand: to stand here today on two legs and say how truly grateful I am. I was just so lucky to have been brought to this most wonderful place. Here's to St Thomas'!'

Everyone clapped and cheered, then Joe took my hand and helped me down from the stage. He walked with me all day as Sir Jonathan and I went to every stall and spoke to every department that was exhibiting.

It took over three hours to complete the tour – I hadn't walked for three hours or even stood for three hours before that day, but there was no way that I was going to request a wheelchair or take a break. I wanted to show them all just how fantastic their work had been: I had to be a model for their brilliance.

To have met both the Chairman, Patricia Moberley, and the Chief Executive, Sir Jonathan Michael, was a great honour for both Joe and me. We said goodbye, waving just as we had when I had left as a patient only nine months earlier. When we got into the car we sat in silence for a good five minutes. I looked over at Joe and he was crying; I was crying too. He squeezed my hand and we both said, seemingly for the millionth time, how lucky we were. They had done it again: St Thomas' had made me feel like the most special, most treasured person in the world.

...

'One Unknown' was certainly not unknown any more.

It was and is wonderful to be recognised and appreciated by a wider group than I would ever otherwise have been. I have become tangible evidence of what is possible, against all the odds.

The experience of being approached in the street by someone who holds my hand and tells me how pleased they are that I am alive, or that they prayed for me every day, or that I have inspired them in some way, adds to the wonder that I see everywhere in Life Two.

I guess it was always there, it's just that now I can see it because my eyes are open and I'm taking the time to look.

Chapter 10

In Sickness and In Health, 'til Death Us Do Part

'In illo tempore: Accesserunt ad Jesum Pharisaei tentantes eum, et dicentes: Si licet homini dimittere uxorem suam, quacumque ex causa? Qui respondens ait eis: non legistis, quia qui fecit hominem ab initio, masculum et feminam fecit eos? Et dixit: Propter hoc dimittet homo patrem et matrem, et adhaerebit uxori suae, et erunt duo in carne una. Itaque jam non sunt duo, sed una caro. Quod ergo Deus conjunxit, homo non separet.'

'At this time: the Pharisees came to Jesus and put him to the test by asking, "Is it right for a man to put away his wife, for whatever cause?" He answered, "Have you never read, how he who created them, when they first came to be, created them male and female; and how he said, 'A man, therefore, will leave his father and mother and will cling to his wife, and the two will become one flesh?' And so they are no longer two, they are one flesh; what God, then, has joined, let no man put asunder."'

. . .

The actual date when Joe first proposed is etched clearly in my memory. It was December 19, 2004, on our old red sofa. He was nervous, as was I. We both knew that the moment he uttered those words, 'Will you marry me?' there would be no going back.

I had almost given up on the thought of us getting married. I'd even stopped dreaming about the proposal – how it would be, where it would happen, whether the huge diamond ring would be suspended in an ice cube, floating in a glass of champagne, that sort of thing. I had my work and life just bowled along. I was Joe's partner and Lily's 'step'-mum – Lily had only been ten when I came into her life, so by the time she was sixteen, the ties were strong; I loved her as if she were my own daughter and worried about her as any mother would – we just hadn't made it all 'official'.

Joe and I were comfortable with each other. We'd been together for six years. We had shared all manner of ups and downs and had grown familiar with the newly emerging lines, greying hair and thickening waistlines. But I wanted to be a wife and to have a husband. That was how I had been brought up. And I wanted to have children with Joe.

I had always been the 'mothering' type. Even as a small child I would invariably have a doll or two in tow and there would be a routine: I'd get them up early for breakfast and dress them, then at night before putting them to bed, I would sit and 'read' them a story (or maybe I just showed them the pictures or even made up a story). Yet somehow, in spite of this – and this has always puzzled me – I chose to follow an extremely demanding career path and pursued it relentlessly; I didn't settle down in my twenties and have my six children.

Joe already knew first hand what it was like to have a baby, the sleepless nights, the financial constraints – not to mention repeating the sleepless nights through worry when that baby becomes a teenager! It was a commitment he needed to feel very sure about.

Poor Joe, he would suffer! There was always the mandatory 'nagging' and 'sulking': every time I received an invitation to a friend's wedding, or heard news of the birth of yet another child, it would send me into a fury. The clock was ticking and I was still no closer to even contemplating my first child. I still held on to my childhood dream of home, family, maybe a dog – at the very least a goldfish or a hamster!

It's amazing how busy you can be – how the days, weeks, months, even years can just whirl by so that in the blink of an eye, or so it seems, another one has gone. Everyone always said that life speeds up as you get older, which seems quite a cruel trick, but as I put another candle on the cake each year, I began to see that. Conveniently, I would justify not having all the things that I had dreamt of and held so dear. It wasn't my fault, it wasn't anyone's fault – time had just 'sucked' them all up. Damn that 'time'. Damn it.

Joe knew that time was running out. He knew that I was increasingly worried that I would miss my chance. He knew he had to decide what he wanted from life and whether that life included a wife and kids ...

Our old, 'comfy' red cord sofa, worn bare around the edges, dominated our lounge. I used to cover it with throws and coloured cushions, making it look and feel inviting. We really were quite fond of the old thing. It was a little out of place in our home because both Joe and I are big fans of modern furniture, so the rest of our home is largely slick and white, very 'architectural' with lots of clean lines and just a hint of 'ordered' colour. But not the sofa. And as we sat together on it one evening, Joe suddenly picked up the remote control and turned the television off. 'Hey, I was watching that!' I squawked.

'I need to ask you something. It's serious Gill – I need to ask you something.' I couldn't imagine what it was. Perhaps he needed to know where his socks might be, or had he mislaid his football tickets? But then Joe went down on one knee, tears welling up in his eyes, and he said: 'Gill, will you do me the great honour of being my wife?' I cried. He cried.

I couldn't talk (a very rare occurrence for me!) so I just nodded, motioning a 'Yes'. Then we just sat there, holding each other, crying and crying. We were going to get married, we were getting married.

Hoping and suspecting that I would say yes, Joe had put some champagne in the fridge, but before we toasted our union there was something else Joe said he had to do. 'I'd better ring your brother and ask him first. What's the number?' As Dad wasn't alive, Graham was next in line to be asked for 'permission' for Joe to marry me and for his blessing. Joe was a traditionalist and everything had to be done in the 'correct' way, even though Joe and Graham had never met. Naturally Graham agreed saying that if this was what I wanted he would be happy.

The next call was to Joe's parents, Antony and Elizabeth. They were thrilled, absolutely thrilled as this was a piece of news that they had been waiting to hear for many years!

Our next mission was to find the perfect engagement ring. It was the week before Christmas and the shops were mobbed – it wasn't a great time for us to be hovering at counters seeking expert advice on the diamond purchase of our lives. So, like two little teenage kids, we went to a high-street fashion store and chose the biggest, brightest most gaudy ring they had (well actually they had a whole rack of the things, designed as they were to be disposable fashion items, a mere snip at £5!).

With our Joe 'n' Gill humour, we did our best to convince the shop assistant that this was my genuine engagement ring. What must she have thought of two grown adults standing there saying, 'Are you sure we can afford it darling?' 'Anything for you pumpkin.'

And so there it was. I had my huge, heart-shaped fake diamond engagement ring and wore it into the office the very next day. With a straight face I told anyone who asked, 'Yeah, I'm so lucky. My Joe spent a fortune on this beauty.'

We wanted to get married in winter as we both love Christmas, snow, singing carols and so forth. We contacted the church and the date – December 10, 2005 – was put in the diary.

I started sketching ideas for dresses – my own and the brides-maids' – and thinking of colour schemes. I loved antique gold, bronze, silver – colours that reflected that Christmas feeling. Oh and the reception, the food, the place settings ... There was just so much to think about. I bought one of those books on how to create the perfect wedding in however little time, but it terrified me – it appeared that I was already behind and most things should have been organised by what seemed like years before the proposal!

The two main parts of the wedding were booked though: the church and the venue. And the great thing about our choices for these was that they linked our two most special places in London.

Our reception was to be held at the Wapping Hydraulic Power Station. This is an extraordinary and unique institution in the East End of London. It is part-theatre, part-art gallery, part-meeting place, part-restaurant, all housed in a magnificent Victorian industrial building, the brainchild of an amazing woman, and, as it happens, fellow Adelaidian (albeit resident for many years in London). It was actually the Australian connection that led us to be introduced to Jules and her husband Josh (who was architect to the project) and we had the privilege of witnessing, and latterly contributing to the transformation of what was an abandoned wreck of a building into one of the most magical spaces in London, or indeed any other city.

In its early years Joe and I were happy to help build the reputation of this place that we'd come to love. We would lead walking tours that started at a particular London landmark and ended at the Wapping Power Station. We never tired of watching people's amazed faces as they approached the venue. I would wear a hat with a big 'W' on it so that people would know who to follow and Joe, never missing his cue, would say, 'Gee, where's Wally today, ha ha ha.'

Anyhow, I digress. Time was whizzing by; it was nearly June and I hadn't done a thing in terms of organising a dressmaker, a cake maker, or going to the bank for a loan to pay for it all! As for invitations – we knew we wanted Alan Kitching (specialist in the pure graphic art known as letterpress) to design them, but again, nothing was organised. Still, there was plenty of time, I reasoned. I would get on top of things at work and then 'Project Wedding' would be my focus over the summer.

I wasn't expecting our plans to be thrown abruptly into chaos. I wasn't expecting to be involved in a bombing, to lose both my legs or to face my greatest fear – that of dying alone. I was just a normal person, a bride-to-be, on her way to work one morning in July ...

We made the decision to keep the date, regardless, just a few days after I woke up in intensive care, following the revelation from Dr Luff that I would actually walk again. The problem was that we had planned to use the summer to get the whole event organised and even that had been cutting it fine. The unspoken fear that we should have postponed, that we were taking too much on hung between us. But at the same time, knowing that we had a goal, something to work towards within an incredibly rigid timeframe, provided us with an extraordinary incentive throughout the difficult and daunting months of rehabilitation.

My friends all rallied around. When news went out that Joe and I were going ahead with the wedding, just as planned, everyone went into action. I think it was an extremely positive signal, something for all those who had been so distraught over my ordeal, to hold on to. It was a sign that I was ok – that I would emerge from all this, still their Gill.

The hospital became 'Wedding Headquarters'. I held meetings in the Day Room, in my room, by the fountain and in the coffee shop. There were three and a half months until the big day and I still only had one leg fitted! I wasn't overly worried though – the greatest lesson that I was taking from this experience was that nothing is worth getting too stressed over; nothing that isn't about life or death.

Amongst the many who signed up to help, two Helens – Helen E and Helen T – proved to be the driving forces, ensuring that all the essentials were covered: a wedding dress, bridesmaids' dresses and naturally a wedding cake. And there was something else I needed too: 'I want a tiara; I have to have a tiara. If I have something amazing on top, then I won't worry so much about what's happening at the bottom.'

I couldn't imagine being able to wear a traditional dress now – the sketches that I had done by the fountain, well they had all the elegance of Audrey Hepburn or Grace Kelly, my idols, but I couldn't imagine exuding that sort of elegance or poise, not now. It's funny, just thinking about all those meetings, discussing fabric swatches and colour palettes, all conducted from within the hospital – a part of me felt that it was all imaginary, I was in my hospital bubble and all these 'things' were happening outside, out there, somewhere. It was surreal, I couldn't believe that it would ever be possible to create my dream, to the very detail.

But Helen E, who was in charge of the dress, found the ideal designer, Laura, whom I immediately loved. What was lovely about working with Laura was that she grasped my vague concepts and instantly transformed them into reality. It was very heartening during such a stressful process to find someone with whom I had a natural empathy and this made working with her to realise my dream a real pleasure.

But whilst designing a fantasy dress was all well and good, how on earth was I going to be able to wear it? I would have to be trained to walk in a gown. Enter Matt, Nichola and Carol. Matt surprised us all by becoming a designer supremo, creating the 'dress of all dresses', made entirely from hospital sheets. *Très chic*! I used an old hand-wash dispenser as a posy, Nichola and Carol stood in as bridesmaids, and with the St Thomas' physio' gym as a backdrop, the lessons began.

I could hardly walk as I held onto Matt's arm, doubled over with laughter. Matt was humming, 'Here comes the bride', but I don't know how he managed to get a single note out, we were laughing so much. We did eventually calm down though and Matt taught me how to brush aside the fabric of the 'dress', to place my foot down, then again, taking small steps each time. 'Up straight Gillington. Eyes ahead, no looking down. This is your wedding day!' Matt's words played over and over in my mind, but not looking down was very difficult – when you can't feel the ground the only reassurance that you are not heading for a fall is to see where you are stepping and to know what's coming up. But I could do it. I knew I could – it was all about practice. So that's what I did. I practised walking down a pretend aisle, wrapped in a sheet, with my head held high!

The theme for the wedding was to be a winter wonderland. I would wear a heavy cream silk coat with a jewelled clasp to match my tiara; the bridesmaids would wear thick, crushed velvet wraps over chocolate/bronze dresses.

Once I was discharged from hospital the fittings began with just eight weeks to go. Lily and Maddy were to be the bridesmaids, and whilst it would be difficult to fit Maddy because she was back in Adelaide, I knew it would all work out and would not allow myself to get stressed about it. I was thrilled, deliriously happy that I had come this far – that I would even be seeing this day at all.

Helen T was making the cake and was also in charge of collecting me from our 'trainer home' in Richmond and taking me to all the various shops and venues to make final decisions. This included several trips to the tiara maker. The tiara designs were sketched and discussed to ensure that it was the perfect headdress for me – it couldn't be too heavy as I would have to be able to stand and walk with it on.

The *City Hospital* crew were always on hand, filming snippets of all the activity for the documentary. They were never obtrusive though and just blended into the scenery. We all got along so well – it was a pleasure having them there and was just one more thing to add to all the bizarre changes in my life.

The day for the final tiara fitting came and was captured by the film crew. It was amazing – just as I had always dreamed it would be. It had a mixture of stones – in golds, blues and diamonds – and when it was placed on my head it was like a scene from a royal coronation! I stood up – even in my jeans I looked like a princess! – then sat back down. I was completely overwhelmed. Helen squeezed my hand. 'Look at you Dame Gill, or Ma'am,' she joked, to lighten the mood. She knew what all this meant to me as only a week earlier I had broken down in her arms when she'd taken me out to try on some wedding dresses.

I'd been desperate just to get a feel, just to see what I might look like whilst my dress was being made. We went into several shops, I'd pointed to the ones I liked and the assistants, often quite snooty, had brought them to me. But faced with the reality of trying the dresses on I was worried about how I would cope in the changing room. I wasn't confident about undressing or taking my legs off unless Joe was there – he just knew what to do and how to hold me upright. That's not to take anything away from Helen but we were just out together, doing 'girly' things, and it's hard when you have always been a friend, to be suddenly forced into the role of carer. So I just held a dress up to myself and looked in the mirror. This was the first time I'd seen myself in a long mirror – I hadn't seen this Gill before. I didn't recognise her. I was bent over on my crutches, I looked tired, drained and the sparkle was gone. I looked like a patient, someone who had been blown up; I didn't look like a bride. I sobbed.

We went back to Helen's car and I cried and cried and cried. She didn't say a word, just held my hand and drove me home, well, back to Richmond.

Helen and I had known each other back in Adelaide, and she, like me, had now made a life for herself here in London. She's a positive, 'can-do' sort of person – the kind you want on your team. She would always come to the hospital with a basketful of cakes and all my favourite foods; most Sundays she'd be there with a fresh batch of banana cake. She was proud of me, proud that I was strong and that I was prepared to overcome any challenge and she vowed to support me in any way she could. She had been a valued friend throughout the whole ordeal.

She was also there to help me try on the first mock dress in calico, to check the shape and for ease of movement. Both Helens were there, in fact. It was a big moment for us. I was so nervous. With only four weeks to go I worried that I had put on weight since my measurements had been taken and nervous that I wouldn't be able to walk.

I got the dress on and the dressmaker held a mirror up for me to get the general idea. Again, I cried, only this time they were tears of joy. If I could have jumped up and down I would have, but instead I just clapped my hands together. It was perfect – exactly what I had imagined and this was just the guide dress!

All the parts of the wedding were now starting to come together. Next, the arrangements for the ceremony and reception would have to be finalised. These were Joe's department.

. . .

Joe is very close to the Church. He worships there without fail every Sunday. The little community at the Church of which he is a part was a source of great strength and hope for him, especially during those dark days when my life still hung in the balance.

Back in mid-November we had gone in a taxi, together with Father Kit Cunningham of St Etheldreda's to meet the Cardinal Cormac Murphy O'Connor. The Catholic Church opened its arms to me and took me to its heart, knowing that I wasn't a Catholic myself, yet recognising me, none the less, as a person of great faith who was to marry a Catholic. (In actual fact, my ambition as a little girl had always been to become a nun, but I clearly remember Mum saying that I couldn't be one because we weren't Catholic. I was absolutely heartbroken!)

The Cardinal had been impressed to hear of all the many miracles that had happened to me, none greater than being given the gift of Life Two. I told him of how certain I was that there must have been Divine intervention for me that day – given how very close I had been to death, how else could I explain my survival? He could see there was no bitterness in me – no hatred nor desire for revenge – and I explained that I felt blessed that I did not carry these feelings and that I was able to find so much enjoyment from life. I think he really understood me and what I was saying. In a message before the wedding he said that I had been 'a marvellous example of courage and faith during these past months' and that Joe had been 'a loving companion and constant support during that time. May the good Lord bless their marriage and grant them much joy and happiness in the years to come.' This meant a lot to Joe and me.

St Etheldreda is a popular choice of church for marriages and from years of practice they truly know how to put on a good wedding. But we know that for us they pulled off something extra special, helping Joe to plan everything and reassuring him that all would be just as he wanted it.

No one could accuse Joe of being a particularly organised person in his daily life, but give him a special project that he's passionate about and somehow or other he'll make sure that every detail is taken care of. The most important element, to him, was the music, which also happens to be an area in which St Etheldreda excels. In the course of a drunken afternoon in the Mitre Tavern (conveniently situated next door to the church!) Joe and Paul, the Director of Music, made the necessary choices. These were a Mass by Palestrina (the sublime *Missa Papae Marcelli*) and motets by Mozart, Elgar and Philips. Most important of all were the *Processional* (played as the bride enters the church) and the *Recessional* (as the bride and groom leave as a married couple). For the first of these Joe made the unusual but inspired choice of Handel's *Eternal Source of Light Divine*, which would mean having a trumpet in addition to the eight singers that had been agreed.

The other details of the service were handled by the Sacristan, Linda, who is one of the most extraordinary of all the extraordinary people at St Etheldreda's! She devotes every day of the week to the church, ensuring that all work carried out is done so impeccably; in her case God is in the detail.

The first time I met Linda was when she came to the hospital to take care of some paperwork (checking birth certificates, christening certificates, and so on). There was such a look of love in her eyes, it's difficult to describe, but I knew from the moment I met her that our wedding would be exceptional – that she would add in a little extra magic to the day. We discussed my flowers – I had set my heart on dark red roses – and she quietly went off and arranged them as her wedding gift to Joe and me. And they were grand prix red roses; this was a truly wonderful gift, a gesture that touched me deeply.

...

'The flowers are here, shall I get them sent up?' Maddy was very excited. She and Lily were all made up, hair done, dresses on, ready and waiting. They looked beautiful.

Jo, Lily, Maddy and I had all stayed at a hotel near the church the night before the wedding. I didn't get much sleep. I was so nervous, but not with the usual pre-wedding nerves. I was worried that I would fall over and just wanted to get through the day without a stumble. Maddy and Lily had helped me get my legs ready the night before – I had special gold tights to cover the plastic casings and my limited edition Adidas chrome trainers! I had never expected to be getting married in trainers, but they were the best fit and had a good grip for balancing. Jo took a picture of them standing on their own, two gold and silver legs! That would definitely be one for the album.

I couldn't help but think about Mum. She would have loved the dress, the girls and all the fuss that was being made of me. I could hear her voice, 'Oh Gilly, are you sure you'll be warm enough? And have you got everything you need – a hankie?' How I wished she was there to say those things to me; those ordinary comments would have meant so much to me. My mind went back to a particular photo' from Mum and Dad's wedding day: they were coming out of the church to a guard of honour – a line of St John ambulance men (Dad was a volunteer for St John and they gave him this tribute for all the work he had done) all in uniform, holding their hats in the air ...

...

The actual ceremony wasn't until four o'clock, when the sky would be changing, hovering between afternoon and evening, yet with just enough light to appreciate fully the candlelit ceremony that we had planned. But time passed in a blink and no sooner had we finished breakfast, or so it seemed, than the photographer arrived, then the

City Hospital crew and suddenly there were people everywhere – no more time for quiet reflection or contemplation.

It was almost time to go. Jo did her best to play the role of Mum, even though there's only three years between us (she being older, of course!). She made sure that my dress was perfect, that the girls were happy, and that all the behind-the-scenes jobs were going according to plan. Jo's final touch before we all left was to help me put on Mum's necklace.

Mum would have been proud to see me – to see how far I had come in only a few short months.

There was a knock at the door. 'Can we come in?' It was Si and Berni – Si would be taking Graham and me to the church in his beloved, dark blue Citroen. This had become a very special car to me and this was to be my second important journey in it – the first having been when Si took me to Richmond for a weekend release and trial from hospital, an important mark of returning to the world and becoming independent. This time though, the journey would take me on a new path, one that was joined to another's in a new life. I still had the same fears though – the feeling of travelling into the unknown. For as exciting and promising as it all was, it would still be new. Being married, being Mrs Kerr would all be new.

'Gill, Gill, look at the crowd. It's unbelievable. This is absolutely unbelievable – I've never seen so many photographers!' As we were approaching Si could see the gathering of press and television crews outside the church gates. Graham and I strained to see from the back seat, but as we passed through the gates, the flashing of all the cameras gave me a pretty good idea of just how many were there. I could also see a line of police as we drove by and remember feeling so thrilled that they were there. I didn't know them, but they represented the entire force to me and I felt that we were sharing this day with them – with all the police forces in London and across the whole of the UK.

Father Kit was there at the church to greet me, wearing a beretta (the old-fashioned hat that priests wear only rarely nowadays). Joe had asked him to wear it as it would fit in with the historic and traditional feeling of the purity of the Latin Mass.

Graham helped me from the car and held my arm as I steadied myself, then we followed Father Kit inside the building. A hush swept across the congregation as a theatrical dimming of the lights gave way to the flickering of hundreds of tiny flames, all burning from candles that filled the entire church. It was absolutely magical.

In the soft, glistening light a single voice began to sing, signalling my first step, followed by the trumpet, at which point, as several people later confessed to me, they could no longer hold back the tears. I deliberately placed one step after the other. I couldn't feel the ground but I was still upright and moving forward. I felt like I was gliding along the aisle, supported by Graham, carried by the love of all who were watching my every movement, willing me to walk unaided and weeping as they watched me fulfil this dream. This would be the single most symbolic and powerful walk that I would make, for every step I took was a step towards the future; every step forward was a step further away from the pain and the tragedy I was leaving behind.

I felt such strength. I carried the physios' voices in my head, saying 'Squeeze, head high, squeeze, weight over, head up,' and it was as though I could have walked for miles, if that's what I'd needed to do. But it wasn't, because there, beside me, was Joe, tears streaming down his face. Graham passed over the responsibility. He handed me to Joe.

We could have been the only two people in the world, as the ceremony began. I was lost in the emotion of the music. I could forget how triumphant I was to have walked up the aisle, I could forget that I was wearing prosthetic legs – this was my wedding. I was a bride. My tears were tears of joy, a sign of understanding how fortunate I was to have this day, to have this moment and to be alive.

Father Kit began the Latin Mass. We made our solemn vows to love one another, to cherish and respect each other and to stand by one another in sickness and in health, until our death. We knew what that vow meant. Already we knew we could do that. We knew that we had a unique strength together and that we would overcome whatever else life threw at us. It was a very powerful moment – there was a sense of being indestructible, invincible, knowing that as long as we were together we would prevail.

There was a change to the traditional end of the Mass in which Father Kit presented us with a special wedding blessing from the

Pope. Linda and Paul from St Ed's had organised it when Paul was last in Rome. It was just yet another one of those special touches that seemed to characterise Life Two, making it so extraordinary.

I was now Mrs Kerr, Mrs Gill – Gillian – Kerr. Joe and I walked down the aisle as husband and wife to the cheers of all. I couldn't look left or right, only straight ahead as I had been taught, which was just as well because I didn't want to cry and knew that if I saw anyone, or caught anyone's eye, that would set me off! Alex discreetly passed me my cane and I walked out of the church with Joe on one arm, the cane in the other. I didn't think about walking – I felt like I was walking on air, as though that was why I couldn't feel the ground.

Outside the church two large Routemaster buses awaited us – one red and one gold – courtesy of Arriva, the company Joe drives for. We ushered everyone who wasn't driving their own car onto a bus, but then there was a twist as Joe pulled out a high-visibility vest and put it over his beautiful wedding suit. He was going to drive the bus to Wapping! No one had quite expected that!

As we drove through the gates the photographers were all clicking madly, flashes blazing brightly. I really couldn't believe that this was happening and one of our guests yelled out of a window: 'You know it's not Jordan and Peter Andre, don't you?' I think the guests were just as stunned as we were at all the media attention.

Our friend Josh had to take the choir from the church to the reception at Wapping. It was a bit like a scene from a comedy film – Josh needing to beat us there so that the proceedings were seamless and Joe taking the scenic route, across Tower Bridge, past all the familiar landmarks, to give Josh as much time as possible. But amidst all the nerves and tension, Joe gave his passengers a bonus memory as he drove his double-decker bus down a one-way street! Suddenly all we could see were the headlights from oncoming cars, followed by furious beeping. Joe, mortified, had to do a tricky three-point turn to get the bus back on track. He has never lived that down and I'm sure it will come up at every anniversary!

We finally reached the Wapping Power Station where heavy red drapes were pulled back to reveal the most fantastical sight – Jules had created the most enchanting winter scene, as if it were straight out of a film set. A towering pine tree, the size of something you might see in a town square (Jules searched most of Europe to find it!) was placed on a salted floor (which gave the appearance of snow) and draped with large red ribbons and apples attached to the ends. The choir (who miraculously arrived before all the guests courtesy of Josh's driving skills) were singing and the champagne and mulled wine were flowing. I felt like I had stepped into my very own fairy tale.

We had 150 guests for dinner, including Aaron, Ray, Andy, Jon and Steve. They'd all been there in that tunnel, desperately trying to carry me out, and now here I was, standing before them wearing a tiara and an ivory silk gown. This was how I wanted them to see me. Prof was there too, like a proud father with his arm around me. Who would have thought that five months after operating on me he would be standing at my wedding, champagne glass charged?

We didn't have a seating plan. We wanted our oldest, dearest friends to blend with our newer friends. I could see work colleagues sitting with nurses, family sitting with police and friends with rescuers; it was personally a very moving observation. So many people there wanted the chance to say 'Thank you', to touch or just shake the hand of someone who had been so brave on that day.

Time again. The evening was racing by. People were chatting at the long, room-length table that held the feast. They were all getting to know each other and the mood and the air were full of love.

Joe tapped the microphone to indicate that it was speech time. Bill, Joe's brother, was best man. He started with jokes and tales of Joe as a child and the mischief he would get up to. He also had the task of reading out the many letters and cards from those who couldn't be there. The Prime Minister of Australia, the Cardinal, the Chief Executive of London Underground, the Australian High Commissioner, the Premier of South Australia and Maurice de Rohan, the Agent General for South Australia – all of them sent their congratulations and wishes for a long and happy future. Maurice's letter was particularly moving as he had been to the church to deliver it in person. He was gravely ill at the time, but he mustered enough energy to see me walk up the aisle. Knowing that he was there had given me great comfort as he was very much a father figure to me.

Antony, Joe's father, was next. Everyone was transfixed by his words. He is a natural communicator and his speech was carefully crafted to highlight the importance and significance of our union. In keeping with tradition, Graham then stood to offer words of thanks and to congratulate both Joe and I on our strength and determination to go through with all our plans, and so spectacularly! He then passed the microphone over to Joe who, like his father, is also a brilliant speaker:

'Dearest family and friends

I can't begin to tell you how overjoyed we both are that all of you, the people that we love the most in the world, are here to share this most precious day with us and to be our witnesses to the solemn pledges and vows that we have made today. Pledges to a future built on love and hope, a future that you have all helped to build. And we do mean all of you, because be assured, every single thing you have done for us, even simply sending a message of support and encouragement at the right moment, has helped us on our way to here.

Today is not the happy end to our story, but a happy beginning; from now we want to be able to say that the truly important day for our new lives was not a date in early July, but today, December 10.

However, there's no doubt that the last few months have transformed the way we have planned today's celebrations, not least because it's a unique and wonderful opportunity for us to offer you our heartfelt thanks for helping us to achieve this moment. And we wish to do that publicly, so right now I need to beg your patience whilst I both offer the expected and necessary thanks for such an occasion, but following that we then wish to honour and applaud those of you to whom we owe a special debt.'

Joe went on to name each person who had done so much to ensure that I had survived and who continued to support us both. There was a standing ovation. Everyone was cheering, applauding, crying, screaming with thanks directed to all those who had made a difference, who saved lives that July day – and indeed every day. No one cheered louder than me. One hundred and fifty people kept up the applause for over fifteen minutes and even then we had to gesture everyone to quieten down because there were even more speeches! I smiled, looking over at Ray and mouthed 'Thank you' to him. He winked and nodded then looked around the room at everyone clapping and cheering. The cheers were for those who were there at the reception, but also for those we didn't know – those people in the emergency services who deserved praise for the work they do every day, all the unsung heroes, the train drivers, the station staff, the volunteers.

Our wedding was a triumph over adversity and we were all sharing and basking in that triumph. But for me, it was also a triumph for love – not only the love and union of two people but also a global love and solidarity between strangers.

Next, breaking with tradition, I took the microphone. There was something I needed to add to Joe's beautiful and poignant words.

'How wonderful and brilliant it is to be alive,
to have had this day, with you all.
I am truly very grateful and humbled by this experience.
My words of thanks are to you all, especially those who have done
so much to help us over the past months.
But to Joe, my husband, my rock,
I know just how difficult these past months have been for you
and you have stayed strong for me.
And your love has kept me strong.
I am so thankful to have you by my side
and I love you so dearly.
Please, everyone raise your glass and join me in a toast to my
husband, Joe.
While you are standing, another toast, if I may.
This is to life, to making a difference where and when you can.
In the words of my father-in-law, to leave more than you take,
and to never forgetting the wonder that is all around us every day!
To life!'

I didn't want the night to end. I wanted to be cradled by this emotion forever. It was wonderful to be surrounded by so many dear friends. I only wished I could have invited everyone I held dear and who had supported me, but I couldn't.

Then, out of the blue: 'I didn't know you were married before Gill darling?' said one of Joe's relatives, remarking on having just met my first husband. 'I haven't! Who on earth was that?' At which point my friend Ian popped up. Ian and I share a particular sense of humour, and even though he is clearly gay, we would often pretend that we were just an old married couple. I later found out that all evening he'd been introducing himself to people as my ex-husband. He'd then gone on to tell them that our divorce wasn't really finalised, which meant that the marriage they'd all just witnessed was probably not legal!

It was clearly time for us to go – I couldn't face any more relatives asking about my delightful ex!

Helen T was ready to drive us to our surprise gift – a night at a private, members-only London hotel. As I turned my head to look out through the back window of the car, I saw a sea of faces, champagne smiles and mascara-streaked cheeks. I saw Michelle waving – we had been friends for over ten years and she'd been the first to the hospital the moment she'd heard, distraught and traumatised at the possibility that my life could end. I saw Margaret, Bill, Diana and Halle, all of whom had flown in from America to be with us; Antonio and Sara from Italy; Debs and all the dear, old friends along with newer ones – Jamie, my nurse, Kat and Jon. They were all waving and hugging; the celebration of that day was like a flame that would continue to burn within them.

...

We arrived home the next day to find the family all sitting at the kitchen table reading the papers! The front cover of nearly every one of the Sunday papers featured either a picture of me, or one of me and Joe! Lily and Maddy were looking at pictures of themselves: 'Look, look here we are. Page four in this one; no, look it's page two in this one. Wow.'

The headlines read, 'Brave 7/7 Bride Walks Down the Aisle' and

'35 Steps of Agony as 7/7 Bride Walks'. Mostly the reports were of the triumph over terrorism, of how we had gone ahead with our plans regardless. We were stunned! It just didn't relate. It couldn't really be our wedding. Once again, I looked at all the papers with a sense of being removed – it was someone else I was reading about. I even felt happy for 'them'! It is a most peculiar sensation, unimaginable; it's neither bad nor good – just bizarre. Once again I was reminded that I certainly wasn't 'One Unknown' any more.

. . .

Qantas were flying us home, business class, for our honeymoon. Joe hadn't been to Australia before, so he was very excited at the very idea of the world being 'upside down, back to front' and the peculiar prospect of swimming in December and having his first sweltering summer Christmas!

The flight was worrying me though. It would be another first and I didn't know what to expect. What would my stumps do? Would they swell in the same way that feet do during a long flight? If that happened I wouldn't be able to get my legs back on. Then I'd be completely stuck – I'd have to crawl to the bathroom in front of all the other passengers. But if I left my legs on for the flight, how would that affect them. Would I need to keep them elevated? Also, my ears – would it be harmful to fly with so much damage done to the eardrums?

The medical staff I'd consulted saw no reason why I shouldn't travel and Joe, already in husband mode, responded to my concerns with a 'You worry too much' comment. Nevertheless I called Qantas customer care to see what they thought was the best option: leave the legs on, take them off, or maybe leave them on for just part of the flight? I can't believe it now but I actually said to the woman on the phone: 'I don't really feel that comfortable with the idea of placing my legs in the overhead locker!' She went absolutely quiet. I bet that was one she hadn't heard before!

Joe was right, I needed to calm down and accept this as yet another first. Whatever happened we would deal with it.

...

Our friend Andrew, a photographic artist, wanted to drive us to the airport. This was just one way in which he expressed his devotion to us both: he had kept a photographic record of Joe's bachelor party and our wedding reception (including a frame-by-frame account of Joe's wrong turn down the one-way street) and the ride to the airport would complete this.

The Qantas crew recognised Joe and me immediately. They were very professional but, at the same time, they each made a point of coming up to us throughout the flight – they would kneel down, squeeze my hand and say just how thrilled they were that we'd been able to keep our wedding date. Then a bottle of champagne would be placed on Joe's tray. By the time we got to Singapore we were both quite drunk!

Singapore ground crew were waiting at the plane doors with a wheelchair, a very welcome form of transport as I wasn't sure how I would manage to walk the distance within the terminal. I wasn't yet skilled in walking with prosthetics whilst under the influence! I was treated like royalty, like precious cargo and everyone was going out of their way to be helpful.

In the lounge Joe noticed the newspapers. 'Gill – guess who's on the front page of the newspaper?' And there we were – but this was Singapore! No wonder everyone was smiling and waving at us.

Once we'd landed in Melbourne, a driver from one of the television stations, Channel Nine, was waiting to collect us. It was all part of the service as Joe and I were due to do an interview – our first in Australia – with the *Today* programme. (I'd met the presenter, Karl, when he was in London.) It was true TV glamour – the driver took us in a black limousine to the Crowne Plaza Hotel where we would spend our first nights. It was all so abnormal that it was almost normal, if that makes any sense. We were both starting to realise that Life Two was even stranger and more wonderful than we could ever have predicted.

Everyone was friendly and happy and smiling. Joe even heard a few 'G'days' which put a smile on his face. He was eager to see some of the Melbourne sights and as we only had a few days there we had a lot to cram in! Tram rides, restaurants, eating seafood, museums, shopping – just soaking it all up. But I wasn't used to walking long distances in the heat. I had my stick and my hat, but the high temperatures, along with the effort of trying to swat flies and walk at the same time were all very wearing.

'Taxi! Taxi!' Every taxi was taken and I was desperate to get back to the hotel and take my legs off. We lined up in a queue; there was nowhere to sit and I was starting to feel the pain shooting up my thighs. From the corner of my eye I could see a couple hailing a cab. I couldn't believe it – the cheek, the nerve – we'd been waiting such a long time. Then the taxi drove up to me and stopped and the couple raced over and said, 'We think you are amazing. Here's a taxi – we got you a taxi. Welcome home, oh and congratulations – the wedding looked great!' Joe and I were speechless. And this was just the first of many such encounters.

The Australian public weren't shy in coming up and talking to both Joe and I as if they knew us. I loved that freshness – it's what I was like all those years ago when I first came to London, smiling and starting up conversations with my fellow commuters on the tube or the bus.

...

In keeping with honeymoon tradition, Joe booked a cabin – not just any cabin but a Gold Kangaroo class – on an overnight train from Melbourne to Adelaide. Getting on the train and indeed into the cabin wasn't exactly a breeze for a newly disabled person, but in the spirit of the occasion we drank our complimentary glasses of bucks fizz and laughed for most of the journey. I awoke to the sight of the familiar trees of the Adelaide Hills – we were near our final stop.

The family were all there on the platform, waving as we came to a halt in the station.

I hadn't been home for over five years. I didn't know all those years ago that I would never again set foot on Australian soil ...

...

Being a lover of good wine, Joe was eager to see the wineries, so we spent some time in the Barossa Valley. I, of course, had been there several times, but this time it was different. I was seeing Australia and all its beauty and splendour through Joe's fresh eyes. I watched as he soaked up the experience, as he did everything else that the summer sun offered – swimming in the sea and playing with the kids on the trampoline, chasing them around.

I longed to feel the sand beneath my feet just one more time. It makes me upset even writing about it; but then I catch myself and remember that yes, there are many things that I will never again do, but there is also so much that I can do and that is where I need to focus my energies and attention.

Shopping was something we could both enjoy and I was happy being in familiar places. It was different now though, as everywhere we went we were recognised. 'Joe, Gill, it's you! Oh, what a lovely wedding – bless you both! The flowers – they were stunning, and you looked beautiful, let me give you a hug.' Joe looked at me and asked, quietly, if I knew this person. 'No,' I replied, 'I thought you did!' And we both laughed. The woman was insistent that Joe should apply to teach at Adelaide University and that we should settle back in Australia – London was too dangerous she said, and she would hate for anything else to happen.

Another woman walked past and, realising who we were, she interrupted and clasped my hand in hers. Looking deeply into my eyes she told me that she'd prayed every day for my recovery and that it was a real miracle for her to see me, standing before her in the centre of Adelaide.

I found these sudden bursts of affection extremely touching, if not slightly overwhelming. I was once a complete unknown, blending and merging into the constant sea of faces you pass through each day. Now I was Gill, a new bride, a survivor – someone that people felt they knew.

...

My high-school friends all came to see me for lunch at Graham and Jo's place. I hadn't seen some of them in eight, maybe ten years, and understandably, they didn't know quite what to expect – what I would be like. They had all dutifully followed the news reports and interviews that had been featured in Australian magazines and papers, so they had some idea but they were all still a little apprehensive. Within minutes of meeting though, the tears turned to laughter as the old jokes started coming out and, soon, any anxieties were forgotten – I was still 'their' Gill, we were still a gang and we were all still the same souls, just a bit wiser. One of the things I have enjoyed watching and being a part of is just this: the melting away of worry and fear of how to be around a disabled person. People are concerned about things like whether I can drink or eat rich food and other things that may seem silly to me but are serious considerations for them – until they see me and all their angst disappears.

. . .

During our visit Joe and I had the real pleasure to meet two prominent South Australian figures. The first was Her Excellency, Governor Marjorie Jackson Nelson, whose name is instantly recognisable to anyone with a knowledge of Australian sporting history. For the Lithgow Flash, as she was known in her youth, is an Aussie legend. Competing in the 1952 Helsinki Olympics, she became the first Australian woman to hold a world record and the first to win a gold medal for running. Over half a century on from these sporting triumphs she is still an extraordinary woman and a celebrated and much loved figure in South Australia. I'm sure that the irony was not lost on either of us that this legendary runner was meeting a woman with no legs!

We met at her residence, the stately Governor's House in the heart of Adelaide. She greeted us with such warmth that we immediately felt at ease in her company. We chatted away whilst drinking tea and nibbling cakes; she was a generous and gracious host. As we drove out through the gates, I remembered how as a small girl I would ask Mum who lived in that big house whenever we passed by. I had never been inside it, never even been beyond the gates before this day. But we were both very touched to meet the Governor and treasure our growing friendship.

We were also fortunate to meet the Premier of South Australia, Mike Rann. He was born in London and he was a soccer man, so Joe was very much looking forward to this meeting – at last he would have something in common with an Australian (although he was, in fact, raised in New Zealand)! Mike shared with us all the exciting developments that the state had been making, especially in education and science. I could have listened to him talk about South Australia for ever as he was so animated and enthusiastic. Like Maurice and the Governor, he welcomed both Joe and I and made us feel very much a part of the larger South Australian 'family'. As a parting gift, he gave us a lovely bottle of Coonawarra Cabernet that we decided to save to drink back in London on a special occasion. In fact, we shared it over dinner with Maurice, his wife Meg, and our dear friends Josh and Jules Wright – fellow Adelaidians residing in London.

· · ·

Once again it was time to go through the pain of saying goodbye and, this time, knowing there were no plans in the immediate future for us all to be together again and having had my family with me for so many weeks, I couldn't imagine how I would cope going back to the old routine of phone calls. The distance is just too great.

I couldn't climb the steps up to the plane, so I went in a wheelchair and then a small crane that lifted me up to the doors of the plane. Waving and crying, waving and crying all the way, it was tearing my heart apart – this was my family, my beloved brother, sister-in-law, niece and nephew. But my life was in London; Joe's life was in London.

We were both hurting – Joe hadn't expected to miss my family as much as I was – and we were mostly silent until we reached Singapore. On landing at Heathrow I could hear piped music playing in the plane as we taxied on the runway; it was '*I Still Call Australia Home*' and that was it – I was completely choked. I said to Joe that this was a sign; a sign that we should get on the next flight and just go back. I guess I knew I was being ridiculous though.

Helen T was there at the airport to meet us. She knew that I would be upset, having been through it so many times herself. It never gets any easier when your heart is in two places. Helen had knitted me a scarf, worried that I would be cold coming back from the heat!

As we drove into London and I saw buildings and familiar signs I began to feel more at ease. I loved London. I loved living in London and there was so much that I had to do. I decided then that Life Two would have to be split – I would spend as much time as I could with the family, but still be based in the city that meant so much to both Joe and me.

We were happy; we'd be happy wherever we were. I guess the question for the future was whether we would want our kids to sound Australian or British? Either way, one thing I do know is that their god-parents will all be here, in London, still saving lives, as they did mine and upholding the law because that's what they do.

Chapter 11

Remember to Live

REMEMBERING TO LIVE is, for me, intrinsically linked with making a difference and making life count.

I've asked myself many times, 'Is it good enough just to be alive?' or is life about what we do, what we all do to leave our mark, to leave the world a better place than when we arrived in it?

Not a day passes when I don't wish that the bombings on July 7 hadn't happened. If I could turn the clock back, I would, without hesitation. I used to think, but I have now stopped for fear of driving myself insane, that it was all in the timing: if I had been just two minutes earlier or later I would have been spared. But I wasn't. Not a day passes either when I am not filled with despair watching the news of my fellow man killing and dying in similar attacks. There is one day, July 7, that 'we', London, can mark as our 'black' day, but in some places in the world, every day is a July 7. Every day. The tears I cry now are for all those who are killed or left maimed, like me.

But just wishing alone doesn't make a difference. It doesn't make things change. Sometimes we have to create the change ourselves, within ourselves.

As I see it, I had no choice on *that* morning, I wasn't asked by Germaine Lindsay before he detonated his bomb if I was his enemy. He took away my choice by assuming that I was, assuming that we all were. But whilst I didn't have a choice at that precise moment, I feel that I have been presented with many choices since.

I could have chosen to let hatred for this act and for the person who committed it to consume me. I could have chosen to curl up in a ball and cry, asking, 'Why me, why me?' I could have done many things, all of which I was entitled to, but I didn't. From the moment I was given the option of choosing life, I made a vow: that if I did survive I would live a full life, a good and rich life. I vowed I would never take anything – all that I have – for granted again. I would never forget how precious every single day is.

I have stayed true to that promise and I believe it is a major contributing factor to my miraculous recovery – the ability to recognise just how fortunate I am even to be here. Once you adopt that attitude and apply it in all areas of life, everything starts to look different. That memory of desperately wanting to drink a cup of water when all I could do was have water dripped from a large cotton bud into the side of my mouth, is never far away. I still make a point of delighting in every mouthful of water, relishing every drop of coffee or tea, savouring every morsel of food, and taking pleasure in every glass of wine. Everything that passes my lips is appreciated (I just wish I didn't appreciate chocolate so much!).

Being slow – physically moving at a slower pace – has been an extraordinary experience. I have seen so much more, just by being able to stop, look and absorb. I've left the 'rat race' because I have chosen not to compete; because I no longer feel the need to 'win'. I don't enjoy life any less because there is less of me, because I am restricted or disabled. To the contrary: I now understand it's what you make of life. It's about how you read it, how you edit it and what role you cast yourself in: like my decision to be a survivor and not a victim of the bombings.

Being 'high on life' gave me and continues to give me the ability to cope and find the positives in nearly all situations. I am still so surprised by this new simplicity I have found: everything is clear, every problem has a solution and, most radical of all, most things don't really matter. I no longer look for complications and they don't come and find me. It's amazing! All the rubbish of life has just slid away. I feel liberated.

I don't fear death, although I wouldn't choose it. And I don't fear life either. I'm not afraid to make mistakes and try new things. It's true, my life did flash before my eyes and I concentrated on the 'good bits' – the highlights and the happy memories – and that is what I now intend to do more of. That is what is important – to me: making more great memories.

I am always excited by the breakthroughs and the triumphs. I am in constant wonder at what my body has achieved, this amazing 'machine' – how it has healed itself and adapted to having its limbs missing. I am just in awe. The tasks that may seem everyday and ordinary to some are monumental to me, and the achievement of conquering these, well, that's my version of climbing Mount Everest. It's exhilarating, brilliant and often extremely emotional – like carrying a hot drink up the stairs, going out on my own and crossing a main road, creating a technique to roll into our bath tub so that I can shower on my own, dancing, making the bed, pushing a trolley at the supermarket, being in a department store buying clothes, managing, adapting to situations where you have to literally 'think on your feet'.

I am encouraged, excited and impressed at witnessing my progress at the hospital where I now go for rehabilitation. My physiotherapist, Jennifer, is teaching me how to jump, jog and anything else she can think of beginning with a 'j'! She, like Matt and Nichola, has the ability to make me believe that I can achieve a task – like walking without staring at the ground, or walking over mounds of earth without my cane – things that I would never have imagined being able to do, but have done, thanks to her coaching.

I can feel myself beam with sheer delight when I am on the treadmill or the exercise bike. It's funny how these things have become 'rewards' now: if I achieve something new or difficult, I can spend a bit longer on the equipment. Who would ever have thought!

But none of this would be possible if I didn't have properly fitted legs. Ollie, my prosthetist, works closely with Jennifer to achieve a greater understanding of both my needs and my potential. He has customised sockets that offer me greater flexibility so that riding a bike, walking on a treadmill or even walking around at home is as comfortable as possible. The relationship with the prosthetist is an important one. Their role can be likened to that of a mechanic: they are crucial to your mobility and, for me, without well-fitting legs, I'd be stuck and could go nowhere. Ollie watches when I try a new pair of legs, like a parent watches their child take its first steps. He stands by as I walk up and down the parallel bars, making adjustments with his tools as I go – a bit of a turn to the ankle joint here, a tightening of the foot there (although, of course, it's all much more technical than that).

At a recent check-up my consultant, who is warm, gentle, considered and always reassuring, told me that he was puzzled as to why I don't take any painkillers, at least for the phantom pains, and given that I didn't take any medication, why was I so happy all the time? I smiled and explained that I am still in a state of absolute euphoria – I am so appreciative, so happy just to be here, to be alive and to be 'me' – legs or no legs. I don't take any drugs because I have been lucky enough not to need them – whenever I get phantom pain in one or both 'legs' I just go with it: I breathe in and out, slowly and deeply, then tell myself that I should 'enjoy' the sensation it gives of having a leg.

Admittedly, it's not great when you are kept awake with an imaginary itch on the imaginary sole of your foot and you can't scratch it, but luckily those times are rare and when they do happen I close my eyes and remind myself that this is what it felt like to have a foot, to have an itch. That's a nice memory to have.

I knew that I would never allow myself to be consumed by my job again. Well, they do say 'never say never', so I should qualify that by saying, *not unless* my job or my role was making a real difference to the world. The only way I felt able to make any sense of what happened to me was by doing all I could to stop more suicide bombings happening. For me, July 7 was much more than a 'wake-up call', because I had thought I was already awake. I thought I was doing my bit for peace and ending wars – I wore the T-shirt and bought the badge; what else could I possibly do?

Today I am still formulating my beliefs and my ideas and am committed to trying to understand the mind of a nineteen-year-old boy (Lily is now the same age as Germaine Lindsay was) who would choose a terrorist path. He thought he was right. He thought God was on his side. And I think I am right and that God is on my side. I didn't know there were two sides. I didn't know I was his enemy. Can two sides both be right?

Remembering to live can also apply to someone who chooses the path of the suicide bomber. Where there is life, there is always hope, but how can we change the things that trouble us when we are not here to do it? We can't discuss and talk and make our point of view heard if we have no voice. Neither can we see or experience the benefits of change if and when change is made, if we are gone.

In many ways, I'm very fortunate. I have found a clarity that I never expected or knew could exist. Life is now simple. I listen to myself, I trust myself and I act on my instincts. I have discovered a strength that I never knew I had – not just physical, but mental and spiritual. If someone had told me that I would live through a bombing and lose both legs as a result, I would have found it unimaginable. Being disabled is one thing I never contemplated happening to me. I had thought about my death and the many ways in which I could die, but I had never thought about living my life in such a drastically different way. Nothing could have prepared me for this, but strength and faith have got me through.

. . .

With my new mindset, continuing my work as Head of Curation at the Design Council was no longer as important to me as it once had been. It just didn't feel right and did not seem to allow me to be true to myself – to my vow to make a difference.

Despite this, though, it was important at least that I returned, that I came back after July 7. For me, it was important to finish unfinished business and to take back the space that was left in my absence. It was symbolic. I wanted to be back, to show them all that I was still their 'Gill', the Gill they all knew and, I hope, loved. I still had the same gags, the same giggle, the same determination – everything was the same. Well, almost.

My first day back was like revisiting a crime scene or the home of a missing person. Gemima, a close friend in the communications team, had everything on my desk perfectly positioned, carefully placed just as it was when I'd last been there eight months earlier. Only there was a 'coldness' about it all and, although familiar, every item there seemed alien.

I picked up the huge 'URGENT' file that had pride of place in my in-tray. This is what I had spent my life, well, Life One doing. Everything in that file defined every hour of every day right up to July 7, 2005. I read through some of the papers, remembering late nights at my desk, writing sections of those papers, weekends researching, breakfast meetings, dinner meetings, lunch meetings, working through lunch and leaving the office only because the security guard needed to close up and go home to his family.

I threw the entire file in the bin and, just like that, a chapter had been closed. I remember thinking that I should feel more hurt than I did – this was the evidence, proof that I had existed, that I had lived. It was all there, dated and detailed in that file. But I also recalled the mad puffing of cigars, copious quantities of coffee to keep me awake, the chest and stomach pains brought on from the anxiety of wanting everything to be perfect. It didn't mean anything now. Nothing had happened with that file for eight months, yet the world hadn't stopped turning. It simply didn't have the value that I'd once placed on it. I could see that very clearly and I knew that day that I would have to leave.

It was difficult saying goodbye to my colleagues and friends (although for those who had become close friends, of course it wasn't goodbye). The Design Council had been very supportive throughout my ordeal. When the newsletters from Joe's sister, Bella, had first been circulated to the Design Council, Gemima and Nicola, who are both very close to me, decided that they would set up a team to generate ideas and create events with the sole purpose of raising money for my St Thomas' fund. The entire staff got behind them, joining in with such crazy events as 'Hawaiian day', special screenings of films and raffles. The in-house chef, Mark Hallard, even created a special recipe book; it sold for £5 a copy and was so popular they had to reprint it several times over! (One of my favourite recipes from Mark's book can be found on page 239 of this book.)

The Design Council had been the centre of my world and my colleagues there, in turn, made me feel as though I was leaving a gaping hole in the organisation – one that couldn't be filled. I was taking a leap into the unknown, out of the security of my position at the Design Council. But I wasn't scared. Every minute of every day had to count and I could feel time slipping through my fingers. (That, incidentally, is the only thing that does scare me – losing time.)

They organised an all-team lunch to say goodbye and Mark made sure all my favourite foods were on the menu (particularly his beetroot salad!). The Chief Executive took the opportunity to make a speech and talked of his observations: how on many occasions he had encountered my 'unique' character, how he was struck by my 'method-in-the-madness' approach to work but, above all else, how he was most impressed with my ability to unite people.

I stood and responded, fighting back the tears whilst looking into as many faces as I could. 'Live every day to the fullest. Appreciate everything, because you never know what will happen,' I said. I then told them how much their cards and letters had meant to me, as well as all their fundraising activities. 'Watch this space,' were my final words. I would carry with me all their encouragement, their support, but most of all their wishes for me to be well and happy.

. . .

My path is being laid and being lit every day. I can see so clearly where I am meant to be going, where I am headed – it's like an airport runway, where the bright lights along the strip guide the planes in. Call it serendipity or a pre-determined destiny, but the brightest lights for me have been and are those people who have come into my life or become a bigger part of it since July 7. They have all helped to shape and define my next steps.

. . .

In the days and weeks that followed my resignation I was kept busy with writing the early outline for this book, going to rehabilitation twice a week at the Royal National Orthopaedic Hospital in Stanmore and with beginning my journey into the unknown.

Contacts were being made with amazing and interesting people all over the world – people whose work was all about 'making a difference'. My story was being read and heard by many who immediately identified with my expression and my overwhelming desire to give back and do all I could to make my life count. There are two women, in particular, whose wisdom and experience in conflict resolution and peace-building have been shaping and informing my work now. They are Dr Pam Ryan, a fellow Adelaidian who founded IDA (Ideas Deliberations Australia and America), and Dr Scilla Elworthy, who founded Peace Direct.

I was asked to speak at an annual conference/gathering called 'Be the Change' – a symposium of inspiring speakers whose common aim was to make the world a greater place by unlocking the potential in each and every person to create a better world. Naturally, this was of interest to me and I felt honoured to be asked to speak at such an event. After I agreed, I discovered that one of the 'Be the Change' founders, Colin, was killed on July 7 at Edgware Road. I brought up his picture on a website and sat staring and staring at his face.

Colin's wife Ros was in the audience at the conference. She approached the stage and introduced herself before I started to talk. She was then the first person I had met who had lost someone on July 7 and it was a memorable and very moving moment for me.

Then I gathered my thoughts and began to speak. I said in a croaky, shaky voice that I wished the world would stop. I wished it would stop long enough for us all to take a good, hard look at what is happening – the innocent lives being lost, people being maimed. And for whom? For what? I spoke from the depths of my heart, trying to express just how quickly life can be taken. I clicked my fingers to demonstrate what it had been like for me, for those in my carriage – in the blink of an eye they were gone. I went on to explain that I was committed to trying to understand the motives, the act itself, and that I wanted to listen – because if I understood then maybe I would have a chance of doing something. Maybe I would be able to deter someone else from following that path.

I ended, abruptly – I just couldn't speak any more. The audience rose to give me a standing ovation.

It was at that conference that I met Dr Scilla Elworthy. Meeting Scilla was a 'runway' moment. It was like finding a soul mate. She could see right through me, into me, around me and she knew that my intentions were sincere and pure. I wanted, above all else, to put an end to terrorism and do all I could to build a bridge to peace and tolerance – that was the end goal.

My views echoed those of Scilla and Peace Direct in the belief that the cycle of violence has to end with each of us. We all have within us the power to say, 'No – I will not retaliate', or 'I will not seek revenge' and should exercise it because revenge is a continuing cycle in which no one 'wins'. One of the most powerful things that Mahatma Gandhi said was, 'An eye for an eye will make the whole world blind,' and that, for me, sums it up.

Scilla and I knew instinctively that we could work together, so I was appointed Ambassador for Peace Direct, an active body that deals with grass-roots conflict resolution – getting to the very core of a problem and helping to enable a solution. My job was to do anything and everything within my power to create peace in any area where there is conflict.

The Leonard Cheshire Foundation also got in touch with me. They invited me initially to a dinner, then left it to me to decide whether theirs was an organisation that would be suited to me – to work with or to connect with at any level I wanted. This was all part of the whole other world that goes with being 'registered disabled'. Yes, it is a part of Life Two, but it is by no means all of it and is not how I identify myself. I am not ashamed to call myself disabled – legally, that's what I now am – but I just don't think about it. I don't give who or what I am a label – I am just Gill. I am happy not to be 'defined' in any way so that Life Two can be flexible; so that I can 'do' in many areas and not be confined only to one. The reason why I chose, in the end, to support and do all I can for this charity is because they help disabled people to regain their independence. I know only too well how important it was and still is to feel 'able' to make choices and not be totally reliant on others to do things for you. Obviously this isn't always possible, but dignity can and must be.

Whilst visiting me in hospital, a dear friend of mine, Martyn, had suggested that I might be interested in something he was involved with called the Forgiveness Project; he was taken by my wish to even try to see the bombers' point of view, to put myself in their shoes, so to speak. The 'F' Word (as the project is also known) was founded and is run by an amazing and passionate woman called Marina. Originally a journalist, she began by exploring the idea of forgiveness and 'told' the stories of those who had been wronged but who had found a path to some sort of serenity.

The very idea of being involved in this project certainly made me think about and question my stance: Did I forgive? Could I forgive? I knew that I wasn't angry. I wasn't bitter or consumed with hatred – actually I didn't feel anything. I felt nothing for the bomber. I have stared at a pictures of him and read all I could on his past, his life, his family, and realised that actually I did feel something: I felt pity. But did I forgive him? That was the greatest question that I had to answer. I didn't forgive the act, no. And as for Germaine Lindsay – the person – well, he was dead. I couldn't forgive him as there was no one I could face, no eyes to look into and see regret in order to forgive. The only picture I had of him was from a newspaper cutting. I would have liked the opportunity to listen to him, for him to tell me why, in his own words, why he would commit such a crime. Why he hated so deeply. Why he hated me.

Mine is now included in this incredible collection of people's stories, people whose world has been ripped apart but who have managed to find a way to piece it back together, with courage, dignity and strength. I am privileged to appear alongside them in this project.

· · ·

Do we need constant reminders to remember to enjoy life? Maybe we do.

I know that if I had my legs back I would be doing so much more than I did before. If I'd known, if only I'd known that one day they would be gone, I would have cherished them more when I had them. I miss so many things associated to Life One. Often I indulge in a daydream; it's called: 'If I had my legs back and my old life back for one day, what would I do?' Each time I have this fantasy, I add new things to the list, so really, I would need longer than twenty-four hours to do everything on it!

On my current list are: jumping out of bed in the morning; standing and having a long shower and turning around in the shower so that the water washes over my back, then my face; getting dry with fluffy towels whilst standing; wearing skinny jeans with 50s pointed shoes; oh, standing up to brush my teeth; paddling, in sea water preferably; learning to swim; running, jumping, cycling, climbing, gymnastics, yoga, martial arts, kick-boxing, anything sporty involving the use of legs; painting my toenails after soaking my feet in a foot spa; rushing; going to a great concert and 'getting down'; salsa dancing, ice skating, skiing, roller blading; just strolling in a park and not worrying about the ground; skipping; getting excited and jumping up and down; climbing onto a chair to change a light bulb; climbing onto a chair to reach something on a high shelf; driving a sports car; doing anything I wanted to do, unsupervised or unaccompanied; going to the movies and putting my feet up on the chair in front; curling up on the sofa with woolly socks on; walking on grass barefoot; doing most things barefoot; walking on sand, on carpet – thick shag-pile carpet – and squishing my toe into the loops; wearing my beloved black Prada back-zip boots; wearing any pair of shoes I liked; buying a diamond toe ring; running for a peace charity ...

My fear is that if I don't constantly remind myself I will forget what it was like to have legs; that my 'new normal' will become, well, normal and all the memories will fade. I don't want to forget. I don't want to ever forget all the wonderful sensations that having legs and feet gave me.

But what I do appreciate now is the ability to even be Gill; to have the essence of Gill back – to be vibrant and strong and so thrilled that I can see the faces of those I love and hug them. 'Remember to live' is my daily mantra – a reminder to never let other 'stuff' get in the way of what I value and the beauty of life.

October 2, 2006

Big Peace... little piece ...

Welcome to the first Practical Peace Newsletter. We are delighted to be sending this out to you in countries as far removed as the Philippines, Vanuatu, and Iceland. This just demonstrates the power of Gill Hicks' words and the desire of so many people to make the first moves towards a sustainable peace.

We're sure you found Gill's film to commemorate the International Day of Peace as moving and affecting as the team here at Peace Direct did.

In tribute to her spirit and courage in overcoming adversity as well as her commitment to peace and understanding, we have come up with practical ways in which we can all implement some of her ethos into our everyday lives.

1. Education in your lunch breaks! You can visit The Forgiveness Project www.theforgivenessproject.com to get a really fresh, innovative and creative take on forgiveness and conflict resolution. Also sign up for the email newsletters from www.opendemocracy.net for some inspiring lunchtime reading.

 2. Go and see "An Inconvenient Truth", Al Gore's documentary film explaining climate change and the need to take immediate action. Note the mention of the dramatic shrinking of Lake Chad, which is affecting and exacerbating conflict in surrounding countries. www.aninconvenienttruth.co.uk.

3. Day of Action to shut DESO: Monday 16th October*. The Defence Export Services Organisation is a UK government department dedicated to promoting exports for private arms companies. A broad coalition of political parties, campaigns and advocacy groups are calling for its closure.

*For our international friends please visit www.caat.org.uk to find out about similar arms campaigning activities happening across the world.

4. Demonstrate Goodwill at all times. Practise putting a smile on your face first thing in the morning and you will be surprised at how quickly it becomes your default approach to the first few hours of your day. Take travelling to work: the fractiousness of others is much easier to bear if greeted with a grin!

Even we at Peace Direct are not always paragons of peaceful virtue, and some of these will be ideas we have just come up with ourselves. However we are all firm believers in small steps at a time and if you have any comments or suggestions we'd be delighted to hear them.

Please forward this message to everyone for whom it may be of interest and some for whom it won't.

More from us next Monday,

The Peace Direct Team

www.peacedirect.org

www.peacedirectblog.typepad.com/

Everyone can do something about Peace.

October 9, 2006

Big Peace...little piece...

Welcome to the second Practical Peace Newsletter. Next week we'd love to include some of your suggestions so any thoughts you have on everyday, practical things we can all do for peace, then please drop us an email. Thanks for all your feedback so far. The Peace Direct team is based in the UK, so if you do things differently in Nigeria, Australia, Morocco, America, or wherever you are in the world, then let us know. We'd love to hear from you.

You can read the first email in the series at http://www.peacedirect.org/latest-news/Practical_Peace.html

And remember you can still view the film featuring 7/7 survivor Gill Hicks that inspired these emails at www.peacedirect.org/messagefromgill or on YouTube at http://www.youtube.com/watch?v=LU3V2suLEbU . Over seven thousand people around the world already have!

Here are four things you can do this week.

1. Do you have a pension? If so, is your pension invested in companies making weapons? If the weapons are used, the majority of casualties are likely to be civilians. Is this really how you want <u>your</u> money to be used? You can get advice on how to clean up your pension at http://www.eiris.

org/. It's easier if you have a personal pension, but if you are in a company pension scheme you might end up changing its policies for the whole company!

2. Try some media that doesn't necessarily reflect your view: http://english.aljazeera.net/HomePage, http://www.foxnews.com/, http://www.ynetnews.com, http://www.arabnews.com/.

3. People say that non-violent approaches are fine in theory, but when did they ever really work? Get your answers from War Prevention Works, 50 stories from every corner of the world, costed and quantified, of how non-violent approaches have turned conflict into lasting peace. Available from Peace Direct at a special price for October only of £5 including postage and packing. Or else ask your local library to order it in from us, that way many more people will be able to read it too. Contact susanna@peacedirect.org.

4. Forgive yourself and extend that forgiveness to someone else too. A staff member's confession:

'The last time I directed anger towards a loved one was when I had behaved like a spoilt child, and was chided for it. My reaction on being reprimanded was acute embarrassment which then became extreme defensiveness and then red-hot anger towards the person who loved me enough to want to help me. So the next time it happened I managed to think about it, swallow my pride and say sorry. We were both happy, because he got an apology, and I knew he didn't think badly of me for longer than a few painful, silly moments.'

As always, please forward this message to everyone for whom it may be of interest and some for whom it won't.

Until next Monday.

Love,

The Peace Direct Team

www.peacedirect.org

Everyone can do something about Peace.

October 16, 2006

Big Peace...little piece...

Wherever you are in the world, hello and welcome to the third in our series of Practical Peace emails. It's incredible to think that over seven thousand people have viewed the Gill Hicks film that inspired this project, and that number is growing every day. It's also great that you're coming up with some of the suggestions for these emails. Can we say a big thank you to everyone who got in touch, and please keep them coming!

The previous two Practical Peace emails are also now online if you've forgotten one or two of the suggestions! http://www.peacedirect.org/latest-news/Practical_Peace.html. In the meantime, here's what you can do this week.

1. If you have a friend or colleague fasting for Ramadan, fast for a day with them. We did it last week in the office with Mohamed, our International Liaison. It was incredibly rewarding and a great bonding experience (even if tempers did get a little frayed towards the end of the day!)

2. Take care of a piece of the earth: find a bit of land to restore to natural health. In most cities you can rent an allotment for a few pounds a year, and it's fun to see your seeds coming up. And even more fun to eat your delicious organic pesticide-free lettuce. If you prefer water, find a river to clean up, there are plenty around full of plastic bottles, and kids love to help.

3. If you work with young people, in school, faith groups or anywhere else, encourage them to think critically, to question what they receive from the media against their own experience, and to consider what other points of view there might be.

4. Use any of a multitude of ways available now to develop wisdom: www.integralinstitute.org or www.transcend.org or www.wisdomuniversity.org.

And here are a couple of your suggestions. We'll have more next Monday...

5. 'Something I learned (late in life!) was to take the emotion out of your arguments. It is very easy to dismiss someone's views if they are expressed over-emotionally. If you remain calm and use straightforward language, it is harder for people to avoid what you are saying.'

Similarly, learn to look past the emotion in the way somebody expresses their grievances. People generally get upset when something means a lot to them, not always because they are upset with you.

Here's another...

6. 'Cut your use of fuel, especially air travel, in half every year. If everyone did this the fuel/energy shortage would be history.'

A reminder that you can view Gill's film at www.peacedirect. org/messagefromgill or on YouTube at www.youtube.com/ watch?v=LU3V2suLEbU.

As ever, please forward this message to everyone for whom it may be of interest and some for whom it won't.

Until next week,

The Peace Direct Team

www.peacedirect.org

October 23, 2006

Big Peace...little piece...

Hello and welcome to the fourth in our series of five Practical Peace newsletters during the month of October.

Some of you have been energetic enough to send us your suggestions for practical peace; we'd also like to hear your feedback. Here is some already received:

'I found the Aljazeera web fascinating, particularly the art Israeli/Palestinian exhibition. Quite something.'

'It was indeed interesting reading the Fox News website and Al Jazeera. Fox News is awful!'

'Good suggestion about cutting your fuel use in half every year. If you have to fly, get on these sites before you go! www.climatecare.org www.carbontrust.co.uk and www. carbonneutral.com.'

If you've just signed up you can see the previous three newsletters here. And here's what you can do this week...

1. If someone in your school or workplace is from a different country, take the trouble to learn a few words of greeting in their mother tongue. Konnichiwa ... Bonjour ... Salam wa Alaikum ... Ola ... Ciao ... Namaste ... it doesn't take much effort and means a lot.

2. Let Coventry inspire you. Their fourth Peace Month is now under way with events across the city. Learn more about the festival here and try and find a way to get your community to adopt something similar.

3. This week's essential reading: 'Unarmed Heroes.' Compiled and edited by Peace Direct, it is full of personal testimonies and essays on the peaceful resolution of conflict. 'An emotional journey where you can feel the heart and soul of the protagonist being poured out onto the page.' Dame Anita Roddick.

4. And a couple of websites for your lunch break. www. timebank.org.uk and www.imagine-life.org.

5. Finally, something easy you can try that makes a real difference. Take two minutes at the end of each day to simply reflect on what you have achieved. In a world that moves fast, there is rarely time to appreciate all we do for ourselves, each other and our work.

A reminder that you can view Gill's film at www.peacedirect.
org/messagefromgill or on YouTube at www.youtube.com/
watch?v=LU3V2suLEbU.

As ever, please forward this message to everyone for whom it
may be of interest and some for whom it won't.

Until next week,

The Peace Direct Team

www.peacedirect.org

October 30, 2006

Big Peace...little piece...

 Welcome to the fifth Practical Peace Newsletter full of
practical things you can do for peace. The thoughts of Gill
Hicks, the person who inspired these emails later, but first
this week's offerings...

1. Choose your own bite-sized peace initiative and become
part of Peace Direct's work. It takes just 35 people to
support a team of peacebuilders for an entire year and all it
takes is ten pounds (15 Euros/19 $US/25 $AUS) each a month.
Choose from Champions projects in Colombia, Kenya and the
Congo here.

2. Peace Direct's Champions Programme funds and supports
just a tiny proportion of the thousands of groups doing
amazing grassroots peacebuilding work around the world. This
week's website choice gives you a chance to find out more about
similar groups www.changemakers.net/journal/peace/

3. Whether it's in a war zone, your own living room or
workplace, the same models of resolving conflict apply. These
concepts are explored in a new book by Charlie Irvine called
Cash In On Conflict. You can learn more about the book here.

Here's more on the cycle of violence...

In a prolonged conflict, be it in the living room or across a minefield, a deadly cycle of violence is experienced that ensures one misdeed leads straight into another, often involving more and more hurt, and sometimes killing.

The cycle of violence has eight stages and it works in the human psyche, at the level of emotions. It starts with an atrocity (a hurt or misdeed in the case of a family) the immediate reaction to which is shock and fear, followed by grief, followed by anger. If nothing is done to break the cycle of violence at this stage, the anger hardens into bitterness, followed by feelings of revenge and then retaliation, which precede another atrocity.

So let's say someone you know has hurt you. If nothing is done to alleviate your feelings, you may well go and hurt them back, or hurt someone else. Think about how abuse gets passed down from generation to generation if nothing is done.

<u>Do let us know about your own experiences. How have you intervened in a cycle of violence? What happened?</u>

We've absolutely loved compiling and sending these emails over the last few weeks – so much so that we want to keep going. From November we'll start sending out a monthly Practical Peace Newsletter, so please keep sending your suggestions and feedback.

Finally, as promised, the thoughts of Gill herself:

'It didn't matter on July 7, 2005 if I was a man or a woman, Muslim, Jewish, Christian or agnostic; it didn't matter if I was rich or poor. All that mattered was that I was a life, a precious life that needed to be saved. The men and women of the police and ambulance services and the team of doctors and nurses who saved me showed absolute dedication; they risked their lives to save mine and never gave up, even when my prospects looked very bleak, they never gave up. One medic said that I had reinforced his belief that "where there is life, there is always hope".

'It is these actions and his words that have instilled my firm belief that humanity can overcome conflict, that we all, each one unknown person can change the world. Please don't just "get the T-shirt" - make Peace a part of who you are, a part of your everyday life!'

 Please forward this message to everyone for whom it may be of interest and some for whom it won't.

Until next month,

The Peace Direct Team

www.peacedirect.org

Chapter 12

This Is Just the Beginning...

Dear Friends

The first anniversary of the London bombings is fast
approaching, and we're sure that you will share our desire
to mark that moment appropriately. The day itself will no
doubt be a complex affair, and people will wish to spend
it in their own way, which might mean participating in
the officially arranged events, or perhaps observing some
private act of commemoration, or even jetting off as far from
London as possible.

However, we feel very strongly that it would a good and
positive thing if as many of us as possible were able to come
together around that time for a mutual act of fellowship
and of remembrance. Therefore we have decided to organise
a service for the evening before, on July 6 at 6.30pm, to
be held at St Etheldreda's RC Church, Ely Place, Holborn,
where we were married last December. The service will take
the form of a solemn Catholic mass, to be celebrated by the
parish priest Father Kit Cunningham, but it is intended for
people of all faiths and persuasions. This is a very formal
form of service, of a kind unfamiliar to some people, but it
is our belief that sometimes ancient and beautiful rituals
are the most appropriate way of marking such extraordinary
and profound occasions.

The service will be dedicated both to those who died on July 7 and also to the many brave survivors, and we hope that although it will be an emotional affair, it can also be a hopeful and affirmative event. It is our desire to be surrounded on that evening by Gill's fellow survivors, by members of the emergency and medical services who performed such miracles on the day, and by friends, family and colleagues upon whom the burden of that day fell so heavily.

We really do hope that you will be free to join us. We only ask that you contact us fairly soon to let us know if you are intending to come, as we will be laying on drinks in the crypt afterwards, and need to anticipate demand.

With love,

Gill and Joe

A Votive Mass for Peace and Justice
A reading from the letter of St James 3:13-18

'If there are any wise or learned men among you, let them show it by their good lives, with humility and wisdom in their actions. But if at heart you have the bitterness of jealousy, or a self-seeking ambition, never make any claims for yourself or cover up the truth with lies – principles of this kind are not wisdom that comes from above: they are only earthly, animal and devilish. Wherever you find jealousy and ambition, you find disharmony and wicked things of every kind being done; whereas the wisdom that comes down from above is essentially something pure; it also makes for peace and is kindly and considerate; it is full of compassion and shows itself by doing good; nor is there any trace of partiality or hypocrisy in it. Peacemakers, when they work for peace, sow the seeds which will bear fruit in holiness.
    This is the word of the Lord
    Thanks be to God'

...

'I can't sleep, I think I'll get up. Sorry to wake you, Boo Boo – go back to sleep.'

It was 5am, July 5.

I couldn't sleep anyway. Seeing images in the press in the lead-up to the anniversary was bringing back many vivid memories. There is something about first anniversaries that is more significant than any other – I don't know why. It didn't feel like a year on; the events of July 7, 2005 are timeless for me – they could have happened an hour ago or ten years ago – they are with me every day.

I was restless, hoping that the service at St Ed's that we had planned (well, that Joe had planned) so meticulously would be well received.

I put my legs on and went downstairs to make some tea. 'Joe, Joe do you want some tea? Joe?' He wasn't there. Where was he at 5.30am? Something wasn't right. I rang his mobile. No reply. I rang again – still no reply. Where on earth was he? I knew something was up. Something was wrong; he'd been secretive. I sat in the lounge waiting for him to return. God, what if he's had an accident? Why isn't he answering his phone?

I was just putting some coffee on when Joe walked in. 'Where have you been? It's 7am! Where have you been for the last two hours, Joe? What's going on?'

Suddenly a head popped around the kitchen door. 'Hello!' – it was Graham ... and Jo! 'What? Aaahhhh!' I was absolutely shocked, here they were, sadly without the kids, but here they were. The Australian Government had flown them over for the anniversary. They could only stay for four days, but that was enough for me – just to have them here for that one special day meant everything.

The anniversary now took on a different shape for me – my brother and my sister-in-law (or 'Party Girl', her special London alias) were here! They'd come all that way just to spend four days in London – it was mad! But that's what I loved the most; that mad behaviour was the new normal for us all now. Nothing really mattered to us except each other and Graham and Jo didn't want to be anywhere but here, with Joe and me on the anniversary of that day in July. The two Jo's had been plotting and planning for months, trying to make the visit a surprise for me. It worked!

On July 6, 2006 – the eve of the first anniversary of the bombings – we held an evening mass at 'our' church, St Etheldreda's. It was our way of marking this occasion with importance, dignity, formality and unity.

The church was packed, just as it had been at our wedding, with a mix of new and old friends: those who had saved my life and the lives of many others; those like me who had survived; those who had been there, supporting Joe and I on the journey to recovery; and those we'd met who had lost a loved one in the bombings. It was so important to us that our families were there and unfailingly they all were. Aunt Mary had come from Canterbury, Antony and Elizabeth made the long journey from Herefordshire to London, Anna and Stefan from Hampshire, Bill from Manchester, Bella and Lyndon from South Wales, Lily – everyone who could be was there.

The families sat together near the front row. I smiled and acknowledged people as they came in, like Richard Alston, the Australian High Commissioner and his wife Megs, Inspector Glen, Gary, Andy and Jon. And I looked over at Jo and told her how special it was that she and Graham were here to share this occasion. But it was when Brian and Lisa walked in, down the aisle to give me a hug and a kiss that Jo and I both burst into tears. They had their uniforms on and it was that symbol – so recognisable – that moved us so deeply.

At 6.30pm prompt the Mass bell rang and a procession of servers, with incense, cross and candles walked slowly through the hushed and solemn congregation in the church to the sanctuary, followed by Father Kit in his vestments. As they entered the choir began a sombre Latin chant. The sung service that followed was the *Mass for Four Voices* by William Byrd (1534–1623), perhaps the greatest achievement in the long history of English choral music. Joe had chosen the Byrd Mass in particular because its composer was an English Catholic who lived through a period of intense religious persecution. The sorrow of that era is reflected in the mournful quality of the music. We hoped that using sacred music drawn from such a troubled age would serve as a powerful reminder of the terrible acts that are committed in the name of religion.

Deputy Commissioner, Paul Stephenson QPM gave the first reading. Richard, our dear new friend and fellow survivor, gave the second.

Then we prayed for the 52 innocent victims.

We prayed for those who were bereaved.

We prayed for the injured.

We prayed for all those who showed great courage in the face of danger and for all those who saved so many lives.

Then we sat in silent contemplation, each of us lost in our own thoughts and memories, our emotions intensified by the beautiful but haunting sound of the choir, piercing us all to the core. This was the very same choir that had sung in joy for us a few months previously; it was now giving voice to our grief and sorrow.

My thoughts turned to the hundreds of lives that are ended or left like mine every day, and the effects that this has on those who love them. I was filled with sadness, as deep and as painful as a wound that may never heal. All those people that are killed through acts of terrorism – all just like me; all 'One Unknowns', living their lives, doing their bit, making plans, eating, sleeping, loving, hating – just like me. And just like the people who killed them. All human.

All of us in the church that evening were there to honour and re-member those whose lives were lost and those whose lives have been irreversibly changed by the acts of four men. It was just four men who altered the course of hundreds of lives by the press of a button, in the click of a finger, the blink of an eye.

But the evening did not end with the Mass. Father Kit invited the entire congregation to the after-service drinks that Joe and I had pre-pared and everyone duly moved downstairs into the highly atmos-pheric ancient crypt of St Etheldreda's to drink a glass or two of wine and to listen to some speeches.

Joe stood up on a bench to make his speech. He talked about our friendships, the amazing people that we now have the privilege and honour to know who were there *that* day. He said that we had learnt so much from their example – how no matter what prejudices or personal feelings they may harbour, a life is a life, and they would do everything within their power to save that life. Through them, he went on, we had found hope. Through them we could see that humanity would overcome the most desperate acts of cruelty.

Each one of us gathered there, Joe said, had been affected by the terrorist acts of July 7, 2005 – all two hundred people in that church. But he asked us to think about the fifty-two who hadn't made it, about their lives and about those who mourned them as well as those who were injured. Some seven hundred people had been affected and the lives of their friends and families – a ripple effect that connects so many to a single tragedy. But Joe then suggested that what this gathering of family and friends also represented was an opportunity to express our solidarity and an affirmation of life. We were living proof that the desire to destroy not only human life but human society and unity as well would not succeed in the face of our common humanity.

Joe concluded by saying how he appreciated that the very specific kind of religious ceremony we had provided – a sung Latin Mass complete with incense and bells – might have been difficult or unfamiliar for many of those present, but that he hoped people were happy to be there for the sentiment expressed. Moreover, he said, this was a special Votive Mass dedicated to Peace and Justice, causes to which we could all happily subscribe and to which he then proposed a toast.

We all raised our glasses in unison and loudly echoed: 'Peace and Justice'.

Richard stood and delivered a rousing impromptu speech. His words were filled with passion as he thanked Joe and me for organising an emotional but uplifting tribute to the anniversary of such a dreadful day.

We had arranged for the local restaurant, the wonderful Bleeding Heart Tavern, to lay on canapés and wine for our guests, but the numbers attending far exceeded our estimate and we knew that these modest refreshments wouldn't last long. Luck was on our side though, for hidden in a tiny alley behind the church was the Mitre Tavern, remarkably compact on the inside but with plenty of space outside for us to gather on what was a warm summer's night. We did feel slightly for this cosy, quiet little establishment that was suddenly invaded by an emotionally charged but extremely thirsty hoard. It more than served its purpose though that night.

Thus in typical Joe-and-Gill fashion a solemn and serious occasion was transformed into a happy and relaxed drink with friends. I sat on a bar stool and watched everyone – Graham sharing a joke with Inspector Glen, Jo laughing with Gary, Gemima and Richard, and Poppy in deep conversation with Brian – and I felt proud to be at the centre of all this, connected to each person there.

. . .

That evening eased the anticipation of the coming day.

I had twenty-six white flowers, individual single stems, to take to Russell Square station. I attached tags to the flowers – a mixture of lilies, roses and freesia – and wrote on them the names of each and every person who had died in my carriage. Doing this was important to me and I thought about each of them as I wrote, before tying their tag to a stem with a white ribbon. I thought about their stories – who they were, what they did, what they had planned to do and I spoke private, quiet words to each of them as I tied on their tag.

We were all going as a family to stand in silence at Russell Square station for noon. All of London would stop and remember the events that had taken place that day, the previous year. Joe had already been to mark the moment the bomb exploded at 8.50am.

I stood with Graham and Jo, with Joe firmly clutching my hand. The silence was eerie. Not a word was uttered; there was not a sound to be heard. London had stopped. I didn't want to be anywhere but there at that moment. I wanted to stand on the spot where a year ago I had lain dying. I wanted to feel as close as I could to the place where so many of my fellow commuters had lost their lives. I wanted to be close to a station that I had positive feelings about – this was the place where I had survived, not where I was nearly killed.

The station manager, Lee, was there, standing proud with many of the station staff, like Mo and Roy and Gary, all of whom had been there that day. It's funny because the moment I walked into the station they all acknowledged me; they knew me in an instant. All I could do was smile and shake their hands because I didn't know them – I do now!

As I lay down my twenty-six flowers I was caught by photographers and that afternoon my distraught face was on the front page of several papers, most prominently on the *Evening Standard*'s.

Lee then took me, Joe and Graham and Jo through to a private area where a plaque had been fixed to the wall to serve as a permanent reminder of those who died. I stood and read all the names knowing how fortunate I was that mine was not amongst them.

I tried to convey my feelings in the book of condolence that was just beneath the plaque:

'I was with you down there. I know, and I am so sorry. I am so, so sorry that you lost your life. I lived. The only way I know to truly honour you is to live a very full life, to live twenty-six lives in one and to make the gravity of difference that twenty-six lives would have made – this is all I can endeavour to do.'

...

We had planned to hold an 'open house' day, where all who were involved in whatever way, now considered dear and close friends could pop in and share some of that anniversary together. It wasn't a sombre occasion for us; our home represented celebration and that is how we spent the day – toasting one another, toasting life and being alive! We were all there: Jon, Brian (sadly, Lisa had to work), Dr Luff, Matt and Kristen, Carol, Lynsey, Gemima, Berni and Si, Debs, Kat, everyone. Kat brought with her as many copies of the *Standard* as she could get her hands on, explaining that as she sat on the tube on her way over she'd been faced with a long line of pictures of my very sad-looking face in the newspapers of people sitting opposite her. She knew how horrified I would be that the papers had captured my distress and thought that the more papers she had, the less there would be for anyone else!

There were police vans parked outside, I can't imagine what the neighbours must have made of it all. Gary and Ray were on shift, but popped in – wearing full uniform. Andy then arrived as well, also in uniform.

Aaron came too. He had been doing all he could to block out the memory of that day. He couldn't watch the television or read the papers, which for me, made his appearance at our home that day that much more special, knowing, as I did, how much of an effort it was for him. I didn't want to be for him the manifestation of such a horrible experience; I wanted him to be able to associate me with what is good in the world and with hope. We never said much when we were together; we would mostly just hold each other's hands.

Aaron and I are connected for life – as I am with them all.

. . .

After losing my parents I never expected that I would receive unconditional love again. Yet every person who helped to save me – One Unknown – did so unconditionally. Neither had I ever realised it was possible to be filled with so much love for so many 'strangers' – for people who risked their own lives to save mine, people who gave their all. Perhaps most of all though, I am grateful – so grateful – to have had the opportunity to know them since then and for them to know me, Gill, no longer a body without a name.

Epilogue

What matters ...
... are the people who risked all to save me, to save many. It matters that they never gave up; they never gave up hope that I would live.

What matters ...
... is that I now know most of these amazing people who continue to save lives, to enforce the law, to nurse the sick. They are my friends.

What matters ...
... is what you do. Someone, somewhere is feeling the effects of something you have done or said.

Every second, every minute, every hour, every day – it all matters.

Making your life count, making a difference – big or small – it matters. Creating wonderful and happy memories – things to keep you alive.

Finding a positive in everything and everywhere that you can.

Surrounding yourself with cherished friends.

Believing in yourself and in the amazing powers and abilities of the body and spirit!

Believing in humanity, in the pure love of strangers.

Appreciating EVERYTHING – sunrises, sunsets, clouds, rain, food, water, wine, tea, hugs, smiles, laughing, standing, walking, being hot, being cold, sleeping, waking up, loving, being loved, pain – anything and everything that signals life and being alive!

Letting it go matters ...
... not getting absorbed by life's rubbish, not sweating the little things.

Telling the people you love that you love them matters.

Not leaving the house angry – it matters.

Never giving up matters.

*Being alive; living a full and rich life – **that matters.***

Appendix

Honey-roasted Butternut Squash Soup
(One of my favourite recipes, taken from Mark Hallard of the
Design Council's recipe book, compiled to raise money for
St Thomas' Hospital)

1½ kg butternut squash, peeled and diced

2 tbsp honey

4 tbsp olive oil

25g butter

1 carrot, peeled and diced

1 leek, sliced

1 onion, diced

1½ litres stock (made with 2 vegetarian stock cubes)

salt and pepper

cream for drizzling

sunflower and pumpkin seeds

- Preheat oven to 180°C.

- Place the butternut squash on a baking tray and drizzle over the honey and olive oil. Roast for 20–25 minutes or until golden.

- Melt the butter in a saucepan, then add the carrot, leek and onion and sauté until soft.

- Add the roasted butternut squash and stock, then bring to the boil.

- Reduce the heat slightly and allow to simmer for about 45 minutes.

- Blitz in a blender and season to taste.

- Drizzle with cream and add seeds to garnish.

Mark rates this dish as 'well easy' – pure Londoner-speak for easy to make (on a scale of 1–10, 1 being the easiest, 10 the most difficult, this was rated 2).